D1546369

TO CARE FOR THE SICK AND BURY THE DEAD

To Care for the Sick and Bury the Dead

African American Lodges and Cemeteries in Tennessee

LEIGH ANN GARDNER

VANDERBILT UNIVERSITY PRESS
Nashville, Tennessee

Library of Congress Cataloging-in-Publication Data

Names: Gardner, Leigh Ann, author.
Title: To care for the sick and bury the dead : African American lodges and
    cemeteries in Tennessee / Leigh Ann Gardner.
Description: Nashville, Tennessee : Vanderbilt University Press, 2022. |
    Includes bibliographical references.
Identifiers: LCCN 2021043728 | ISBN 9780826502537 (hardcover) | ISBN
    9780826502544 (epub) | ISBN 9780826502551 (pdf)
Subjects: LCSH: African American fraternal
    organizations—Tennessee—History—19th century. | African American
    fraternal organizations—Tennessee—History—20th century. | African
    American cemeteries—Tennessee. | African Americans—Tennessee—Social
    life and customs. | African Americans—Segregation—Tennessee.
Classification: LCC HS2261.T2 G37 2022 | DDC 305.896/0768—dc23
LC record available at https://lccn.loc.gov/2021043728

Dedicated to

Justin, Hardy, Ellie
My parents, Kay and the late Bob Watson
My in-laws, Gilene and Brooks

CONTENTS

LIST OF ILLUSTRATIONS

ACKNOWLEDGMENTS

I have so many people to thank for their support and encouragement during my research that I will inevitably leave someone out of this list. Dr. Carroll Van West, director of the Center for Historic Preservation at Middle Tennessee State University, encouraged me throughout my time there as both a graduate assistant and later a staff member. He provided me with information about lodge buildings he had seen over the years, shared photographs from cemeteries he visited that had lodge associations, and was the first to encourage me to consider writing a book about these cemeteries.

Various staff members at the Center for Historic Preservation listened to me talk about lodges and offered support and assistance during my time there, including Anne-Leslie Owens, Dr. Antoinette van Zelm, Caneta Hankins, Jennifer Butts, Kira Duke, Dr. Susan Knowles, and Laura Holder. Fellow graduate student and later colleague Amy Kostine travelled with me to several sites and listened to me formulate my theories more times than I can enumerate over the years. I appreciate the fellow graduate students at the Center who listened to my presentations on benevolent groups and provided excellent feedback that allowed me to narrow the focus of my research.

My former supervisor at the Office of Research and Sponsored Programs at Middle Tennessee State University, Jeffry Porter, provided support and encouragement once I began writing, allowing me to take personal time for field visits as well as listening to me talk about these places. Many thanks to the archivists who helped me along the way, including John Lodl at the Rutherford County Archives, and archivists at the Metro Archives of Nashville and the Tennessee State Library and Archives.

My parents and in-laws were also supportive of my interest in cemeteries. Finally, I must express my heartfelt appreciation and thanks for my spouse, Justin, and my kids, Hardy and Ellie. Whenever I doubted my ability to write this story, they always told me that I could do it. They have travelled to cemeteries, endured "quick trips" to see cemeteries while on our way somewhere else (such as the movies), and gamely recorded their impressions of the sites on fieldwork forms. Hardy travelled with me to places in Memphis, to rural Giles County, and to Bedford County in 2020, taking notes and making excellent observations. Without their love and support, none of this would have been possible.

PREFACE

I remember the first time I encountered an African American benevolent lodge. It was the fall of 2010, and I was sitting in my first graduate class, back in college full-time for the first time in twelve years. The years immediately prior to graduate school had been spent as a stay-at home parent, after stints as a archival assistant and legal assistant/paralegal. I was nervous and eager to prove myself as a historian to my newfound colleagues and to the faculty. Sitting in a public history seminar, the professor tasked our class with creating an online exhibit about Cemetery, a local African American community that formed around the Stones River National Cemetery following the Civil War. The government's decision to create a military park (now known as the Stones River National Battlefield) in the 1930s largely destroyed this community.

Our class had copies of the deeds where the United States government purchased land from the families, both African American and white, in the community. Previous classes had identified the African American inhabitants living in the Cemetery community during the early twentieth century, as well as the basic outlines of community life, such as the churches and the school. We were to sift through this information and create an online exhibit highlighting some aspect of life in Cemetery. This is where I learned of the Working People's Labor and Art Association. The federal government purchased the small lot on which this organization had erected their lodge and demolished the building. Intrigued by the name, I asked the professor what was known about this group. The response was that nothing was known about the organization and it was likely unknowable. With those words, I became determined to find out more. Soon I was fascinated by what I learned about the role of fraternalism and benevolence in the local African American community. Diligent research, as well as a lucky break at the Rutherford County Archives, led me to a court case involving the group. Stuck in the files of the court petitions were depositions from group members and a copy of the group's constitution. By December I had linked this group to another African American organization—a local benevolent society lodge. Within months, I leaned about the existence of a local cemetery established by the Benevolent Society in Murfreesboro, as well as a different benevolent society cemetery in Montgomery County. From there, I discovered the rich world of African American fraternal and benevolent organizations that flourished across the state, including the network of cemeteries organized by these groups.

It is a world not yet explored deeply or widely by historians. Some study fraternalism in general, focusing on well-known groups such as the Prince Hall Masons, the Elks, and the Knights of Pythias. Others study the larger benevolent groups, such as the Grand Fountain of the United Order of True Reformers, or focus on women's associations, such as the Order of the Eastern Star. Some researchers study cemeteries with a focus on the differences between African American and predominantly white cemeteries. However, it appears that no one has looked at the world of African American lodge cemeteries, particularly in the state of Tennessee. It is a world I have sought to document for close to a decade.

I approach the work with the knowledge that these are neither my stories nor my cultural heritage. I am not African American, and I do not wish to appropriate these narratives for my benefit. However, the more I work to document African American fraternal and benevolent groups, the more convinced I am of their importance, both within their communities and within the state as well. It is a fascinating chronicle of how members of African American communities across the state created and sustained a mutual aid network that extended beyond life to the grave. It is also the account of how people coped with a segregated, racist society by creating their own separate world, sometimes literally separated from the white community by fences. It is a story I wish was more fully known and widely studied. I approach this work with the hope that others, perhaps those who belong to the communities I study, will take these histories and continue to share them with the scholarly community, that these tales of fraternalism and benevolence, of commemoration and segregation, of community building, will be seen by all as part of the saga of Tennessee. It is a record of how people pooled their resources and worked together to ensure that members of their community would be cared for when sick and properly buried when the time came. This story is ultimately bigger than that of Tennessee or the United States, as it is about the human spirt and a people's willingness to care for their own in the face of segregation. It is a story that continues to unfold across the state, and will continue to be relevant long after I have concluded my research.

Leigh Ann Gardner
Murfreesboro, Tennessee
August 2020

INTRODUCTION

A Time of Change

Tennessee between 1865 and 1930

First, it was presented and defended as
"race" separation, but it was never mere race
separation. It was always domination of
blacks by white officials, white police and
laws and ordinances made by white men.

—W. E. B. DU BOIS, 1935

Tennessee saw enormous changes during the period span-
ning from 1865 to the early twentieth century. The formerly
enslaved gained freedom, Tennessee enacted a new state
constitution that still governs daily life, a public education system was introduced across the state, and the right
to vote was extended to new segments of the population.
To fully understand the history of African American fraternal and benevolent groups in Tennessee, we must first
understand the time and place that created a space for these

groups, delving into life in Tennessee for African Americans as they transitioned from enslavement to freedom and beyond. Please note that this is not an extensive look at this period, but an overview of the time that shaped the people who organized benevolent and fraternal lodges in the state.

Reconstruction (1865–1877)

Following the Civil War, Tennessee requested readmission to the Union in December 1865, having met President Johnson's readmission conditions by ratifying the Thirteenth Amendment (which abolished slavery), repudiating state debts acquired during the Civil War, and rescinding the Articles of Secession. When the Republican-held Congress in Washington required an additional prerequisite of ratifying the Fourteenth Amendment (which defined the formerly enslaved as citizens), Tennessee complied, ratifying that amendment in July 1866. Tennessee thus became the first former Confederate state to be readmitted to the Union.[1]

Tennesseans of all races worked to rebuild new lives following the economic devastation of the Civil War. A congressional committee estimated the non-slave property losses in Tennessee at approximately $89 million, which represented one-third of the total value of non-slave property in Tennessee in 1861. Additionally, recent studies estimate the median value of real estate fell between one-half and three-fifths during the 1860s.[2] In real terms, this meant Tennesseans had to rebuild homes, farms, and communities that had been destroyed or damaged by battles, creating new roads, railroads, banks, schools, and a variety of community institutions.[3] As well as rebuilding the physical landscape, African Americans and whites had to find new ways of working together by making the transition from forced labor to paid labor. Initially, many white farmers negotiated contracts with freedmen that provided wages in return for farm labor; over time, white landowners began to divide their farms into smaller plots and rent those plots out to African Americans to farm. In return, African Americans either paid the farmer rent for the land, or they provided a share of the harvested crop at the end of the season.[4]

The transition from enslavement to freedom in Tennessee meant different things to people. For African Americans, it was both joyous and bittersweet, a time when they took control of their futures and made their own decisions about how and where they would live. It was also a time when people searched for relatives and loved ones from whom they had been separated by slavery and the war. African Americans also legalized the marriages they had entered into while enslaved and took surnames.[5] Some historians state that the transition period was seen by the formerly enslaved in almost mystical terms, as the beginning of a new epoch in their history.[6] It was also an uncertain time, as many of the formerly enslaved struggled to deal with having inadequate food, unsatisfactory housing, and insufficient clothing.[7] For whites, this was not a time seen in mystical terms, which was reflected in their attitudes and behavior toward the formerly enslaved. Seeing them acquire education and make economic progress often reminded poorer whites of their own ignorance, powerlessness, and poverty.[8] This led to random violence by whites against African Americans; these attacks were joined, beginning in 1867, by organized attacks led by the Ku Klux Klan. The Klan, initially formed in Pulaski, Tennessee, in 1866, allegedly began as a "social club" of sorts for young white men. However, by the spring of 1867, this initial Klan had regrouped into a terrorist organization determined to intimidate African Americans, with former Confederate general Nathan Bedford Forrest elected as its leader, or Grand Wizard.[9] What started as attempts to scare African Americans with processions of hooded and silent horsemen was soon replaced by outright violence, with African Americans dragged out of homes in the daylight and beaten or murdered.[10] It is not a surprise that increased violence coincided with African American men receiving the right to vote in 1867, as the Klan attempted to scare them into not voting. Klan activity and violence was strongest in Middle and West Tennessee, particularly in Giles, Humphreys, Lincoln, Marshall, Maury, Dyer, Fayette, Gibson, Hardeman, and Obion counties. In 1868, Governor Brownlow asked the state legislature to formally investigate the Klan, which led to the passage of the Ku Klux Klan Act, making any citizen who was a member of the organization or any other secret group engaged in domestic terrorism subject to arrest, imprisonment, and fines. In February 1869, Brownlow briefly declared martial law in nine counties to root out the Klan, and Forrest called upon the Klan to disband.[11] Although the Klan did cease to be an overt threat against African Americans during this period, neither the risk of violence nor acts of brutality against African Americans abated.

Despite the violence during this time period, African Americans created a number of their own institutions and separate communities freed from the control of white society. The church was one area in which African Americans acted swiftly to create their own institutions. Following the end of slavery, African Americans left formerly biracial congregations and created their own churches, and at times, their own, separate denominations.[12] The Colored (now Christian) Methodist Episcopal (CME) Church, for example, saw its beginnings as a separate denomination in Nashville in 1866, and the formal CME convention was created in 1870.[13] In addition to creating churches, African Americans created a multitude of other institutions in Tennessee during Reconstruction, such as fraternal and benevolent lodges, trade associations, drama clubs, equal rights leagues, and debating societies.[14]

African Americans also participated in politics; as early as 1865, an African American political leader in Nashville declared to Democrats that African Americans would leave the party of Lincoln if the Democrats "would prove a better friend to the Negro than the Republican Party."[15] That same year, African Americans in Tennessee convened the first State Colored Men's Convention, where they gathered to discuss racial conditions; the conventions continued for several years.[16] The 1865 convention, held in Nashville, formed committees to monitor the progress of the formerly enslaved across the state and to fight for their political privileges and civil rights.[17] A number of African Americans were elected to local office across the state, including W. S. McTeer, an African American merchant, to Maryville's board of alderman in 1868, and Edward Shaw, a saloon owner and orator, to the Shelby County Commission in 1869.[18] Some were also elected to the Tennessee General Assembly—Sampson Keeble represented Davidson County from 1873 to 1874; John W. Boyd represented Tipton County from 1881 to 1884; Isham Norris represented Shelby County from 1881 to 1882; and Samuel A. McElwee represented Haywood County from 1883 to 1888, to name a few.[19]

An organization that assisted freedmen in making the transition from slavery to freedom was the Freedmen's Bureau, authorized by President Lincoln on March 3, 1865. This governmental agency served a number of functions in the Southern states, from managing schools for freedmen and negotiating labor contracts between the formerly enslaved and white employers to organizing hospitals, orphanages, and homes for the aged. Perpetually underfunded, the Freedmen's Bureau dealt with hostility from white residents in Tennessee who opposed many of the goals of the bureau. The Bureau began to phase out in Tennessee as early as 1867, when the state took responsibility for the schools; by 1869, the Bureau was no longer serving Tennessee.[20]

In conjunction with the Freedmen's Bureau was the Freedmen's Savings Bank and Trust Company, authorized by Congress in early 1865. The bank began operating in Tennessee in 1865, and branches were located in Nashville, Chattanooga, Columbia, and Memphis. The Nashville branch generated more capital than the other Tennessee branches, with more than sixteen thousand accounts and in excess of $550,000 in deposits. Many of the depositors included newly formed benevolent and fraternal groups. Nationally, the Freedmen's Bank collapsed in 1873 due to a combination of factors including the 1873 financial depression, fraud and mismanagement in the national branch, risky loan policies, and poorly trained administrators.[21] While most depositors received a small portion of their money back after the collapse, some of the larger depositors lost thousands of dollars.

In short, the Reconstruction era in Tennessee was a time of tension and great change. It saw a change in labor relations as the formerly enslaved became paid laborers. It was a time that saw African Americans formally recognized as US citizens, with African American men receiving the right to vote. African Americans created churches and other institutions, and in general, created a society that they controlled. But it was also a time of violence by whites against African Americans. As organized hostilities against African Americans receded, systems of segregation became entrenched across the state in the following decades.

Post-Reconstruction (1877–1900)

The time between Reconstruction and the beginning of the twentieth century in Tennessee is characterized by the rise of white supremacy. This doctrine permeated all aspects of life and created the segregated society one thinks of when considering this period. Some whites viewed segregation as a way to "regulate" race relations in the state. They felt segregation "protected" African Americans from the racial prejudices of poorer whites as well as "protected" whites from the "lower-class crudeness" of African Americans. These "protections" created segregated facilities to keep the races apart, leading, in theory, to racial harmony. Other whites supported segregation due to their mistaken belief in the racial inferiority of all non-whites.[22] Due to these beliefs, segregation of public facilities steadily increased during this period.

Segregation gained ground in Tennessee during the 1880s, spreading haphazardly to hotels, theaters, and public parks.[23] After these facilities became segregated, other aspects of life, such as housing, followed. The African American community did not initially resist all forms of segregation. Having separate churches and lodges allowed African Americans to control those institutions, and it allowed African Americans leadership roles not permitted in the larger, white-controlled society. Leaders in the African American community did protest, loudly and vigorously, separate treatment that was not equal, as well as the segregation of public accommodations.[24] African Americans fought segregation in the 1880s, for example, by pushing against segregation on railroads and interstate transportation and filing lawsuits against individual cases of discrimination.[25] African Americans also resisted outside the legal system. For example, it was not uncommon for African Americans in Memphis to react to segregation practices with resistance and physical violence.[26]

In addition to increased public segregation, life in Tennessee changed in a variety of ways. Railroads became more present across the South and Tennessee and connected small communities to a larger world. By 1890, it is estimated that nine out of ten Southerners lived in a railroad county.[27] These railroads could take Tennesseans from their rural communities to larger towns and cities, where industries such as lumber mills in West Tennessee and coal and iron mining in East Tennessee had cropped up and taken root.[28] Nashville became home to sawmills, liquor distilleries, gristmills, papermills, and a petroleum refinery, and woolen mills were established in places such as Tullahoma and Jackson. Chattanooga became an iron-making center, with nine furnaces and seventeen foundries located across the city by 1885.[29] These industrial gains led to job opportunities for whites and African Americans; however, there was segregation in these opportunities as well. While African Americans were hired into these new industries, they were typically hired as unskilled laborers, even if they had worked in skilled occupations during slavery. These unskilled jobs were low paying and the work was irregular; many companies reserved the higher-paying skilled jobs for whites.[30] This economic atmosphere fostered the need for benevolent and fraternal groups in Tennessee to provide a social safety net for their members.

This period also saw African Americans speaking openly about their experiences in the segregated South. A Tennessee example of this is Sutton E. Griggs, an African American minister who came to Nashville in the 1890s to serve as pastor of the East First Baptist Church. In 1913, he moved to Memphis to become pastor of Tabernacle Baptist Church, remaining there until 1930, when he moved back to his native Texas.[31] Griggs was also a writer, and in 1907 he published *The One Great Question: A Study of Southern Conditions at Close Range*, based on his experiences as an African American living in segregated Nashville. He openly decried the segregated educational system, stating, "The facilities for the accommodation of the Negro children in the city public schools are not now and for years have not been adequate for their needs."[32] He discussed the impact of an unfair judicial system that was more hostile to African Americans: "All elements of the Negro population have grown to regard the Courts as the temple of injustice, rather than the temple of justice. . . . The Negroes have come to the conclusion that, as between an accusing policeman and a prisoner, there is absolutely no chance for the prisoner."[33] After describing Nashville as a place where African Americans were systematically excluded from politics and endured an unequal education system and an indifferent legal system, Griggs elaborated on the reality of everyday life in a segregated Southern city for African Americans. He wrote,

> It is by no means here contended that there are no good white people in the city. There are many who, personally, are as high-minded and humane as can be found anywhere. Nor do we seek to convey the impression that Negroes must dodge bullets every step they take as they walk along the streets. But we do most emphatically assert that the general feeling of the Negro population is one of insecurity; that they regard the government machinery as actively hostile; that they feel that not so much as the weight of a feather can be laid upon any white man of murderous instincts who may see fit to claim a Negro as his victim.[34]

A New Century (1900–1930)

The first decades of the twentieth century are known as the Progressive Era in United States history, a time when individuals and groups worked to correct what they saw was wrong with society, striving to improve social, economic, and political conditions. There was also a Progressive political movement that sought to increase participation in politics by advocating for direct election of United States senators, direct primaries, and the use of the recall and referendum in politics.[35] In Tennessee, the Progressive movement was not a political movement; although some Tennessee politicians supported Progressive goals at times, very few identified as Progressives.[36] One popular reform movement in Tennessee was temperance, or the removal of alcohol from public life. In Tennessee, Prohibition, the ban on manufacturing and selling alcohol, was enacted by the general assembly in 1909, a full decade before it was ratified in the rest of the nation.[37] The Progressive era also saw increased opposition to Jim Crow segregation from both individuals and groups in the African American community. Accommodation to segregation, the approach taken by many African American communities in 1900, had decreased by the beginning of World War I.[38]

In addition to social changes and a growing resistance to segregation, the state's demographics changed during this period. In 1900, the majority of Tennesseans lived in rural areas. Additionally, almost half of Tennessee's African American population, 48 percent, lived in West Tennessee, and of those, almost three-fourths were rural.[39] However, during the period between 1910 and 1930, African Americans began to leave both their rural communities and Tennessee itself in ever increasing numbers. Migration from Tennessee by African Americans was not new, and there had been other periods of migration. The Exoduster movement of the 1870s, for example, lasted from approximately 1869 to 1881 and saw the migration of African Americans from Tennessee to places further west, such as Kansas. A lack of funds, however, prevented many from reaching their western destinations. Those who successfully reached Kansas established several African American communities, such as Dunlap and Nicodemus. Approximately 5,400

Tennesseans moved to Kansas during the Exoduster period.[40] The migration of the 1910s and 1920s, however, was different; it was more spontaneous and unorganized, and more African Americans left the state. Between 1910 and 1920, Tennessee's African American population decreased by 4.5 percent. Of those who stayed behind, many moved to urban areas, increasing the number of African American urban residents by 13 percent.[41]

World War I also impacted the state, and over sixty-one thousand Tennesseans served in the war. Of that total, 17,339 were African Americans, many of whom used the war to demonstrate their loyalty to the United States.[42] More African Americans than whites applied for enlistment at military recruiting stations in Knoxville and Chattanooga. African Americans purchased war bonds to finance military operations, planted victory gardens, and volunteered with the Red Cross. Some African American leaders hoped the enthusiastic embrace of the war effort would entitle their community to receive more fair and equitable treatment following the war.[43] This hope did not bear fruit, as the end of the war saw a rise in racial tensions and a riot in Knoxville in 1919 that began when a group of white men violently searched the Knoxville jail for an African American man falsely accused of murdering a white woman. When they did not find him, the men attacked the African American community, which fought back. The riot lasted two days, resulted in the deaths of both African Americans and whites, and caused the migration of more than 1,500 African Americans from the city.[44]

Following World War I, Tennesseans faced reconciling increased modernization with their rural roots. Under the leadership of Austin Peay, inaugurated as governor in 1923, the road system was expanded and upgraded, allowing for modern culture to expand to more rural and isolated areas. Peay also standardized teacher licensing and created an equalized funding mechanism for schools that resulted in most public schools starting to offer an eight-month school year across the state.[45] In addition to these reforms, Tennesseans increasingly purchased modern items such as radios, which they used to listen to traditional music, such as country or blues, which in turn reaffirmed rural values.[46]

The 1920s saw the resurgence of a menace last seen during Reconstruction. The Ku Klux Klan reorganized in the 1920s and broadened their call for white supremacy by being anti-immigrant, anti-Catholic, and anti-Semitic as well. The Klan attracted support in Tennessee by opposing "immorality" and anything they felt assaulted traditional values. They opposed "wild dancing" and alcohol, destroying moonshine stills. They denounced "loose women," bringing allegations against prostitutes to local police and harassing divorced women on the streets.[47] More than two thousand white men in Knoxville alone had joined the Klan by 1923, and there were members of the Klan across the state. The Klan also became involved in politics, working to help elect Austin Peay as governor and Lawrence Tyson as senator in 1924. Klan membership did begin to decline in the state during the Great Depression.[48]

By 1930, Tennesseans born in 1850 or 1860 lived in a very different world. It was no longer legal to enslave people based on the color of their skin and force them to labor without wages. Although still very rural, towns and cities had grown across the state, changing it in profound ways.

Public education was available to all; however, the system of white supremacy created segregated educational systems that did not provide equal educational opportunities to Tennessee's citizens. Segregation was a way of life, extending to all public accommodations. This segregated system included a separate African American world controlled by African Americans. Fraternal and benevolent lodges were an important element of this world, serving a number of purposes and part of a network that extended across the state and beyond. What follows is the story of these lodges.

CHAPTER 1

The Rise of Fraternalism

Broader, and fully as interesting, is the
fact that in free and democratic America
there are more secret societies and a larger
aggregate membership among such organizations than in all other civilized countries.

—ALBERT C. STEVENS, 1907

A large "For Sale" sign, noting the site's "great potential,"
sits at the edge of a seemingly empty, large lot consisting
of slightly over thirty-seven acres in southwest Memphis.
Small trees and bushes located at the edge of the property
along the road obscure the view, as does a short concrete
fence. The real estate listing notes the great price for the
parcel, offered for sale at $125,000, and notes its potential
development uses: "residential, church, and park." The listing has its present usage as "none/vacant" and notes that
there are no improvements on the property. It is zoned for
single family or commercial usage.[1]

The lot is located on a four-lane road, with a state highway roughly a third of a mile away. To judge by the nearby church congregations, the neighborhood is likely predominantly African American. A CME church is three-tenths of a mile east of the lot, an African Methodist Episcopal (AME) Zion church lies three-tenths of a mile west, and one mile south is a Missionary Baptist Church. One of the churches has a small graveyard located on the property. Judging by the number of churches and homes in the area, this has obviously been a community for many years. The vacant lot is located a little over a mile south of Nonconnah Creek, and was likely part of the Nonconnah community. The interesting thing to note about the property, however, is not its development potential. This piece of property is also listed on the Shelby County Register of Deeds website as the site of the intriguingly named Union Forever Cemetery, established by the Union Forever Society.[2] If the Register of Deeds site is correct, this is the site of an African American lodge cemetery, one of at least three in Shelby County. The Union Forever Society is one of hundreds of African American benevolent and fraternal groups that proliferated across the state beginning in the nineteenth century and were important parts of their communities.

If it is a cemetery, as it appears likely, there is little that can be done to protect those who may be interred here. Native American graves and burial remains are protected by the Native American Graves Protection and Repatriation Act (NAGPRA), enacted in 1990, which provides for the repatriation of items of cultural patrimony, including burial remains.[3] Unmarked graves belonging to other ethnic or cultural groups, such as African Americans, can be excavated without a legal requirement to inform descendants or community stakeholders.[4] In Tennessee, if developers find human remains on a property, they are required to stop work immediately and notify the local medical examiner, law enforcement, and state archaeologist. The state archaeologist will work with the developer to consider how the work can continue in such a way as to avoid the burials; in the event that is not possible, a legal process must be followed to move the graves to a different location.[5] In Tennessee, state law allows for the termination of use as a cemetery of any burial ground that has been abandoned or is in neglected condition, or if it has activities or conditions nearby that do not display reverence for the dead.[6] The most likely scenario for this site, if it is the Union Forever Cemetery, is that if the presence of human remains are detected during development, they will most likely be moved to a different location and reinterred. Although its future is uncertain, the condition of the Union Forever Cemetery is not necessarily indicative of the state of the other lodge cemeteries across the state. Each of the three Grand Divisions in Tennessee contain African American lodge cemeteries, and these cemeteries are important resources for learning more about African American lodges and their members, and how African American fraternal groups continue to endure as community institutions into the twenty-first century.

Alexis de Tocqueville, a nineteenth-century French politician and author of *Democracy in America*, noted as early as 1838 the tendencies of Americans to create social groups both to promote order and industry and as a means of resisting moral temptations. However, Americans began forming fraternal and benevolent lodges much earlier than that, going back to the earliest days of the Republic.[7] Following the end of slavery in 1865, the formerly enslaved took advantage of their newly gained freedom to create thousands of different types of organizations for themselves, including but not limited to debating clubs, fraternal lodges, drama societies, temperance clubs, tradesmen groups, and equal rights clubs.[8] Faced with increasing governmental neglect or outright exclusion from economic and political opportunity, freedmen and -women created their own network of self-help groups, known as fraternal and benevolent groups, to fill the welfare gaps of their society.[9] These groups fulfilled purposes beyond welfare as well, such as the creation of community ties and opportunities for leadership development for their members.[10] They also provided opportunities for African Americans to organize themselves across class and economic lines.[11] Over the years, fraternal and benevolent groups became a place where African Americans could meet as equals, regardless of class, education, or religious differences. What other American institution allowed a laundress and a doctor's wife to meet in the same organization and be equally able to hold office? What are these groups that made up such an integral part of the society and culture of the time?

Sociologists and historians typically divide these lodges in the United States into three groups—fraternal, benevolent, and insurance. Fraternal lodges include groups such as the Masons, the Elks, the Grand United Order of Odd Fellows (GUOOF), and the Knights of Pythias (also known as the Pythians) and are usually the best known to people not terribly familiar with the concept of fraternalism. The primary focus of fraternal groups is the meeting ritual, as well as the regalia that members must wear during said rituals. Fraternal lodges often include graduated levels of membership to allow members to work toward higher rank within the organization. In addition to a ritual and special clothing, they stress the importance of the bonds of brotherhood and/or sisterhood; as such, keeping the rituals of the lodge secret from nonmembers is an important part of fraternal life. These lodges can, and often did, also offer some form of a safety net to their members, such as benefits paid out to sick members or burial benefits; however, these benefits were not the defining characteristics. Fraternal lodges typically limited membership to adult males; however, some groups created auxiliary lodges for females, such as the Order of the Eastern Star (the auxiliary for the Masons), the Household of Ruth (the auxiliary organization of the GUOOF), and the Order of Calanthe (the auxiliary for the Pythians).[12] Many of these lodges and their auxiliary organizations continue to exist in Tennessee and the United States.

Benevolent groups differ from fraternal organizations in a variety of ways. A benevolent organization's primary goal and purpose was to offer an economic safety net to members or to enable members to work to better society in some way, such as attempting to end the consumption of alcohol. In a time before the federal government offered its citizens any sort of welfare or economic safety net, these groups typically offered the only monetary benefit a person could rely upon in times of illness or death. While benevolent groups could have a special meeting ritual or designated regalia for special occasions, the primary purpose did not center on ritual or regalia. Benevolent groups were numerous across the United States, with some beginning in the decades prior to the Civil War. A number of different ethnic groups, such as the Germans or the Irish, started benevolent societies to benefit their members, many of whom were new immigrants to the United States. Examples in Tennessee include the Knoxville Hebrew Benevolent Society, a Jewish organization active by 1869, and the Chattanooga Turn Verein, a German gymnastics organization operating in that city by 1871.[13] Irish groups were represented in Tennessee, with the Friendly Sons of St. Patrick, an organization created in 1771 in Philadelphia, meeting monthly in Memphis by 1868.[14] Other types of benevolent groups present in Tennessee focused on social issues, such as the Sons of Temperance, who worked for the elimination of alcohol in American life; this organization had three lodges in Nashville alone in 1860.[15] Benevolent groups of various types were located in towns and cities across the state, and it is impossible to document the sheer number of these groups or how long they lasted.

The third type of lodge group is best described as insurance societies, and they primarily offered life and burial insurance to their members. Some companies offered sickness insurance, which could be used to pay for medical treatment. The member typically had to undergo an examination of sort, either by a doctor or a visit from the sickness committee, in order to qualify for the benefit. Additionally, there was often a limit to the length of time a member would receive the paid benefit. These organizations differ from benevolent groups in a number of ways. They are not associations of like-minded people united together in a common purpose. Rather, they are businesses founded upon actuarial principles to which people made small payments, and in return, received a financial benefit in the case of sickness or death. There are no meetings or any type of community for members. Fraternal insurance groups in the African American community began in the late nineteenth century, at a time when a number of publications depicted African Americans as poor insurance risks for traditional insurance companies. African Americans started several fraternal insurance companies that flourished.[16] The Grand United Order of True Reformers, a fraternal group based in Richmond, Virginia, is recognized as the first African American society to offer life insurance benefits beyond funeral costs to the membership.[17] The first Tennessean-owned African American insurance organization in the state was the Universal Life Insurance Company, established in 1923 in Memphis, and by 1930 it was one of the eight largest African American insurance companies in the nation.[18] While important to members of the African American community, insurance societies will not be discussed in detail in this work.

For African Americans, finding fraternal and benevolent lodges that admitted them to membership was often difficult; white lodges would not admit them due to members' racism and tightening Jim Crow laws prohibiting members of different races meeting together. In answer to this discrimination, African Americans formed their own fraternal and benevolent lodges, sometimes direct counterparts to white organizations. For example, in 1775 an African American named Prince Hall approached a British military Masonic lodge in Boston and asked to be an apprentice member. This lodge, Irish Military Lodge No. 441, accepted him and fifteen other African Americans into membership, initiating them into the lodge on March 6, 1775.[19] Prince Hall fought for the American colonies during the American Revolution, and following the war, he and his fellow African American members requested a charter to establish a separate lodge. After the local (white) lodge refused the request, Prince Hall petitioned the Grand Lodge in England for a charter, which was granted in 1787, thereby creating the only Masonic group accepting African Americans as members for many decades.[20]

Approaching an English lodge for a charter of establishment was a path followed by several other African American fraternal groups, as the English did not typically refuse a lodge charter on the basis of race. Peter Ogden, an African American freedman, was refused a charter for the whites-only International Order of Odd Fellows (IOOF) in the United States, so he traveled to Great Britain in 1842 and received a charter from the Grand United Order of Odd Fellows (GUOOF), the British branch of the Odd Fellows.[21] This created an American GUOOF organization in parallel to the IOOF. Another approach in the United States involved obtaining a copy of the ritual of a white lodge and using it to create a parallel organization for African Americans. After African Americans were denied admission to a Benevolent and Protective Order of Elks (BPOE) lodge in Cincinnati, Ohio, Arthur Riggs obtained a copy of their ritual that the white Elks had failed to legally protect. Riggs used this ritual to create a parallel Elks organization for African Americans known as the Improved Benevolent and Protective Order of Elks of the World (IBPOEW). Threatened by whites with lynching for his role in starting the African American Elks, Riggs quit his job as Pullman porter and withdrew from public life.[22] This story repeated itself in the case of the

Knights of Pythias. A few African American men who could "pass" as white were admitted to a white Pythian lodge and then shared the ritual with their fellow African Americans, allowing for the creation of a parallel organization.[23] This continued through the twentieth century as one type of African American response to segregation in fraternalism.

Other types of white organizations also typically denied admittance to African Americans, who therefore created separate networks of their own. Although some of these new groups, such as the Benevolent Society of Tennessee, claimed that their organizations began before the Civil War, most of them began during the aftermath of the Civil War, during the transition period from slavery to freedom.[24] During this time, African Americans created a number of organizations designed to help the sick, widows, orphans, and any person regarded as less well-off. This creation of benevolent lodges may represent an extension of the idea of family in African American society, as members of African American communities understood their collective respon- sibility to care for each generation.[25] African Americans worked together in a number of ways in both rural and urban communities, watching each other's children, caring for older relatives in their households, and offering assistance to newcomers who moved to the area from elsewhere. This concept of mutual aid and care for one another extended at times to people refusing jobs from someone who fired a neighbor or relative.[26] Combined with the concept of mutual aid was the idea of "collective self-improvement," which extended into benevolent groups assisting nonmembers facing destitution or a need of some sort.[27] This is shown in some of the published histories and founding documents of several African American benevolent groups. The Grand United Order of True Reformers, an African American fraternal group founded in Richmond, Virginia, stated in a 1909 history of the group that they had an obligation to teach the children "to assist each other in sickness, sorrow and afflictions and in the struggles of life . . . teach them to care for the sick and afflicted, relieve and comfort the distressed, and bear each other's burdens."[28] The Working People's Labor and Art Association, an African American benevolent group originating in Nashville, stated in their constitution their aim was "to elevate, unite, and give employment to the Negro youth, to establish and encourage charitable undertakings, to encourage and foster trades, trade schools and any enterprise that will guarantee the Negro a livelihood, make his labor in demand to all avenues of life, and to be of practical utility to the race and state."[29] The Independent Pole Bearers Association Number 9, whose cemetery will be discussed later, stated in their Articles of Incorporation that one of their purposes was to "hold social meetings *for the purpose of the advancement of each other*" (emphasis added).[30] A thread that ties many of these benevolent and fraternal groups together were their twin duties to care for multiple generations and to offer education and training for the younger members of the community.

What sort of fraternal and benevolent lodge groups existed in Tennessee during the nineteenth and early twentieth centuries? The traditional fraternal lodges associated with African American society, such as the Prince Hall Masons, the Elks, the Grand United Order of Odd Fellows, and the Knights of Pythias, all established lodges in Tennessee in the decades following the Civil War. However, it is almost impossible to calculate the number of different benevolent groups existing in Tennessee in the later nineteenth and early twentieth century. Some were purely local, confined to the single town or city where they were established. Others, however, were part of larger regional or state-wide organizations. Additionally, a few national benevolent groups also established lodges in Tennessee. In my research over the last decade I have found evidence of more than one hundred different African American benevolent societies with more than 756 lodges across Tennessee during this time period. It is a conservative estimate of the number of African American benevolent lodges to say that there were hundreds across the state, consisting of thousands of members, all working to create better communities and offer members opportunities to care for each other. What follows is a discussion of some of the larger groups found in Tennessee.

As stated earlier, Prince Hall Masons date their beginnings in the United States to 1775, but the precise beginnings of Prince Hall Masonry in Tennessee is unknown. By 1871, African American Masonic lodges were located in towns such as Nashville, Knoxville, Memphis, Chattanooga, Brownsville, Columbia, and Lebanon, and there were at least six to seven hundred Masons across the state.[31] Masonic lodges continued to spread during the remainder of the nineteenth and early twentieth centuries. In addition to offering the benefits of fraternalism to its members, Prince Hall Masonic lodges in Tennessee offered leadership opportunities to their members in a variety of areas. A notable example of Masonic leadership occurred in 1908 when the Masons, along with the benevolent Independent

Order of Immaculates, boycotted the town of Pulaski, Tennessee, following the lynching of an African American man by a mob. When officials refused to press charges against those in the white community who organized and participated in the lynching, the Prince Hall Masons and the Immaculates both canceled the state-wide conventions scheduled in Pulaski that year. This cancellation resulted in an economic loss for Pulaski, as hundreds of members would have gathered in the town for the meetings.[32] Prince Hall Masons showed leadership in other ways across the state, such as in 1918 when the Grand Lodge purchased the first Liberty Bond issued in the Federal Reserve district, in the amount of $1,000, as part of the World War I war effort.[33] Masons also worked to register African Americans to vote across the state. In 1957, Charles F. Williams, Grand Master of the Prince Hall Masons in Tennessee, wrote a letter that urged all Masons across the state to register to vote. He stated, "It is especially imperative that Negroes realize and understand the importance of registration and voting. As a minority group, as a neglected group, . . . we must be doubly zealous in the duties of citizens, primarily among which are registration and voting."[34] Considering that this was during a time period when African American participation in voting was discouraged by law as well as by practice, this showed considerable leadership on the part of the Masons. In fact, this insistence on voter registration in Memphis's African American community came nearly two years before the NAACP in Memphis launched a voter registration drive in the community.[35] The topic of Prince Hall Masonic participation in the civil rights movement is one that is ripe for exploration, as it may broaden our view of who was involved in the movement. The Masons continue in existence throughout the state, serving their communities in a variety of ways.

The Improved Benevolent and Protective Order of Elks of the World is the African American parallel organization to the Benevolent and Protective Order of Elks, which only admitted whites to its membership during the nineteenth and early twentieth centuries. By the early twentieth century, the IBPOEW had spread to eight states, including Tennessee, from its home state of Ohio.[36] The history of the organization in Tennessee during its early years was rocky and its growth unsteady, as an incident in Shelby County demonstrates. In 1907, a group of African Americans started an IBPOEW lodge in Memphis; later that same year, a group of white men noticed a group of African Americans wearing their Elks pins on Main Street. Enraged that African Americans had the audacity to create their own lodge and wear the same symbols as they did, the white Elks in Memphis sued the IBPOEW in chancery court to prevent them from using the name, ritual, title, or symbols of the Elks.[37] Although the African American Elks argued that no one could confuse the two groups, as only African Americans were admitted to the IBPOEW and only whites were admitted to the BPOE, the supreme court in Tennessee ultimately ruled in favor of the white Elks, banning the IBPOEW from organizing in Shelby County. This injunction remained in place for more than thirty years.[38] This case hampered the efforts of the IBPOEW to organize in the state, although the group did eventually establish lodges in towns across the state and continues to exist in both the United States and in Tennessee, with five hundred thousand members worldwide.[39]

The Grand United Order of Odd Fellows is the African American parallel organization to the white Order of Odd Fellows. The first GUOOF lodge established in Tennessee may have been the Memphis Star Lodge #1501, organized in 1872.[40] Although a fraternal order focused on ritual, regalia, and ranked membership, the GUOOF also offered some insurance benefits to its members. By the 1910s, it was an extraordinarily popular order nationwide;[41] in Tennessee, membership numbered more than six thousand.[42] African Americans established lodges of the GUOOF across the state in all three Grand Divisions, in towns such as Martin, Trenton, Newbern, Jackson, Clarksville, Cowan, Sparta, Murfreesboro, Dandridge, Cleveland, Jonesborough, and Coal Creek. Although in abeyance in Tennessee for a number of years, the GUOOF is working in 2020 to re-establish lodges in Tennessee.[43]

The Independent Order of Good Samaritans and Daughters of Samaria, known better as the Good Samaritans, began as a gender-integrated benevolent group in 1847 focusing primarily on temperance. Not only did they work to ban alcohol from all aspects of American life, the group also promised aid to "distressed families" that pledged to abstain from "intoxicating drinks." Their ritual was based on the Biblical story of the Good Samaritan, and their emblem was a dove and olive branch enclosed by a triangle, with the words "Love," "Purity," and "Truth" on each side of the triangle. In addition to being gender-integrated, the Good Samaritans were racially integrated as well, allowing African Americans to join separate lodges; however, African Americans were not allowed to hold any national leadership roles.[44] In addition to not allowing African Americans to hold leadership positions over white members, individual lodges could not have African American and white members meeting together. African American members were allowed to participate in the national convention, but they could only vote on matters pertaining to African American lodges. By the 1870s, however, African Americans made up the majority of the membership and began moving into national leadership roles; whites then withdrew from the organization. The year 1877 was the last year that the Good Samaritans was a racially mixed organization.[45]

It is unclear when the first lodge of Good Samaritans was established in Tennessee, or the true reach of the organization within the state. An 1870 Nashville newspaper mentioned the group, stating, "The Samaritans, a colored benevolent association of this city, gave a large supper at No. 78 Cherry Street, last night, which was numerously attended."[46] The group was mentioned again in Nashville in 1874, although that event was not so well attended. The *Nashville Union and American* reported, "The Colored Women's Good Samaritan Society No. 2 gave a festival at the Courthouse last night. . . . The managers had thought of holding the festival two nights, but the attendance was so small last evening that they were uncertain whether to repeat the entertainment tonight."[47] There were at least two Good Samaritan lodges in Knoxville, as the *Knoxville Daily Chronicle* reported on the anniversary of Good Samaritan Lodge No. 2, which was "composed of a large number of the most respected and influential colored men of our city."[48] A lodge no. 2 indicates that there was also a Good Samaritan Lodge No. 1 in that city. The Good Samaritans do not appear to be in existence at present.

In 1869, African Americans in Philadelphia established the Knights of Pythias of North and South America, Europe, Asia, and Africa, the parallel organization to the white Order of the Knights of Pythias, known more informally as the Knights of Pythias, or just the Pythians. Much like the GUOOF, the Knights of Pythias centered primarily on ritual but also offered social insurance benefits to its members.[49] The Pythians had established lodges in most of the major cities and towns of Tennessee by the end of the nineteenth and beginning of the twentieth centuries. Pythians created lodges in Nashville, Chattanooga, Jackson, Columbia, Clarksville, Memphis, Morristown, and Pulaski. By 1892, the Pythians were a major presence in Memphis, where there were seventeen lodges and seven courts in that city alone.[50] However, by 1911, the Pythians were under attack from the white parallel organization in both Tennessee and Georgia. White Pythians in both states filed injunctions against the African American Pythians to prevent their operating in those states. *The Crisis*, the publication of the National Association for the Advancement of Colored People (NAACP), reported in March 1912 that "the Knights of Pythias of Tennessee have succeeded in getting a final court decision, restraining the colored Knights of Pythias from operating in the State."[51] In May 1912, the US Supreme Court intervened, issuing a Writ of Error against the supreme court of Tennessee, allowing the African American Pythians in the state to continue.[52] The Supreme Court decision helped the growth of the African American Pythians, and by 1912 there were 22,200 members of the Pythians and 475 lodges in Tennessee.[53] The Knights of Pythias continues to exist in a number of states across America.

It is believed that an AME clergyman named Moses Dickson created the Knights and Daughters of Tabor (also known as the Taborians) in Independence, Missouri, in 1872, although others claim the organization dates to an anti-slavery secret society created in 1846 known as the Order of the Twelve.[54] Whatever the origins, there were Taborian lodges in Memphis by 1880, and by 1908, there were seven hundred Taborians and eighteen Taborian lodges in that city alone.[55] Taborians were also found in Jackson and Nashville.[56] In 1913, the Taborians in Franklin moved to a new home in south Franklin and invited the public to a banquet and public installation of officers at their new location.[57] The Taborians designated male members as knights, who met in Temples, and they designated female members as daughters, who met in Tabernacles.[58]The Taborians were especially numerous and popular in neighboring Mississippi, where they opened Taborian Hospital, staffed entirely by African Americans, in Mound Bayou, Mississippi.[59] The hospital closed in 1983, but in 2007, the organization reformed and now works in that area to preserve the history of Mound Bayou, with a mission to use the remaining buildings of the Taborian Hospital to tell the town's story.[60]

In 1892, Chester W. Keatts of Arkansas and J. E. Bush, a Tennessee native, established the benevolent organization known as the Mosaic Templars. The group originally began as a local group that assisted widows of men living in Little Rock, Arkansas; however, branches of the group quickly spread to other states.[61] As with other benevolent organizations, the Mosaic Templars offered both sickness and burial benefits to its members.[62] Women and men could both join as members, with female members organized in Chambers and male members organized in Temples. If a town had no organized Temple lodge but did have an organized Chamber lodge, men could join the Chamber lodge. The extent of Mosaic Templar membership in Tennessee is unclear due to a 2005 fire at the headquarters of the Mosaic Templars in Little Rock, Arkansas, that destroyed membership records of the order. I have documented Mosaic Templar lodges in Fayetteville, Jackson, Grand Junction, La Grange, Moscow, McKenzie, Trenton, Nashville, Winchester, and Vildo, and found Mosaic Templar tombstones in other towns as well. The state headquarters were located at 419 Columbia Avenue in Franklin, Tennessee.[63] The Mosaic Templars did not survive the Great Depression, but a museum dedicated to the history of the order is located in Little Rock at the site of the former national headquarters.

The Benevolent Society (also known as the Colored Benevolent Society) was established in Nashville in the 1860s, offering members both sickness and burial benefits. Some historians assert the group was established in 1865 and incorporated in 1866, and the articles of incorporation registered with the state were revised in 1868 to allow the Benevolent Society to create lodges across the state.[64] However, the 1890 Constitution for the group states that the group was organized on August 15, 1853, while a sign in a Benevolent Cemetery in Nashville has an establishment date of 1862.[65] In short, the exact date of the organization of the Benevolent Society is unclear. To join this group, members paid an initiation fee of one dollar and monthly dues of fifty cents, and agreed to abide by the society's rules.[66] The Benevolent Society flourished in the state, particularly in Middle Tennessee, and lodges could be found in

Nashville, Fayetteville, Port Royal, Jackson, Murfreesboro, Shelbyville, Sparta, and Memphis. Several Benevolent Society lodges also organized cemeteries for the burial of their members, a number of which are still in use. While most of the Benevolent Society lodges appear inactive, at least one, the Port Royal Benevolent Lodge No. 210, continues in operation as an active presence in its community. Although a white supremacist group burned their lodge hall in 1994, the group raised funds and built a new building on their property in 2001.[67]

In 1868, a group of young men in Nashville created a benevolent organization known as the Young Men's Immaculate Association. Despite its name, the Immaculate Association admitted both men and women to the group, and members received sickness, accident, and disability benefits. In 1872, some of its members created a successor organization named the Independent Order of Immaculates.[68] This group spread to other states, and by 1907, one could find lodges in Tennessee, Alabama, Mississippi, Georgia, Arkansas, Kansas, Kentucky, Texas, and Ohio.[69] It is not surprising, given its origin in Tennessee, that lodges of the Immaculates flourished in the state. Different sources often praised the Immaculates as an excellent organization. The *Pulaski Citizen* reported on the group in 1878: "This order, which was instituted entirely by colored men, is composed of the most intelligent young men of the race." It went on to further state that the membership in Pulaski was "very large and composed of the most intelligent and enterprising colored people."[70] A newspaper in Milan, Tennessee, praised the organization in 1882 for paying the widow of a recently deceased member a death benefit of $1,000. The paper stated, "The order of Immaculates thus proves itself to be honest and well managed."[71] In 1884, during an annual meeting of the Immaculates in Memphis that drew attendees from several states, the *Memphis Daily Appeal* reported, "Though the streets have been crowded with members of the order for two days, no accident or unbecoming conduct on their part has been reported, and the fact that such is the case shows not only the good influences which the order exerts, but the excellence of its management."[72] By 1908, Memphis was home to three lodges of Immaculates with a membership of more than five hundred. In his book about African American life in Memphis published that year, G. P. Hamilton stated that the Immaculates "numbers among its members some of the best and most progressive people in Memphis. It has done much good in the past and its prospects for the future were never brighter than now."[73]

For an organization that grew into a national organization, no archival repository appears to house the records of the Immaculates, and it is difficult to ascertain when the group stopped operating. They appear to have survived World War I, as Nashville listed ten lodges being active in the 1924 city directory.[74] Alabama's *Annual Report of the Commissioner of Insurance* in 1920 stated that the organization had 1,156 members in that state; however, the report raised concerns about the financial situation. The report stated, "its financial condition is fairly satisfactory, however, it is very necessary that its rates should be revised upwards and upon a more intelligent plan in the place of the makeshift that they are using at present. . . . The system of accounts in use is not entirely satisfactory."[75] The organization existed in Arkansas as late as 1920, when the state lodge held a convention in

Little Rock with more than five hundred attendees.[76] The *Chicago Defender* reported in 1945 that the Immaculates lodge in Gallatin, Tennessee, had recently celebrated their annual Thanksgiving sermon at First Baptist Church.[77] In 1952, the Alabama grand lodge held a state convention in Tuskegee and reported that they looked forward to a great future.[78] It does not appear that the Immaculates continue to exist at present, and little trace of them can be found on the landscape.

The Independent Pole Bearers Association began in Memphis as a semimilitary organization allowed by the civil authorities to bear arms in the years following the Civil War. The fact that the group bore arms clearly worried whites during the period, as there are several references to the group as being "insolent," "bullies," and other racist terms. The *Memphis Daily Appeal* reported on the group on August 25, 1870, "The mokes had a picnic yesterday. As usual the pole bearers (better polecaters) were out in force, with Masonic aprons and other toggery. The procession was headed by a band of n*** music, and had every mackerel in town at its heels."[79] In 1871, it was noted that "Two hundred negroes, armed with pikes, and styling themselves 'Pole Bearers,' paraded through the streets to-day. . . . The society of Pole Bearers is a branch of the Grand Army of the Republic, and is a well organized military battalion."[80] The *Public Ledger* in Memphis on June 5, 1874, noted,

The Pole Bearers Association is composed principally of negroes who served in the Federal army. It is a military organization, about six hundred strong, and they are regarded as bullies and fighters by the other colored

associations. Indeed, other colored organizations have
but little use for the Pole Bearers, who are a terror to their
own people. Those arms should be taken from them as a
precautionary measure. Should the insolent Pole Bearers
ever start a riot not one of them would be left to tell the
tale on the bluffs. We give them this advice gratis.[81]

By the time the Pole Bearers invited General Nathan
Bedford Forrest, General Gideon Pillow, Congressman H.
Casey Young, and Memphis Alderman Henry G. Dent to
speak at their July Fourth celebration in 1875, their reputa-
tion in Memphis was mixed.[82] This event, however, was significant, in that the Pole Bearers seemingly wanted an event
that highlighted reconciliation between former Confederates
and the formerly enslaved. On July 3, 1875, the program for
the event was printed in the newspaper, and one of items
highlighted was to be the "presentation of bouquet by young
colored ladies to General Forrest, as a memento of peace
and reconciliation."[83] Local press acknowledged the concern
over this meeting between these former Confederates and
the local African American community, stating, "There was
no little anxiety as to the probable result of this meeting
and conference."[84] Forrest addressed those gathered at this
event, stating, "I am your friend, for my interests are your
interests, and your interests are my interests . . . [I] shall do
all in my power to bring about peace. It has always been my
motto to elevate every man—to depress none."[85] He made
no mention of the hundreds of enslaved he had sold through
his work as a slave trader prior to the war, of the hundreds
of United States Colored Troops (USCT) massacred by men
under his command at Fort Pillow during the Civil War, or

of his role as first Grand Wizard of the Ku Klux Klan, an organization that terrorized African Americans across the state.[86] Having Forrest speak before at the July Fourth celebration likely did make the group seem more palatable to whites living in Memphis.

At some point within a few decades of its organization, the group abandoned its militaristic origins and operated primarily as a benevolent group.[87] For example, the 1879 Articles of Incorporation for Independent Pole Bearers Association No. 2 stated the purpose of the group was to "establish a means whereby we may secure for each other exemption from neglect, in the exigencies of sickness, want and death."[88] The group amassed enough resources to erect a lodge hall at the corner of Second and Washington in Memphis by 1872.[89] In addition to their benevolent work, the Pole Bearers also held celebrations for their members, as on New Year's Eve 1873, when they held an officer installation, emancipation celebration, comic pantomime, and masquerade ball on the same evening.[90] By the early twentieth century, G. P. Hamilton, an African American principal of Kortrecht High School in Memphis, noted that the Pole Bearers had seventeen different lodges in Memphis with six hundred members. Hamilton noted, "It has no endowment but it takes proper care of its sick and gives its dead a respectable burial."[91] Several Pole Bearer lodges still exist in the Shelby County area. Pole Bearers Lodge No. 9 is still an active presence in Memphis, and although a fire destroyed their hall in December 2018, the cemetery is still in use.[92] Pole Bearers Lodge No. 12 continues to own property in Shelby County, and Pole Bearers Lodge No. 6 also currently owns a lodge building in Shelby County.

Multiple African American groups bore names with the word *Zion*, such as the Sons of Zion, the Daughters of Zion, the Sisters of Zion, or the Sons and Daughters of Zion. It is unclear if there was one overarching group made up of all these groups, or if each of these groups was a separate and distinct lodge. Wilson County saw the establishment of a Daughters of Zion group that held a Christmas fair at the Wilson County courthouse in Lebanon in 1867. The newspaper noted, "We are pleased to see the colored people here turning their attention to things useful, and would recommend those at a distance to follow their example. By this means they will make friends of all good citizens, who will then take pleasure in assisting them."[93] Clarksville in Montgomery County was home to the Daughters of Zion No. 1 in 1876, whose purpose was "taking care of the sick members of said society and for the purpose of burying such members as may die, and for the purpose of mutual assistance to the members of said society."[94]

Memphis was home to a number of groups with the term *Zion* in the name during the later nineteenth and early twentieth centuries. In 1867, Daughters of Zion in that city joined with the United Sons of Ham, the Sons of Zion, and Benevolent Society No. 2 to celebrate the Fourth of July with "speechifying, singing, dancing, eating and drinking, and holiday enjoyment generally."[95] The Daughters of Zion No. 3 organized in 1869 in Memphis, met at the Providence AME church, and had a bank account in the Freedmen's Bank.[96] The 1874 *Boyle & Chapman's Memphis City Directory* noted that the Daughters of Zion had a membership of 270 that year.[97] There was a Sisters of Zion lodge meeting in 1874 with a membership of 150.[98] Some historians note that both the Sisters of Zion and the Daughters of Zion in Memphis primarily drew their membership from the city's working class.[99]

In addition to the Daughters and Sisters of Zion, a Sons of Zion existed in Memphis and was possibly one of the older benevolent groups in the city.[100] There may have been two different groups with a similar name. In 1874, the Sons of Zion met on Rayburn Avenue with a membership of 200, while the United Sons and Daughters of Zion No. 1 met at the Beale Street Church with a membership of 270.[101] It is unclear if the two lodges are connected. In 1873, the United Sons of Zion purchased land and established the Zion Christian Cemetery in Memphis, and began using the burial ground in 1876.[102] This cemetery will be described in more detail later.

An interesting group originating in Tennessee that spread beyond the borders of the state is the Ancient Order United Knights and Daughters of Africa, founded in Nashville in 1888 by Dr. D. L. Martin. Martin founded the group "upon the principles of race pride and the general elevation of the negro race." Using pride in being of African descent, something that the larger American culture derided, likely propelled the group's growth, as it was reported that the organization had 138 lodges within two years. The organization was described as being "purely benevolent and nonpolitical."[103] By 1900, a mere twelve years after its foundation, lodges could be found in Tennessee, Alabama, Missouri, Kansas, Illinois, Arkansas, Pennsylvania, and New York. There was even a travelling representative of the order based in Africa, who reportedly established a lodge in Monrovia, Liberia.[104]

The Knights and Daughters of Africa mixed teaching pride in being of African descent with the ideals of "knighthood" to promote moral uplift in their communities. They also had separate juvenile lodges for children and youth, working to promote their values to a younger generation. For the juvenile lodges, the group worked to teach "the principles of unity, race pride and morality."[105] The Knights and Daughters also avoided politics at all costs, as the governing laws of the organization forbade all political discussion in the grand and subordinate lodges. It is as if the group had decided that the mixture of teaching racial pride with ideals of Victorian respectability and avoiding "politics" would most help African Americans advance in American society, as well as make the group more palatable to white society.

In the early decades of the group's history, leadership of the national organization was dominated by Tennesseans. Dr. D. L. Martin served in a variety of leadership positions, including Supreme Master. He was also the editor of the *Palladium*, the organization's monthly newspaper.[106] Another prominent Nashvillian, Dr. R. F. Boyd, served in leadership roles, including the Supreme Secretary of the Order.[107] In 1904, the organization voted to purchase property on South Cherry Street in Nashville to create a home office.[108] It does not appear that the property was ever purchased by the group, and following the deaths of Boyd and Martin, leadership of the organization no longer belonged to Tennesseans. By the 1930s, the group was dominated by those who lived in St. Louis and Chicago. It appears the group may have faded from existence in Tennessee.

The Sons of Ham were a major presence in both Memphis and Nashville in the years following the Civil War and possibly earlier. The Memphis Sons of Ham predates the Civil War, and they remained active in the city throughout Reconstruction.[109] Newspapers of the period mention them taking part in parades and other official processions on multiple occasions, though typically ones that were not celebrated by white residents in Memphis. In 1866, the Sons of Ham led a procession in Memphis to commemorate the anniversary of the capture of Memphis by Union forces in 1862.[110] The lodge also organized an event in Memphis in 1866 to celebrate West India Emancipation, where "speeches were made, and eating and dancing and other forms of merrymaking observed."[111] West India Emancipation refers to the August 1, 1838, anniversary of the end of slavery in British colonies in the Caribbean. For many of African descent living in North America, this emancipation gave hope that slavery in the Americas would eventually end, and it was celebrated as a holiday for decades in communities across North America.[112] In 1875, the Sons of Ham observed Independence Day with a picnic at Humboldt Park attended by over two thousand African Americans. Sons of Ham No. 2, a second lodge, also held a picnic that same day at Alexander Park, a popular picnic ground in Memphis located on the south side of Vance Street, west of the Memphis & Charleston Railroad.[113] In 1880, when former president (and general) Ulysses S. Grant visited Memphis, the United Sons of Ham No. 1 acted as marshal for the welcome parade and United Sons of Ham No. 2 was part of the procession, with more than two hundred members taking part in this parade.[114] While it is unclear when the organization ceased to exist in Memphis, references to the group are found as late as 1891, when the Sons of Ham Hall was located at the corner of Beale and Hernando Streets.[115]

Davidson County was also home to a group called the Sons of Ham, and in 1869, the Sons of Ham No. 1 of Edgefield Junction was incorporated "for the purpose of raising funds for the systematic relief, protection, and education of its members; and for the care of the sick and burial of the dead."[116] It is unclear if the Nashville and Memphis Sons of Hams had any type of connection or if they were part of a larger organization of Sons of Ham. In 1872, the Sons of Ham in Nashville held a procession during an African American fair, with more than one hundred lodge members taking part in the procession.[117] As with other groups, it is not clear when and if the Sons of Ham in Nashville ceased to exist.

Multiple African American groups with the term *Relief* in the name existed in Tennessee, such as the Sons of Relief and the Daughters of Relief. Nashville was home to the Sons of Relief before the end of the Civil War. The *Nashville Daily Union* mentioned on March 21, 1865, that the Sons of Relief celebrated the end of slavery in Tennessee:

The colored people of Nashville yesterday held high festival in a celebration of their deliverance from slavery through the ratification, by the people of Tennessee of the amendment of the Constitution abolishing and prohibiting slavery. . . . At half past ten the procession entered the public square . . . then boys, more music, the extensively represented order "The Sons of Relief," in the white collars of their order.[118]

The Sons of Relief in Nashville organized as a benevolent organization with the intent to assist widows and orphans, feed the poor, help the sick, and bury the dead. In 1869, their charter was revised to allow the group to purchase or lease real estate.[119] Perhaps not coincidentally, that same year the Sons of Relief joined with the Colored Benevolent Society to organize Mount Ararat Cemetery in Nashville.[120] It is unclear when the group died out, but by 1920, the group was no longer listed in the *Nashville City Directory*. There were other Sons of Relief lodges across the state, and it is not clear if they were connected to each other. Wilson County was home to a Sons of Relief lodge in 1878, whose purpose was to "bury the dead, provide for the sick and needy, and to encourage industry & good citizenship."[121] Dyer County, in northwest Tennessee, was also home to a Sons of Relief lodge in 1876.[122] In April 1870, Sons of Relief lodges from the towns of Nashville, Franklin, Murfreesboro, and Gallatin participated in a celebration of the ratification of the fifteenth amendment held at Fisk University.[123] There was also a Sons of Relief lodge in Sand Hill, a community in Rutherford County.[124]

The United Brothers of Friendship was created in Louisville, Kentucky, in 1861, by a group of African Americans consisting of both freed and enslaved members. The Civil War disrupted the group, and William H. Gibson reorganized it in 1868.[125] Gibson, born in Baltimore as a freedman in 1829, moved to Louisville in 1847, where he worked as a teacher in Freedmen's Bureau schools and as a cashier in the Freedmen's Bank.[126] He was always serving his community in some way, so it is not surprising that Gibson took the opportunity to re-form an organization dedicated to helping others. The organization established a women's auxiliary, known as the Sisters of the Mysterious Ten, in 1878.[127] By 1871, the United Brothers had spread across Kentucky, and by 1875, into neighboring states. A benevolent organization, the United Brothers offered sickness and burial benefits to its members.[128]

Although it is unclear when the first United Brothers of Friendship was organized in Tennessee, there were at least four lodges in the state in 1897, located in Memphis, Nashville, Jackson, and Clarksville.[129] In 1910, the *Nashville Globe* reported that West Tennessee was home to more United Brothers of Friendship lodges than any other section of the state.[130] In 1913, Mr. P. F. Hill, the Grand Master of the group in the state, established lodges of the order in Pulaski and Mount Pleasant.[131] Historians believe the national organization did not survive the Great Depression and World War II.[132] The full extent of the reach of the United Brothers of Friendship in Tennessee is not known.

Perry G. Morton and H. H. Bains organized the Working People's Labor and Art Association (WPLAA), a benevolent organization, in Nashville in 1890 because "they had borne the sting of oppression until they could hold out no longer."[133] The group not only offered sickness and burial benefits to its members, it also opened membership to men, women, and juveniles. The Sick Committee visited unwell members to determine whether they would receive the sick benefit. In addition to checking on the health of the member, the committee inspected the sanitary condition of the household. If the committee decided that unsanitary conditions contributed to the illness, the committee could require improved living conditions before paying the full amount of the benefit. Sickness benefits were available after a member was ill for seven days. The local lodge had the authority to determine the exact amount of the sickness benefit, but it could not exceed one dollar per week.[134] The burial benefit amount also varied by lodge, but it was not to exceed thirty dollars if the member had been in good standing for up to ten years; those who had been members for more than ten years were eligible for a thirty-five dollar burial benefit. Families of juvenile members were eligible to receive a burial benefit not to exceed fifteen dollars.[135]

The group openly rejected the use of regalia and ritual in their lodges, wishing to appeal to "the learned and unlearned for the city and the country."[136] This desire to remain open to all classes may be due to the working-class backgrounds of both Morton and Bains. Morton, according to the 1890 *Nashville City Directory*, was a grocer, while Bains was a stone mason.[137] In addition to offering a social safety net to its members, the group also had strong temperance leanings, and no one who sold alcohol was eligible for membership.[138] The WPLAA grew steadily, and by 1909 representatives from more than fifty lodges attended the annual convention held in Murfreesboro, Tennessee.[139] By 1914, the WPLAA had a membership of between eight hundred and nine hundred across the state.[140] However, a split occurred within the group in 1914, when delegates to the annual convention voted in favor of changing the name of the organization to the Sons and Daughters of Cyrene.[141] A rival faction created a new organization, known as the Working People's Labor Aid Association.

The split caused dissension within and between the lodges of the organization, with factions in Murfreesboro, Tennessee, suing each other for control of the lodge and its funds. The name change signified a desire by the leadership to rise above the working-class origins of the group and to strengthen their appeal to the middle class. James Bumpass, treasurer for the Supreme Grand Board of Directors, shed light over why the WPLAA changed their name during a court deposition. He stated, "I with others thought it would be a more suitable name and it would not be likely to create the wrong impression between employers and employees of the same places." When asked in the same deposition if the name change had hurt the group, he stated, "We have lost the worst element of members that we had in the order. We have lost but very few of the better class."[142] Despite the assertion of Bumpass, both the Sons of Cyrene and the Working People's Labor Aid Association (consisting of mostly working-class former members of the WPLAA), struggled to recover from the split, and neither survived the Depression.

In addition to the bigger fraternal and benevolent lodges mentioned so far, there were numerous smaller lodges throughout the state that were tremendously important to their local communities. Examples include the Royal Sons and Daughters of the Temple, who met in Briersville (near what is now Madison in Davidson County), about which little is known except that they held an annual sermon.[143] The United Sons and Daughters of Charity in Bolivar in West Tennessee cared for the sick and buried the dead in their local community. In 1909, the group built a lodge hall in Bolivar, and when it burned down in the 1920s, they rebuilt a building that served as the heart of the African American community, a place where several church congregations met to worship, as they could not afford to build their own buildings. It was also home to numerous social gatherings for the community as well as being used for fundraising events.[144]

African American fraternal and benevolent lodges created a vast network across Tennessee, linking people across
economic, class, religious, and gender lines. They were an
important part of their communities, in which they served
a variety of purposes. As important as they were, however,
discovering the full extent of their history and importance is
difficult. There are no archival collections of papers belonging
to the larger organizations in the state, such as the Benevolent Society, the Independent Order of the Immaculates,
the Sons of Ham, or the Knights of Pythias. The rituals of
the local and regional groups either were not published or
the published books are not available in public reposito-
ries. The written records that survive exist mainly in the
form of newspaper articles, filed articles of incorporation,
deed records, and legal records such as trial transcripts
and depositions. Occasionally one can find proceedings or
constitutions in files related to lawsuits between various
lodges. To study fraternal and benevolent lodges and their
importance in the African American community, you have
to turn to the effects lodges left on the built environment
in the form of cemeteries and lodge buildings. While some
lodge buildings continue to stand, many have fallen victim
to urban renewal, development, or demolition. Cemeteries,
many of which still exist, represent the best opportunity to
learn about fraternal and benevolent lodges, their importance in Tennessee, and about the people who made up the
memberships.[145]

These cemeteries highlight the importance of providing
a place for proper burials to the members of the organizations. In a time of increasing segregation, few cemeteries were open to African Americans, so they created their

own. By banding together and pooling financial resources, lodges could raise the necessary funds to purchase land to provide burial space for their members and their families. Additionally, cemeteries were a place where African Americans could maintain a black identity separate from the larger white society.[146] They could bury their dead in the ways that mattered to their community and without having to defer to the white community.

Lodge cemeteries also show the role of commemoration in the African American community. They often contain a monument to the lodge itself, the purpose of which was to hopefully ensure that the lodge and its work would not be forgotten by future generations. Lodge cemeteries also contain numerous examples of folk art and hand-carved tombstones, which will be examined in greater detail to see what these stones tell us about African American life. Also, the presence, or in some cases, lack of historic markers at sites clearly important to their communities highlights the ways African American historic places are often overlooked by historic marker programs.

The geography of lodge cemeteries is also important as it often illustrates the segregation of the era in which they were established. Some lodge cemeteries sit adjacent to white cemeteries, separated by a fence or a no-longer-visible boundary, mute testimony that the impacts of segregation continue to be felt today. Some are located in the heart of a community, while others are relegated to the outskirts of town. It is also important to look at the placement of cemeteries in relation to the African American communities they are part of, as this highlights information about the spatial layout of those communities and enclaves across Tennessee.

The cemeteries are also sometimes the last remaining evidence of once-vibrant African American communities that have disappeared.

The silences of the cemeteries are of note, as these silences tell us things about specific communities. Silences are looked at in the context of unmarked graves, and what this might mean about lodges and their communities. Other silences considered are the absence of signage designating these cemeteries as lodge cemeteries and what this lack might mean. This lack of signage can also put a cemetery at risk to loss to development. "Unmarked" graves and areas not recognized as cemeteries point to the possibility of disinterment by developers or authorities.[147] Also explored is the bias implicit in regarding a grave as unmarked because it lacks a stone marker. In cemeteries across the state, there are many unmarked graves that actually are marked by some sort of vegetation, such as yucca or buttercups, or by some other nontraditional marker.

Lodge cemeteries also demonstrate the importance of fraternalism and benevolence to the African American community. Organizers traveled by train across the state to small towns and larger cities, organizing new lodges and checking in on established ones. As a result, fraternal and benevolent groups underwent a growth spurt during the later nineteenth century, particularly among the African American community in the 1880s.[148] As lodges grew, it was not uncommon for them to buy property for one of two reasons: to build a lodge hall or to establish a cemetery for the benefit of the members. However, as seen in the burials of the people in the cemeteries, people were often members of multiple fraternal groups; many of the cemeteries contain burials of people who belonged to fraternal lodges other than the group that established the cemetery. In several cases, multiple groups established joint lodge cemeteries, and the ways different lodges worked together to achieve their goals will be examined.

Finally, the persistence of these lodge cemeteries is of interest, as it is a common belief that most of the fraternal and benevolent groups ceased to exist by World War II. If this is true, why have the cemeteries persisted? Why do burials continue in these places? Have the cemeteries somehow transformed into community cemeteries? The question of the possible persistence of benevolence will be examined in this work.

While these specific cemeteries continue to exist, African American fraternal cemeteries are increasingly at risk at being overlooked, especially in a region known for rapid population growth in the last decade. Between 2000 and 2018, the population of Tennessee on the whole increased by 6.26 percent. In some counties, the growth has been even more pronounced and rapid. Rutherford County, home to several lodge cemeteries, had an 18.43 percent population increase during the period, and Wilson County, also home to multiple lodge cemeteries, had a 17.41 percent increase.[149] This growth has led to increased real estate development, a very real threat to the continued existence of some of the cemeteries. As Lynn Rainville stressed, "the burial grounds of underrepresented groups may be the most valuable because theirs is a largely forgotten or silenced history. Moreover, these groups are less likely to be represented in the documentary collections of historical societies, and their homes, in most cases, have not been saved or preserved."[150] The time to document and tell the stories of lodge cemeteries and their importance to the State's history is now, before some of them are swallowed whole by development.

CHAPTER 2

Lodge Cemeteries in Tennessee

The common expectation for a cemetery is
neat rows of stones and markers on a well-
mowed green lawn. Afro-American graves
in rural areas do not conform to this norm.

—JOHN MICHAEL VLACH

On an early August morning in 1908 just outside Murfreesboro, Tennessee, a teenage white woman walked home after
having spent the night at a friend's house. Also walking that
morning was a young African American man named George
Johnson. During the course of these separate walks, their
paths crossed, and George Johnson, for reasons unknown,
allegedly came up behind the woman and grabbed her arm.
The woman screamed, and given that this was the South
in 1908, Johnson ran away. Unfortunately for Johnson, the

woman's screams attracted attention, and soon a group of people began searching the countryside for the young man. The search committee was joined by Sheriff J. W. Primm and other deputies. The crowd soon found him, and he was taken into custody by Sheriff Primm. Primm hustled George into his buggy to drive him to the county jail in Murfreesboro. By this point, it was obvious that the crowd was not looking for a tame and "legal" end to the matter, as they began to follow the buggy in order to take justice into their own hands. Sheriff Primm managed to get George to the jail, and a mob, estimated at one thousand people, soon circled the jail. Primm had had previous experience dealing with Murfreesboro's mob mentality. Four months earlier, in April 1908, a mob had attempted to lynch a man accused of murdering of a highly respected man in Florence, a small town north of Murfreesboro. In that instance, Sheriff Primm had taken the accused to Nashville in order to evade the mob.[1]

Johnson, the sheriff, and the deputies soon realized the mob wanted nothing less than Johnson's life. At no point does it appear that anyone in the mob questioned why a man should lose his life merely for grabbing someone's arm. The sheriff, to at least his partial credit, did not turn Johnson over to the mob, instead wanting to "follow the law" and allow for Johnson's death to occur in approved, legal fashion. Sheriff Primm attempted to place Johnson in a car and take him to Nashville for safety, but the crowd was expecting this maneuver and blocked it. Several prominent men, such as newspaper editor C. C. Henderson, addressed the crowd in an attempt to disperse them, but to no avail. Sheriff

Primm spoke to the mob and told them he would not surrender Johnson, but the crowd continued to demand the keys to Johnson's cell. Finally, the sheriff and his deputies dressed Johnson as a woman and placed a wig on him. They rushed him to a buggy and started driving toward Nashville. However, men with white handkerchiefs on their faces overtook the buggy, overpowered the deputies, and took Johnson into their custody. Johnson was taken to a nearby tree, shot, and then hanged. A placard was placed on the body stating that Johnson's remains were to stay there until 10:00 a.m. the next day as warning "of the same fate to all the negroes guilty of a like crime." The crowd then dispersed and returned to their homes.[2]

Following the crime, Johnson's body was taken by the coroner to a local undertaker, and a coroner's jury was held. The jury found that Johnson had died "by hanging by unknown parties."[3] Following the coroner's jury, it was time to bury Johnson. Reportedly, more than two thousand people came to view Johnson's body the morning prior to his funeral. If true, that is a staggering attendance, particularly as the total population of Murfreesboro around this time period was approximately 4,500.[4] After the funeral, a procession consisting of the undertaker's wagon, two buggies carrying the family, and a procession of people on foot made its way through the public square and the one mile to Benevolent Society No. 11 Cemetery, an African American lodge cemetery that had been established in 1897.[5] George Johnson's death at the hands of a mob for doing no more than grabbing a woman's arm is beyond tragic. His story is unfortunately too familiar for any who study the history of the South. When something so incomprehensible happens, the family left behind has to find a way to properly bury their dead. In the case of George Johnson, his family was able to turn to a local organization, Benevolent Society No. 11, to find a final resting place for their loved one. Just as in Murfreesboro, lodge cemeteries across the state became the final resting place for many in the African American community, both those who were murdered and those who lived a long life. Johnson, and all the members of the larger African American community, deserved a final resting place. In Benevolent Society No. 11 Cemetery, George Johnson found his final place of rest. There are similar stories of lynchings that took place across the state, and it was not uncommon for the victims to be offered final resting places in African American–controlled cemeteries, where their bodies were safe from further abuse from the white community.

What follows is a brief description of identified African American lodge cemeteries. Please note that these cemeteries may not be the only ones in the state of Tennessee. Rather, these cemeteries have a positive identification of having been established by an African American fraternal or benevolent lodge. Some may no longer have an active lodge, but all are bound by the commonality of organization by a fraternal or benevolent lodge.

West Tennessee

In the nineteenth century and beyond, West Tennessee was regarded as a prime agricultural location in Tennessee. Joseph Killebrew described the region in 1879: "Its soil is rich, mellow, and fertile, and the southern half is peculiarly well adapted to the growth of cotton."[6] Memphis, established in 1819 by Andrew Jackson, John Overton, and James Winchester, experienced slow growth initially but was a rapidly growing and thriving city by the 1870s. However, yellow fever epidemics in 1867, 1873, 1878, and 1879 decimated the city's population. Following these calamities, the city rebounded in the later nineteenth century, with its population reaching one hundred thousand by 1900.[7] Much of this population growth was due to people moving into Memphis from nearby rural areas and from the annexation of neighboring towns. Since it drew from a rural population, in some respects Memphis retained a rural feel, with rural customs and attitudes.[8]

Memphis contained several African American communities, many of which were located in the worst areas of the city. Early communities were known as "Slippery Log Bottoms," "Queen Bee Bottoms," and "Shinertown," all located near the central business district. In northern areas of the city, African American communities were pushed to the swamps along the Wolf River, and in southern areas of the city, to areas near the railroad lines or warehouses.[9] Blair Hunt, principal of Booker T. Washington High School and a member of Memphis's African American community following World War I, remarked on this residential segregation.

> Whenever you had seemingly a residential area of blacks, it was close to a bayou or a railroad track. I suppose because the land was cheap or cheaper, and no doubt, that's why we settled. But we lived in patches. There was no big black belt, no solid black belt anywhere in this city of Memphis. Then in the course of time, the Negros began to expand their residential areas.[10]

Memphis was home to a number of African American lodges and at least two African American lodge cemeteries. Lodges were located in the areas outside of Memphis as well. Writing of Dyersburg, W. L. Miller noted, "There is in Dyersburg a network of lodges—Masons, Odd Fellows, Pythians, U.B.F., Mosaics, Sons of Tabor, and ladies' auxiliaries connected with each. It is easy to see that in health, sickness or death the colored brother is prepared for any emergency."[11] Jackson was home to Masonic, Odd Fellows, and Knights of Pythias lodges.[12] Somerville, in Fayette County, contained the Seventh Star Lodge No. 47 of the Knights of Pythias.[13] Despite evidence of lodge activity throughout West Tennessee, the only lodge cemeteries that I have positively identified are located in Shelby County. More work is needed, particularly in rural West Tennessee, to identify both African American cemeteries and lodge cemeteries.

ZION CHRISTIAN CEMETERY

Zion Christian Cemetery is possibly the most well-known African American cemetery in Memphis or Shelby County. As the population grew following the Civil War, the need for an African American cemetery became increasingly apparent to the community in Memphis. The United Sons of Zion established this cemetery in 1876, just outside the city limits of Memphis on what was then Grand Municipal Drive, now South Parkway East.[14] In addition to the cemetery, by 1872 the organization also owned Zion Hall, a one-story building located on Beale Street.[15]

Zion Christian Cemetery is fifteen acres in size and is divided into eight separate named sections: Morris Henderson, Emmanuel Square, Felix Square, Zion Hill, W. M. Ramier, Mt. Ninevah, Shephard Hill, and North Shephard

FIGURE 2.1. View of Zion Christian Cemetery in 2020. The internal roads of the cemetery are barely visible.

Hill. There are approximately thirty thousand burials in the cemetery. Burial registers for the cemetery are not complete, and the registers for the years 1876 through 1894 were either lost or destroyed.[16] The cemetery remained under the ownership of the Sons of Zion until 1893, when the members of the lodge created the Zion Cemetery Company, a for-profit company, and the deed transferred to the new company. In 1986, the deed was conveyed to the CME church by the widow of George Christian, the last owner of the Zion Cemetery Company.[17]

Zion Christian Cemetery is in fair condition. A fence surrounds the property, and a large iron sign with the name sits on stone pillars at the entrance. The cemetery is bounded on one side by the railroad. The graves are arranged in rows oriented east to west. In addition to the rows, roads enable access to the different cemetery sections; however,

vegetation has somewhat obscured them. There are numerous unmarked as well as marked graves, as well as a number
of large, mature trees. A Tennessee Historical Commission
state historic marker is present at the site, located on South
Parkway East. In March 2019, a National Park Service marker
was erected to commemorate the victims of the People's
Grocery lynching of 1892 at the gravesite of Thomas Moss,
one of the victims.[18] The last burials took place in 1974.[19]

NUMBER NINE HALL CEMETERY

The Independent Pole Bearers Lodge Number 9 established
the Number Nine Hall Cemetery south of Memphis in a
semirural location, approximately 1.5 miles from the Mississippi border. The Independent Order of Pole Bearers
Number 9 lodge received its Charter of Incorporation from
the State of Tennessee in 1896, and the object of the group
was to "establish a means whereby we may secure for cash
other exemption from neglect in the exigencies of sickness,
want and death; to secure for each other employment, and to
hold social meetings for the purpose of advancement of each
other."[20] The incorporators of the Independent Pole Bearers Number 9 included Joseph Burns, Chas. Wilson, Pierce
Holmes, Albert Matlock, and Frank Jackson. Mr. Burns was
a farmer, aged twenty-two at the time of incorporation, who
rented a farm in the area.[21] Mr. Holmes, also a farmer, who
lived in the area and rented the farms that he worked, was
approximately forty at the time of incorporation.[22] This
lodge appears to have been, at the time of incorporation,
made up primarily of farmers, indicating the area was rural
at the time the cemetery was established.

FIGURE 2.2. Number Nine Hall Cemetery in 2013. The lodge building can be seen in the background, to the right.

The Number Nine Hall Cemetery measures approximately one acre and is still in the ownership of the Independent Pole Bearers Lodge Number 9. A lodge building that sat adjacent to the cemetery burned in 2018, but the members built a replacement pavilion in 2019. Trees border the rear and side of the cemetery, and the plan of the cemetery appears haphazard. There are no internal paths or roads in the cemetery, which sits adjacent to a church and retains a rural feel.

UNION FOREVER CEMETERY

The intriguingly named Union Forever Society was established in Memphis and Shelby County during the early years of Reconstruction. One historian described the group as one of the larger benevolent groups in Memphis that drew its diverse membership from both skilled and unskilled laborers, including river workers, blacksmiths, levee workers, carpenters, day laborers, and bookkeepers.[23] It is believed that the group was formed to provide proper burials to members.[24] It is clear that the group was active by the early 1870s, as they took part in ceremonies in Memphis in 1874 that marked the death of abolitionist Charles Sumner, marching as part of a procession through Memphis.[25] The group may have spread into northern Mississippi, as there is a Union Forever Society No. 3 of Arkabutla, organized in 1878, and Union Forever Society No. 4 of De Soto County, organized in 1881.

Prior to 1911, the Union Forever Society in Memphis established a cemetery on Horn Lake Road, south of the railroad yards.[26] Cemetery websites, such as Find a Grave, indicate that the cemetery is overgrown and not easily accessible. When attempting to document the cemetery, I was unable to find a point of entry for the cemetery. On the Find a Grave website, more than one hundred burials have been noted based on information taken from death certificates indicating Union Forever as the cemetery. A note on the summary for the cemetery on Find a Grave also notes that satellite images of the property indicate that there may be some tombstones present.[27]

Middle Tennessee

An 1869 book about emigration praised Middle Tennessee for "the rich and fertile soil, mild winters, and prevailing healthfulness of Middle Tennessee, with its cordial and hospitable people, its well organized system of schools and churches, and other attractions, [that] offer the emigrant great inducements to come and participate in its advantages."[28] Joseph Killebrew described Middle Tennessee in 1874 as "by far the most valuable division of the State. It embraces forty counties and has a superficial area of 18,000 square miles. . . . It contains 245 towns and villages. It has 550 miles of railway, and nearly 500 miles of navigable rivers."[29]

Approximately 39 percent of Tennessee's African American population lived in Middle Tennessee in 1900. The dominant city in the region was Nashville, which was home to several African American colleges, two African American publishing houses, and at least fifty-seven African American congregations.[30] In addition to Nashville, the region contained a number of small cities and towns with vibrant African American communities, such as Clarksville, Columbia, and Murfreesboro. Winchester was home to lodges for the Knights of Pythias, GUOOF, and the Masons, while nearby Tullahoma was home to the Independent Order of Immaculates, Masons, and Odd Fellows in 1910.[31] The *Nashville Globe* noted Murfreesboro's lodge network in 1910, stating, "This town boasts of all the leading fraternal orders thus insuring the visiting brother good fellowship. Among the leading organizations are the Masons, Odd Fellows, Knights of Pythias, Household Ruth, Calanthe Court, Eastern Star and several others which we cannot recall."[32] To date, the greatest number of lodge cemeteries has been identified in Middle Tennessee. It is unclear if that is due to increased lodge activity in this region, or if it is due to my living in Middle Tennessee, making it easier to find and confirm the lodge cemeteries in this region.

FIGURE 2.3. Agnew Benevolent Cemetery. St. Paul-Agnew AME Church is visible in the background.

AGNEW BENEVOLENT CEMETERY

Agnew Benevolent Cemetery is located in the Agnew community of rural Giles County, west of the county seat of Pulaski and approximately fifteen miles north of the Alabama border. It was established by the Agnew Benevolent Society, who purchased the property in 1903 from W. D. Reynolds, a white farmer in the community, and is approximately one acre in size.[33] The Agnew community is an old community in Giles County, established on Agnew Creek in 1808 or 1809 by John Agnew. From its earliest days, the community was made up of both whites and African Americans.[34]

The earliest marked grave dates to approximately 1928. The cemetery is well maintained and sits adjacent to the St. Paul-Agnew AME Church. Most of the graves are arranged

FIGURE 2.4. Odd Fellows Cemetery Elkton sit atop a hill in rural Giles County.

in rows oriented north, but the graves themselves all face east. In the rear right corner are located several graves not in rows. This section is overgrown and unmown, and some of the markers appear to be older than the markers laid out in rows. The cemetery remains in use, and a sign was erected between 2015 and 2020 marking this as the Agnew Benevolent Cemetery.

ODD FELLOWS CEMETERY (*Elkton/Ardmore*)

Odd Fellows Cemetery is located between Elkton and Ardmore in Giles County, Tennessee, approximately one and a half miles north of the Alabama border. The age of the cemetery is unclear, but the oldest marked grave dates to 1912. It is also located roughly two hundred yards south of Elliot Cemetery, a white cemetery. Both cemeteries are within eyesight and earshot of Interstate 65. It is unclear which Odd Fellows lodge established this cemetery.

Odd Fellows Cemetery is located atop a small hill, with an unpaved path leading from the road to the cemetery at the top of the hill. Burials are arranged in rows and graves are oriented east to west. There are several depressions indicating the presence of unmarked graves. The cemetery contains a number of deciduous trees, as well as several cedars. A large white sign with "Odd Fellows Cemetery" is located on the edge of the property at the road.

BENEVOLENT LODGE NO. 210 CEMETERY

Benevolent Society Lodge No. 210 Cemetery is located in the community of Port Royal, in Montgomery County. The Benevolent Society lodge in Port Royal was organized in 1872 in a log cabin school. By 1890, trustees of the lodge had purchased a lot in the town of Port Royal and built a lodge building. Within eighteen years, the lodge sold their property in Port Royal itself and purchased three acres outside of town, on Port Royal Road. On this property the members built a lodge hall in 1908 and established a cemetery. The lodge continued meeting in the building until 1994, when a fire set by white supremacists destroyed the lodge building as part of the wave of church burnings that swept across the rural South in the early 1990s. The lodge raised funds and erected their present building between 1999 and 2001, and the lodge remains an active part of the Port Royal community.[35]

The Benevolent Society Lodge No. 210 Cemetery is approximately 2.4 acres in size. There is some fencing present in the form of wood posts with iron chains between the posts, although some of the chains are missing. The cemetery is adjacent to the current lodge hall and picnic pavilion.

FIGURE 2.5. Benevolent Lodge No. 210 Cemetery is shown here along with several of the cedar trees present in the cemetery.

A number of large cedar trees marks the site. The arrangement of burials appears somewhat haphazard, with some areas arranged in rows and others scattered more randomly. However, most graves appear to be oriented east-west. A monument to the lodge, an obelisk, is located beneath a large tree in the eastern section of the cemetery. The obelisk has fallen but is leaned against its base. The cemetery and lodge are marked by not only a large sign at the property, but also by a directional sign on the highway that points the way to the "Port Royal Benevolent Lodge." A large white, wooden sign is located at the cemetery property line fence detailing the history of the order. It was erected in 2014-2015 as part of an Eagle Scout project.

KING DAVID LODGE CEMETERY

The King David Lodge #187 established a cemetery in the Cedar Hill community of Robertson County during Reconstruction. The lodge was established not long after emancipation, and by the beginning of the twentieth century, the group had organized Eighth of August celebrations, an event marking Emancipation, for Robertson County.[36] The group remained active well into the twentieth century, taking part with other Robertson County organizations in a fundraiser for the Vanderbilt University children's hospital as late as 1986.[37] The group may have been a Masonic organization, as a search indicated a number of Masonic lodges across the nation operating under the name "King David Lodge."

The cemetery is located south of Highway 41 in the Cedar Hill community. A 1987 work, *Robertson County Cemetery Records*, noted that the cemetery was "full of row after row of sunken graves with no tombstones and many marked by fieldstones."[38] As of the date of this writing, I have been unable to positively identify the cemetery. Although a 1987 book with Robertson County cemetery transcriptions provides directions for the cemetery's location that state the "cemetery is on the south side of Hwy 41 after going through Cedar Hill & crossing Sturgeon Creek," two attempts to locate the cemetery have proven fruitless.[39]

ODD FELLOWS CEMETERY (*Springfield*)

The Odd Fellows Cemetery is located on South Main Street, adjacent to a tobacco processing facility, in Springfield in Robertson County, approximately one and half miles from

67

FIGURE 2.6. Large oak trees dominate the Odd Fellows Cemetery in Springfield.

the center of town. The Lend-A-Hand Society, which, judging by the name, was likely a benevolent group, originally established the cemetery at some point before 1910. For unknown reasons, the cemetery purchase was not completed by the Lend-A-Hand Society, and the Grand United Order of Odd Fellows Lodge No. 2806 purchased the property in November 1916.[40] The Odd Fellows was one of several African American benevolent and fraternal lodges in Springfield in the early twentieth century, along with the Masons, the Knights of Pythias, and the Independent Order of Immaculates. In addition to the cemetery, the Odd Fellows also owned a lodge building in Springfield, likely located at the corner of Cheatham and Holman Streets, near the AME church and an African American Baptist church.[41] The city of Springfield took ownership of the cemetery in 1993 at the request of the remaining owners.[42]

The cemetery is approximately 4.5 acres in size, and it is oriented west to east. A chain-link fence surrounds

FIGURE 2.7. The sign at Benevolent Society No. 16 Cemetery indicates that the Benevolent Society was established in 1862. It also features a dove, a symbol of the group.

the property. A white wooden sign is located outside the fence, at the street, designating it Odd Fellows Cemetery. The cemetery contains a number of large, old oak trees, and there are also a few cedar trees at the western edge of the property. Hail and Cotton, a tobacco processing plant, borders the cemetery to the south. The burials are mostly arranged in rows. Not all graves are marked, and there are several depressions indicating unmarked graves.

BENEVOLENT SOCIETY NO. 16 CEMETERY

Benevolent Society No. 16 Cemetery is located in Goodletts-ville, in Davidson County, directly across the street from the First Baptist Church, an African American congregation. Trustees purchased the property for the cemetery in 1885 for the sum of $50.[43] Benevolent Society No. 16 lodge had eighty-nine members and met on the second and fourth Monday nights of the month in 1926. The lodge also owned property valued at $1,500, which was likely the cemetery.[44]

The cemetery is marked by a large stone sign at the entrance inscribed "Benevolent Cemetery Lodge #16 Est 1862," and there is a dove, one of the symbols of the Benevolent Society, on the sign. The cemetery is well maintained, with no fencing. Most of the burials are grouped on the north side of the cemetery, and there appear to be few or no burials in the south part of the cemetery. Graves are arranged in the northern section in three partial rows, but more haphazardly through the rest of the cemetery. The graves arranged in rows are from the later twentieth century to present, as it continues in active use with recent burials. The cemetery is also immediately adjacent to the largely white Cole Cemetery.

SONS OF HAM CEMETERY

The Sons of Ham Cemetery is located in the Dry Creek community of Madison, in Davidson County. The first Sons of Ham lodge in Nashville was organized in 1868.[45] The Sons of Ham lodge in Dry Creek was organized in 1873 or 1874, but the lodge became inactive following the collapse of the Freedmen's Bank, likely due to loss of any funds belonging to the lodge.[46] At some point the lodge at Dry Creek reorganized, and members were holding monthly meetings by the early twentieth century.[47] In addition to the cemetery, the Sons of Ham also had a lodge hall on their property. The hall is not extant, and it is not clear what happened to the building.[48]

FIGURE 2.8. Sons of Ham Cemetery in Davidson County slopes down to Dry Creek. The cemetery is sometimes referred to as Dry Creek Cemetery.

The Sons of Ham Cemetery is approximately 1.77 acres in size and is well maintained. A stacked-stone fence marks the eastern boundary of the cemetery on Gallatin Road. Dry Creek runs immediately adjacent to the northern edge of the cemetery. A brick sign stands left of the entrance with the inscription "Dry Creek Cemetery Lodge Suns [*sic*] of Ham No. 1 1869." This sign is located in the southern section of the cemetery, which also seems to contain the oldest burials. The oldest observed tombstone, located in this section, dates to 1869. A very large cedar tree is present in this section of the cemetery, possibly marking a burial site. There are also older burials on the other side of the driveway on the northern side of the cemetery, although none as old as in the southern section. The most recent burials are congregated on the west side. The cemetery contains a number of trees and rock outcroppings.

FIGURE 2.9. Benevolent Society No. 79 in Madison is located in the middle of a suburban neighborhood.

BENEVOLENT SOCIETY NO. 79 CEMETERY

Benevolent Society No. 79 Cemetery sits in a residential subdivision in the Briarville community of Madison, in Davidson County. Trustees of the lodge purchased the land for a cemetery in 1904 from Alex Pettis and his wife, Parillee, also trustees and lodge members.[49] Mr. Pettis was a minister and an important member of the Briarville community. Born into slavery in Alabama, he served in Company A of the 17th Reg. United States Colored Troops during the Civil War, rising to the rank of corporal. Active in politics, he was a delegate to the state Republican convention several times. In addition to being a charter member of Benevolent Society No. 79, he was also a member of the Grand United Order of Odd Fellows.[50] The lodge continued in the decade following his death in 1913, and by 1926, the lodge had at least seventy-two members.[51]

The cemetery sits in the middle of a suburban subdivision and contains no signage to indicate its name or lodge affiliation. It is well maintained, and there is a stacked-stone fence at the eastern border of the property, at Briarville Road. The older burials are located in the southern front quadrant of the cemetery, and newer burials are located at the northern front quadrant and the rear southern quadrant. There are few to no burials in the rear northwest quadrant of the cemetery. Arrangement of burials varies, with some rows containing three to five marked burials while other areas appear to contain marked graves in no discernible row or pattern. Burials primarily face eastward. There are some depressions in the cemetery, indicating unmarked burials.

MT. ARARAT CEMETERY (*Nashville*)

Mt. Ararat Cemetery is located in Nashville, in Davidson County, near Murfreesboro and Elm Hill Pikes. Established by the Sons of Relief No. 1 and the Colored Benevolent Society, it may be the oldest African American cemetery in the city of Nashville.[52] From its establishment in June of 1869 to October of that year, there were ninety-two interments in the cemetery, highlighting the need for an African American cemetery in the community.[53] It has enjoyed a long, varied, and interesting history. In 1885, it was discovered during an investigation of the state prison, located at that time in Nashville, that it had a contract with the management of the cemetery to bury convicts at Mt. Ararat.[54] It is not clear if these convicts were African American or white. During the testimony about whether the coffins conveyed to the cemetery contained bodies, it was also revealed that the

FIGURE 2.10. Mt. Ararat (Nashville) Cemetery covers nine acres. A Purity Dairy processing plant can be seen to the rear left of the image.

cemetery struggled to stop "body snatchers" attempting to rob the graves. It was alleged that these body snatchers were students from local medical schools trying to get bodies to use in their anatomy classes.[55] By the 1970s, the cemetery was no longer the only burial option for Nashville's African American community and it fell out of popularity. An article in the *Nashville Tennessean* in 1973 described the place as "once a proud cemetery. But that was long ago. Today, everything has changed—for the worse—and the cemetery has become an eyesore."[56] In 1982, the cemetery passed into the ownership of the National Christian Missionary Convention.[57]

Mt. Ararat occupies approximately nine acres and is bisected by Orr Avenue. One part of the cemetery is immediately adjacent to the Greenwood Cemetery annex.[58] This section contains a stone gate with a metal sign at the entrance.

Each stone pillar has an inset stone with the name of the two groups and their trustees in 1914, presumably when the gate was installed. The arched metal sign contains the name of the cemetery and is topped with a cross. There is a dirt road through the cemetery, which is divided into sections. Parts of the cemetery appear to be planned, with burials in neat rows, while other parts contain less orderly arrangements. A state historic marker sits adjacent to the cemetery as well. One section of the cemetery is located across Orr Avenue and is immediately adjacent to a Purity Dairy processing plant. This section contains several older graves, with many of the marked burials dating to the later nineteenth century. The burials in this section are more haphazard in arrangement, with few rows. It is unknown exactly how many burials took place at Mt. Ararat, which continues in use today. Both sections of the cemetery contain many large, old trees, bearing silent witness to the cemetery's long history.

BENEVOLENT SOCIETY NO. 84 CEMETERY

Benevolent Society No. 84 Cemetery is located on Hamilton Church Pike in Antioch, in Davidson County. The surrounding community was once known as Hamilton or Hamilton Hill but is now a suburb of Nashville. The exact age of the cemetery is unknown, although there are mentions of the lodge in the *Nashville Globe* dating back to at least 1909.[59] In 1926, the Benevolent Society No. 84 lodge met on the first and third Saturday nights, included thirty-eight members, and owned property valued at $1,200.[60]

The cemetery is approximately 1.8 acres in size and there is no sign indicating the name or lodge affiliation of

FIGURE 2.11. Benevolent Society No. 84 Cemetery contains only a few marked graves.

the cemetery. There is metal fencing around the cemetery. There are approximately twenty marked graves and several unmarked graves as well. The graves are oriented west to east, and burials are mainly located at the western and eastern edges of the property. There are more tombstones at the rear of the cemetery, in an overgrown section that appears to extend into the residential subdivision behind the cemetery. When I first visited the cemetery in December 2012, a concrete lodge building remained on the property. This building is no longer standing, having collapsed sometime in 2014 or 2015, and the debris from the collapsed building remains on the site.

FIGURE 2.12. The abandoned lodge hall for Benevolent Society No. 84 as it appeared in 2012. The building no longer stands.

COLORED MUTUAL CEMETERY

The Colored Mutual Cemetery is located in Smyrna, in Rutherford County, behind a large apartment complex and adjacent to the busy Sam Ridley Boulevard. The date of organization for this benevolent group is unknown, although it likely dates to the late 1800s. In 1902, the Mutual Aid Society of Smyrna applied for a charter of incorporation to the Secretary of State. The organizers included Dock Brown, Ab Drennon, Dan Davis, Nath Matthews, and Stewart Ridley, among others.[61] Census records indicate that Matthews, Brown, Drennon, and Ridley were farmers, indicating this was a rural community.[62] In 1905, the group purchased 3.75 acres of land in Smyrna to establish a cemetery.[63]

The group remained active until the 1940s, at which point the cemetery slowly sank into disuse. In 2013, ownership of the cemetery was transferred to the nonprofit Smyrna Cemetery Organization, after a local attorney found that there was no longer anyone associated with the group that had a legal claim to the property.[64] Access to the cemetery is difficult. There was once a gravel farm road that led to the site, but a senior living community was built near the cemetery and now blocks access to the lane leading to the cemetery.[65] I have been unable to access the cemetery in person. The Rutherford County Archives conducted a survey of cemeteries in Rutherford County and has shared a GIS map of all known cemeteries on their website. On this survey, there are two images of the cemetery available that appear indicate the presence of both marked and unmarked graves. There are several trees located in the center of the cemetery.[66]

BENEVOLENT SOCIETY NO. 11 CEMETERY

Benevolent Society No. 11 Cemetery is located in Murfreesboro, in Rutherford County, one mile south of the courthouse square. It is surrounded by warehouses and desolate industrial spaces in a town whose rapid development and growth threaten the existence of this and other small cemeteries. Trustees of the Benevolent Society No. 11 purchased the property from Alfred Miller in 1897 to establish a cemetery for the group.[67] In 1926, the lodge consisted of 130 members with property valued at $3,500. The group met on the first and third Tuesday nights of the month. Interestingly, the leader of the organization in that year was a

FIGURE 2.13. Benevolent Society No. 11 Cemetery in Murfreesboro was established in the late 1890s.

woman, President Sallie Seward, and the secretary was local doctor J. B. McClellan.[68] The last surviving member of the society deeded the property to Allen Chapel AME Church in Murfreesboro in 1988.

Today this cemetery is difficult to access and not noted for a park-like setting. The railroad and the Highway 231 overpass are visible from the cemetery. There is some fencing, but it doesn't entirely enclose the property. There is no longer a sign at the cemetery, although the wooden posts holding the former sign remain in place. The site is approximately 7.5 acres in size and is bisected by a dirt path. Most of the burials are located on the northern half of the property. There are a large number of unmarked graves and many grave depressions. It is difficult to determine the original arrangement of burials as many stones have been knocked off their bases or have fallen over. Bushhogging attempts at the property in recent years may have also resulted in the movement of markers. A pedestal-urn marker dedicated to the lodge and erected circa 1902 is located west of the cemetery path, in the section with marked graves. There are a number of large trees in the cemetery, including some cedar trees. The cemetery has endured difficulties in the last several decades and undergone cycles of neglect and renewed community interest.

MOUNT ARARAT (*Shelbyville*)

Mount Ararat Cemetery (Shelbyville) is located in the town of Shelbyville, in Bedford County, and is immediately adjacent to the older and historically white Willow Mount Cemetery.[69] The exact date the cemetery was established is unclear, but it was established by Benevolent Society Lodge No. 44. Interestingly, Lodge No. 44 was actually a Ladies Benevolent Society Lodge, with leadership consisting entirely of women. The lodge held annual Decoration Day events at their cemetery, as described in the *Nashville Globe* in 1911:

> The annual decoration of graves took place last Sunday evening at Mt. Ararat Cemetery. Addresses were delivered by several prominent citizens. The students of Turner Normal College presented a beautiful floral design for the grave of the late Dr. B. A. J. Nixon, who was one of the pioneers in the work of Turner Normal. They also rendered some musical selections.[70]

The annual Decoration Day events at the cemetery may date to 1894, as the *Nashville Globe* in May 1910 described

FIGURE 2.14. Mount Ararat (Shelbyville) Cemetery sits adjacent to the older Willow Mount Cemetery, which is visible to the left of the image.

the event as the "sixteenth anniversary decoration of the graves."[71] By 1926, this lodge consisted of ninety-nine members and owned property valued at $2,100. The group met on the first and third Tuesday afternoons of the month.[72]

As noted previously, Mount Ararat (Shelbyville) is located immediately adjacent to Willow Mount Cemetery, and a fence separates the two cemeteries. There is no signage indicating the name of the cemetery, which currently has the same owner as Willow Mount and is kept in good condition. The cemetery is primarily laid out in rows with graves oriented east-west. There are a number of large trees present in the cemetery, providing shade and giving an indication of its age. A marker is dedicated to the Benevolent Society with the inscription, "Erected to the sacred memory of the honored dead of the Benevolent Society. Their works do follow them. August 1897."

FIGURE 2.15. The Benevolent Society No. 91 Cemetery sign was erected in the mid-2010s.

BENEVOLENT SOCIETY NO. 91 CEMETERY

Benevolent Society No. 91 Cemetery, also referred to as Lester Cemetery in the Wilson County Property Assessor records, is located on Saundersville Road in Mt. Juliet, in Wilson County. The trustees for Benevolent Society No. 91 purchased the property for the cemetery from Emanuel and Louella Lester, members of the society, in 1936.[73] Benevolent Society No. 91 consisted of thirty-nine members in 1926, and the property was valued at $225. The group met on the first and third Monday nights of the month. The president of the lodge in that year was Emanuel Lester, the same person who sold the property for the cemetery to the lodge.[74]

Benevolent Society No. 91 Cemetery is less than one acre in size, and a white sign was erected sometime after 2015 on the south border of the cemetery, at the street. There is no fencing surrounding the cemetery, and a creek borders the property on the north and east side of the properties. It is located across from a somewhat recently built subdivision and a water treatment facility. It is a well-maintained cemetery, with no broken monuments or grave markers. There are some trees on the property, but overall, there is not a great deal of vegetation present. There are two separate and distinct sections of marked burials in the cemetery, on the east and west sides of the cemetery. The graves are all oriented east to west.

GREENLAWN CEMETERY

The Benevolent Society established Greenlawn Cemetery in the Needmore community of Wilson County, likely in the late nineteenth or early twentieth century. The Benevolent Society had a lodge hall in the community, possibly shared with the Knights of Pythias, that also functioned as a schoolhouse for the community during the 1920s and early 1930s. This building was located next to Williamson Chapel CME church, a focal point of the community.[75] It is not clear which Benevolent Lodge was active in the community.

MAYS CHAPEL BENEVOLENT CEMETERY

The Mays Chapel Benevolent Cemetery is located in the Mays Chapel community of Wilson County, northeast of the town of Mount Juliet. It is located near the Mays Chapel Missionary Baptist Church, and the lodge and the church were the heart of the African American community. The land for the cemetery was deeded to the lodge by the Rutherford family, an African American family living in the community.[76] It is unclear what the lodge number of this particular Benevolent Society was, or the size of the lodge's membership. The cemetery is less than an acre in size, and there is no signage at the cemetery to indicate its name or ownership. When I attempted to visit the cemetery, I could find no pull-off from the road into the cemetery. It appeared to only contain five to ten marked graves. Little vegetation is present. The cemetery blends into the surrounding rural area and is easy to overlook for anyone not familiar with the area.

YOUNG MEN'S AID SOCIETY CEMETERY

The Young Men's Aid Society Cemetery, also referred to as the Laguardo Benevolent Cemetery, is located in the Laguardo community of Wilson County, at the intersection of Creighton Lane and Woods Ferry Road. The Young Men's Aid Society in Laguardo was established in July 1877. According to the Articles of Incorporation for the group, the purpose of the organization was for

> assisting weak & distressed members, visiting & administering to the sick of the order, and burying the dead. To suppress indolence and vice by encouraging its members to honest labor, and to teach the principles of morality & Christian virtue to its members as calculated to the happiness of mankind.[77]

The group met on the first and third Wednesday nights of the month. In addition to offering sickness and burial

FIGURE 2.16. Young Men's Aid Society Cemetery measures approximately one acre in size.

benefits to members, it also allowed nonmembers to pur-chase burial plots from the trustees for $4.00.[78] Trustees of the Young Men's Aid Society purchased the property for the cemetery in 1885 from W. L. Bradshaw, a white farmer who lived in the same district.[79]

The Young Men's Aid Society Cemetery is approximately one acre in size, and there is no fencing surrounding the property. A creek marks the boundary of the cemetery on the south side of the property. A large wooden sign, erected circa 2017, is present at Woods Ferry Road. The cemetery is in good condition and contains a number of mature trees. There are several depressions indicating unmarked graves. The cemetery is primarily laid out in rows, particularly in the eastern section of the cemetery, nearest Woods Ferry Road, with graves oriented west to east, although not all rows are full of marked graves. A large area in the western section of the cemetery contains few marked graves but a number of grave depressions. The oldest marked grave dates to around 1893.

East Tennessee

In 1876, Joseph Killebrew described East Tennessee as the "Switzerland of America," a region with "towering mountains locking up deep, rich and verdant valleys and coves, its succession of ridges and valleys, its magnificent forests, its roaring streams. . . . All conspire to make it one of the most desirable spots in America."[80] Although a lovely spot, only roughly 13 percent of all African Americans in the state lived in that region in 1900.[81] Knoxville was the major city in the region, and by 1880, African Americans accounted for 32 percent of its overall population.[82] African Americans in Knoxville were active in politics, and due to the somewhat equal support among the white population for both Democrats and Republicans, African Americans had leverage as swing voters. Thanks to this, African Americans were able to obtain positions as police officers, firemen, and post office employees before the end of the nineteenth century.[83] However, the Great Depression created population decline in Knoxville, both among the white and African American populations. More than one thousand of the city's African Americans left between 1930 and 1940, dimming the former vibrance and activity of the African American community. The decline continued following World War II, as good-paying jobs left the city, and the population experienced further decline.[84] This declining population between 1930 and 1960 may help to explain why several

African American lodge cemeteries in Knoxville endured long periods of neglect.

Although Knoxville was one of the major cities in the region, there were other African American communities in East Tennessee. Morristown, in Hamblen County, also boasted a thriving African American population, and at least one lodge cemetery. Bristol, in Sullivan County, was home to the Leatherwood Lodge No. 3543 of the Grand United Order of Odd Fellows.[85] Chattanooga was home to at least two African American Knights of Pythias lodges, five GUOOF lodges, and three African American Masonic lodges.[86] Harriman, in Roane County, which only had between five thousand and six thousand total inhabitants in 1910, was home to the Occidental Lodge No. 39 of the United Brothers of Friendship and the Morning Glory Temple No. 40 of the Sisters of the Mysterious Ten, as well as Congress Lodge No. 3737 of the GUOOF, two Masonic lodges, the Junction Lodge No. 103, and the Toussaint L'Ouverture Lodge No. 113.[87] Although East Tennessee did not have as many African Americans residents as other regions of the state, the lodge network was a vibrant one.

ODD FELLOWS / DAUGHTERS OF ZION / GOOD SAMARITAN CEMETERY COMPLEX

The Odd Fellows / Daughters of Zion / Good Samaritan Cemetery is actually a complex of at least four cemeteries, all immediately adjacent to each other and occupying an entire city block on Bethel Avenue in east Knoxville, in Knox County. It is difficult to discern the exact boundaries between the four cemeteries. Four separate lodges purchased property in the 1880s from the same owner, Preston L. Blang, a white farmer living in the Shieldstown community, and created what is commonly referred to as Odd Fellows Cemetery today.[88] Banner Lodge No. 1653 of the Grand United Order of Odd Fellows purchased its section of the cemetery at some point prior to 1881.[89] On June 23, 1882, Banner Lodge No. 1653 held a dedication ceremony for their cemetery. At this dedication, the lodge met at their hall on Gay Street and formed a procession that was led by the Banner Lodge Brass Band. Conveyances such as carriages, buggies, hacks, and phaetons and people on foot followed the procession from the lodge hall to the new cemetery. Once there, addresses and speeches were given by various ministers and lodge officers and music was performed by the lodge band. That night, the lodge continued the celebration by holding a grand festival in their hall in downtown Knoxville.[90]

Trustees for the Daughters of Zion purchased their portion of the cemetery from Preston Blang in 1881 for the sum of $139.35.[91] The group held various fundraisers to pay for the property, such as a supper they gave in April 1881 that raised $47.15.[92] In November 1881, the group held a dedication for their cemetery. The lodge was described as having over one hundred members, all female. In addition to purchasing the one and a half acre property, the lodge had also enclosed their cemetery with "neat fencing."[93] The Daughters of Zion lodge was also well regarded in the community for the care they provided to the sick. In 1882, Lawson Irvin wrote a letter to the editor of the *Knoxville Daily Chronicle* praising the group for the care they gave his recently deceased wife. He praised them "for their unceasing care and devotion," and noted, "from first to last she was attended by them unceasingly, until her remains were removed to their final resting place—the cemetery of the Daughters of Zion, of whom she was a member."[94] It is unclear what happened to the Daughters of Zion lodge in Knoxville. They were active as late as 1927, when they held their annual meeting and celebrated the fifty-second anniversary of the group. At that time, there were still three of the original ten charter members still living.[95] I have not found any mentions of this lodge after this reference.

In March 1881, a Good Samaritan lodge purchased its portion of the property from Preston Blang.[96] In 1887, trustees of the Rebecca Lodge of the Good Samaritans transferred their purchase of the cemetery to the Mt. Calvary Lodge of the Good Samaritans, although the reasons for this transfer are not clear.[97] The Good Samaritans were an active presence in Knoxville and owned a hall on Gay Street in Knoxville. In 1882, the group celebrated their anniversary by holding a parade and a festival at their hall. The newspaper commented, "in more ways than one this organization is accomplishing a noble and good work among our colored fellow-citizens." The paper went on to comment about their cemetery, stating, "Through its workings they have secured a desired and ample site for a burying ground, in East Knoxville, and they have just recently added some more territory to it. They are to be commended for this work."[98] The Rebecca Lodge met at Samaritan Hall on the first and third Monday evenings of the month.[99] As with other groups, it is unclear when the Good Samaritans ceased to exist in Knoxville. In 1934, the *Knoxville News-Sentinel* reported that the group was to hold a wiener roast in Tyson Park with all proceeds to benefit the lodge.[100] I have found

FIGURE 2.17. The Odd Fellows Cemetery complex in Knoxville contains walking paths, shown in this image.

no references to the groups following 1934.

Silver Moon Lodge No. 1803 of the Grand United Order of Odd Fellows purchased the final section of the cemetery from Preston Blang in September 1885.[101] Silver Moon Lodge was established circa 1877.[102] In 1881, the lodge celebrated its anniversary with a procession that marched to the train depot, where the members caught a train to nearby Inskip Station for a picnic. At the end of the day, the members returned to Knoxville for a reunion of East Tennessee Odd Fellows and a festival at the opera house in Knoxville.[103] By 1882, the lodge was meeting on the first and third Monday nights of the month in a building located at the corner of Gay and Main Streets in Knoxville.[104] As with the other lodges, it is unclear when and if Silver Moon Lodge No. 1803 became inactive.

The Odd Fellows Cemetery complex is located in a historically African American neighborhood of Knoxville.

A state historic marker, erected by the Tennessee Historical Commission, is located on Bethel Avenue near Kyle Street. There are many grave depressions within the complex, indicating a large number of unmarked graves. The cemetery contains many large, old, deciduous trees. Graves are oriented east-west. A gazebo has been installed in the cemetery as well. The site has gone through several periods of inadequate maintenance and poor condition. Since 2009, a group of volunteers consisting of community members, University of Tennessee faculty and students, and the City of Knoxville have worked to restore the cemeteries and reclaim the site, cleaning and mapping the cemetery, as well as working on the landscape.[105] The cemetery has a variety of marker types in addition to the unmarked graves.[106] Regardless of the different purchase dates and dedication celebrations, today the complex is generally regarded as a single cemetery. It was noted in 2003 that "it is difficult to discern the exact boundaries between the various cemeteries and all are overgrown with brush and small trees. Several attempts have been made over the years to clean the area, but the block continues to be a community dumping ground. There are probably in excess of 6,000 burials in this block."[107]

Since those words were written, the cemetery and its surrounding community have undergone a rebirth. New housing has been built, and a road added adjacent to the cemetery named Odd Fellows. Walking paths have been added to the cemetery, which is well kept. Broken monuments have either been repaired or placed upright, and some monuments have been stabilized.

MYSTERIOUS TEN CEMETERY (*Knoxville*)

Mysterious Ten Cemetery is located in the Oakland Community of Knoxville, near Foster's Chapel Missionary Baptist Church, an African American congregation. It is almost certain that this lodge cemetery was established by the United Brothers of Friendship and Sisters of the Mysterious Ten, an African American group described earlier. It is known that the Sisters of the Mysterious Ten were active in Knoxville as recently as 1929.[108] In 1956, a newspaper article in the *Knoxville News-Sentinel* referred to the place as a lodge cemetery and noted that the lodge was not active, although the Mysterious Ten "still flourishes in Virginia, and in many Southern states."[109]

Looking at city directories for Knoxville, it appears that the African American community of Oakland centered on Oakland and Beverly Roads in the Fountain City section of Knoxville. While it was not a large community, there were other African American institutions present in this area. There were several churches, such as the Oakland AME Zion Church, Oakland Baptist, and Fosters Chapel Missionary Baptist Church. As early as 1907, there was an Oakland School located in the community, noted as African American and serving an elementary-aged school population.[110] In 1936, this school building was replaced with a new WPA-built school with "one of the most modern cafeterias in any Negro school in Knox County."[111] There was a second cemetery in the community for African Americans, known as Citizens Cemetery, present in 1935.[112]

Mysterious Ten Cemetery may date to the early twentieth century.[113] It is located directly across from Fosters

Chapel Missionary Baptist Church, and it is approximately two-tenths of a mile from the former Oakland School and a church. At the time of my site visit, it was completely overgrown and there was no visible access to the cemetery. There is no signage to indicate the name of the cemetery. Robert McGinnis noted the presence of a handful of gravestones during his site visit in December 2004.

SOUTHERN CHAIN CEMETERY

Southern Chain Cemetery is located in West Knoxville, part of the West View Cemetery district. This district contains multiple cemeteries for diverse groups of people, such as the Lonas Family Cemetery and Middlebrook Cemetery, historically white cemeteries; the New Jewish Cemetery; and a complex of African American cemeteries—Crestview, Longview, and Southern Chain Cemeteries. Crestview, Longview, and Southern Chain were all established in the late nineteenth century and are adjacent to one another.[114] There are paths between the three, as well as a historical interpretive marker outlining their history.

The Southern Chain Lodge No. 4038 was a Grand United Order of Odd Fellows lodge in Knoxville dating to the period between 1870 and 1890. In 1897, the *Knoxville Sentinel* reported that the Banner, Silver Moon, and Southern Chain lodges were celebrating their fiftieth anniversary on the first Sunday in May at the African American First Baptist Church. This was likely the fiftieth anniversary of the GUOOF itself, not of the specific Knoxville lodges.[115] Also in 1897, Southern Chain Lodge No. 4038 held a big picnic at Cedar Grove. One newspaper report of the event described

FIGURE 2.18. Southern Chain Cemetery is part of a larger African American cemetery complex of three different cemeteries.

the lodge as "one of the largest colored lodges in the city."[116] In 1903, the lodge held a New Year's reception, along with the Household of Ruth, at the GUOOF lodge hall on Gay Street. This event included an invocation, musical performances, and recitations. There were several speeches, with titles such as "Welfare of Lodges" and "100 Years Hence." Refreshments served included oysters, ham, chicken salad, turkey, cold slaw, olives, pickles, ice cream and cake, and coffee.[117]

The Southern Chain Cemetery was established in 1898, when the William Bradley family sold the lodge several acres of land to create a cemetery. It is believed that burial in the cemetery was restricted to members of the GUOOF and their families until the early 1920s. By the 1970s, Southern Chain, Longview, and Crestview Cemeteries had fallen into disuse and were overgrown. In 1993, the Tennessee

Department of Commerce and Insurance acquired all three African American cemeteries and then turned the properties over to the West View Community Action Group. This group, along with the Knox County Sheriff's Department, care for the cemetery.[118]

Southern Chain Cemetery is well marked and easy to find. It suffers from some neglect with being slightly overgrown. Trash has also been dumped in several spots in the rear areas of the cemetery which are not easily viewed from Keith Avenue. Some monuments have been broken. There are many grave depressions that indicate unmarked graves as well as a few sunken graves. The cemetery is home to numerous trees, both deciduous and cedar. There are yucca bushes and buttercups marking a number of graves as well. Paths in the cemetery, which also connect to Crestview and Longview, are gravel and in need of repair. The grave placement is irregular in some spots while other areas are arranged in neat rows. Some of the graves are oriented east-west. The area nearest to Keith Avenue seems to contain the most recent burials.

COLORED MASONIC CEMETERY

The Colored Masonic Cemetery is located in Morristown, in Hamblen County. Various sources have called the cemetery by different names. *Love Lives On* by Robert McGinnis identifies the cemetery as either the Rock of Ages Baptist Church cemetery or the Morristown African American cemetery. He also states that there are two cemeteries on the property but no boundary between them.[119] *Cemeteries of Hamblen County, Tennessee*, vol. 3, edited by Marguerite

W. Williams, identifies the two cemeteries as Morristown City and Treece.[120] Several obituaries and death certificates identify the location as the Colored Masonic Cemetery. This cemetery being identified by several different names is not uncommon. Some cemetery transcription books were prepared by people who do not live in the community, who often assign a name to a cemetery, sometimes based on the last name of the majority of the people interred, such as Treece Cemetery, named for the number of Treece family members interred here. Based on the obituaries and other research, I feel that at least one of the cemeteries at this location was likely regarded as the Colored Masonic Cemetery, at least for a time in its history.

Morristown and Hamblen County have an interesting African American history, although the population may not have been as large as Knoxville. In 1910, the total population of Hamblen County was 13,650, 1,610 of whom were African American, representing nearly 12 percent of the total population.[121] The town was the home of Morristown College, an African American two-year college established in 1881 by the Methodist Episcopal Church. In 1901, the school was renamed the Morristown Normal and Industrial College, and it began offering courses in woodworking, masonry, carpentry, agricultural training, and domestic science. In the 1930s, the school switched to a liberal arts curriculum. The school struggled, however, and finally closed in the 1990s.[122] The school also acted as a high school for the African American community of Morristown and the surrounding area. The African American Masonic lodge was established early in Morristown's history, and is known as the Star Light Masonic Lodge No. 16. Its first Grand Master was Mr. Arthur Poe of

FIGURE 2.19. The site of the Colored Masonic Cemetery in Morristown contains two cemeteries with no discernible boundary between the two.

Morristown.[123] In 1907, the *Morristown Gazette* reported, "The colored Masons are erecting a hall on the west side of Cumberland Street near the new A.M.E. Church."[124] At some time in the early twentieth century, the Masons also established a cemetery for African Americans in Morristown. A 1934 article in the *Morristown Gazette Mail* on the death of John Prince, a ninety-year-old African American resident of the town, mentions that following his funeral service "interment will follow in the colored Masonic cemetery."[125] The death certificate for Mr. Prince lists his burial place as the Masonic Cemetery. The cemetery was still called the Masonic Cemetery as late as 1962, when Charles Parrish Dockery, a Mason, died. The newspaper reported that his burial would take place at Masonic Cemetery.[126]

Several sources agree that the site is home to two different cemeteries, and there is no detectable boundary between the two. The graves immediately adjacent to the Rock of Ages Baptist Church, to the west of the building, and those adjacent to the street, northeast of the church, are laid out in orderly rows. The graves at the rear of the property, located directly west of the church, are more haphazard in arrangement. There are only a few trees present in the cemetery, and most of these are located near the edges of the cemeteries. There are multiple grave depressions, indicating unmarked graves. There is no signage at the cemetery of any type. The cemetery is well maintained and still in use.

The above is not an exhaustive list of African American lodge cemeteries in Tennessee, as it is probable that there were others across the state established by fraternal and benevolent societies. There are also a handful of white fraternal cemeteries in the state, such as the Odd Fellows Cemetery in Baxter, Putnam County; the Concord Masonic Cemetery in Concord, Knox County; and the Eastern Star Cemetery in Sewanee, Franklin County. I have not visited some of these cemeteries, so I am unable to make comparisons between them and African American lodge cemeteries. The cemeteries described in this chapter are the ones I have documented as being either being established or currently owned by a fraternal and benevolent group.

CHAPTER 3

The Importance of Fraternalism and Benevolence in the African American Community

No complete account of Negro benefi-
cial societies is possible, so large is there
number and so wide their ramification.

—W. E. B. DU BOIS

In April 1909, members of the African American Knights
of Pythias lodges in Nashville, Tennessee, celebrated the
forty-fifth annual Thanksgiving celebration for the Knights
of Pythias of Nashville. Before the celebration began, organizers of the event realized that it would not be possible to

accommodate the men and women associated with the Pythians in one venue for the annual Thanksgiving sermon. There was reportedly no venue big enough for everyone to gather in the large numbers anticipated for the event. The celebration was therefore split into two and took place in two of the larger church spaces available, St. John's AME Church and Mt. Olive Baptist Church, located on Cedar Street. Two separate sermons were preached, with Missionary Baptist minister Rev. T. J. Townsend preaching at St. John's AME and an unnamed AME minister preaching at Mt. Olive Baptist. Both celebrations had the same program, and members could choose which church celebration they attended. A local paper described the attendance at the event, stating, "for an entire block one solid mass of surging humanity lined Cedar Street, unable to gain admittance to either church." It is estimated that approximately five thousand people took part in this Thanksgiving celebration.[1] Nashville's total population in 1910 is listed as 110,364, and its African American population was 36,523. If five thousand did attend the Pythian celebration, that means that 4.5 percent of Nashville's total population, and 13.7 percent of its African American population attended this event.[2] Given these numbers, this was an important event in the African American community, and shows the interest that it had in fraternal and benevolent events in their neighborhoods.

As this story illustrates, fraternalism and benevolence were extremely important to the African American community during the late nineteenth and early twentieth centuries, and people often held membership in multiple groups. Several sociologists in the early twentieth century who studied African American communities noted this tendency for

African Americans to join multiple fraternal and benevolent groups. Sociologist Howard Odum wrote in his 1910 study on African Americans in several Southern towns that "it is essential that the Negro and his family be protected by his membership in one or more of the lodges. Such membership will insure him against starvation and dire want, at least, will assure him of visits from his people which he would not otherwise get, and render him secure in a reasonable degree."[3] Hortense Powdermaker's anthropological study *After Freedom: A Cultural Study of the Deep South* (1939) also described the tendency of African Americans to join multiple fraternal groups for increased economic security in times of distress: "Most of the local Negroes belong to at least one of the societies, and some belong to more than one. . . . Burial insurance is usually the first to be taken out and the last to be relinquished when times grow hard. It is considered more important by the very poor than sickness or accident insurance."[4]

While the African American lodge and church are sometimes portrayed as two separate parts of the community at odds with each other, it is probably more correct to see the lodge and the church as two mutually supportive institutions that together formed the backbone of many African American communities in Tennessee.[5] The church and the lodge played interrelated roles in the community and worked jointly and individually to address the social, political, and economic problems faced by the members of their communities.[6] Particularly in rural areas, many African American benevolent groups were closely associated with the local church, taking Biblical names for their groups and meeting in the church when they did not own a lodge

hall.[7] Church buildings offered meeting space for a number of organizations in the African American community,
such as debating clubs, drama societies, trade associations,
temperance clubs, and equal rights leagues.[8] The African
American church building was one of the few spaces that
allowed community members to meet with no restrictions.
In some places, particularly as lives became more segregated,
their own churches were one of the few places that were
open to them. African American preachers from a variety
of Christian denominations were invited to speak at and
take part in annual lodge celebrations, preaching sermons
or discussing topics of importance to the community. The
church often represented more than just a physical meeting space for a group; it also provided a communication
network and financial resources for fledging groups.[9] Even
after lodges moved into separate buildings, relationships
between lodge and church continued.

There are numerous examples in Tennessee of lodges and
churches sharing resources, and of lodges holding meetings at churches. The Colored Relief Society in Bolivar, in
West Tennessee, met at the "colored Baptist Church" in 1878
and worked to collect money for the benefit of yellow fever
sufferers.[10] In 1874, the Colored Benevolent Society No. 1
of Nashville, one of the co-founders of Mt. Ararat Cemetery in Nashville, held their ninth anniversary celebration
with a procession that began at a church, Clark's Chapel,
located on Franklin Street.[11] Lodges also held anniversary
sermons, inviting different preachers to speak, as in 1907
when the AME church hosted the annual sermon for the
Benevolent Society in Shelbyville, preached by Dr. J. A.
Jones.[12] At the annual statewide convention of the Knights

of Pythias in 1907, organizers invited "several orators from different parts of the states, *most of whom were preachers,* . . . but the one to make the greatest impression, the one to make the men forget that they were jammed in a hot hall was Rev. Sutton E. Griggs, Nashville's polished preacher and renowned author" (emphasis added).[13] Lodges represented an ecumenical space where people from different Christian denominations in the African American community met together on neutral ground and worked for the betterment of their communities. Once they acquired space to meet, lodges would also offer meeting spaces to church groups when necessary. In 1870, the United Sons of Ham lodge in Memphis loaned their building to the AME Zion church for their annual conference. In thanks, the AME Zion conference printed a resolution in the newspaper to thank the Sons of Ham: "Resolved, that we esteem them as our friends, and will ever remember them to Almighty God, that their Society may live and grow and the blessings of the Almighty God attend them."[14] In 1875, when the building for the Shiloh Presbyterian Church, an African American congregation, was being erected, members of the Masonic lodge took charge of the ceremony for the laying of the cornerstone of the church. The ceremony was described as "well conducted and impressive," and the minister gave a brief history of the church following the ceremony.[15] In 1876, the GUOOF in Nashville held an annual celebration and festival at Spruce Street Baptist Church, with addresses made by two different preachers, Rev. M. R. Johnson of Nashville and Rev. A. Allensworth of Louisville.[16] This symbiotic relationship between lodges and churches is one deserving of scholarship and attention.

Lodges also pulled heavily from Christian belief systems, which formed an important part of the identity of many African American benevolent and fraternal groups. Many lodges took their names from Biblical references, such as the Sons of Ham, Good Samaritans, and the King David lodge. The Independent Order of Good Samaritans and the Daughters of Samaria displayed the biblical story of the Good Samaritan on all their membership ribbons and also used the story of the Good Samaritan as the central piece of the group's ritual.[17] Some of their cemeteries, such as the two Mount Ararat cemeteries organized by benevolent groups, also took their names from the Bible, as Mount Ararat was considered to be the resting place for Noah's Ark. The burial rituals of several groups also borrowed heavily from Christian tradition. In short, the Christian worldview shaped African American lodges in a variety of ways.

Segregation and racism both had a role in why African Americans created benevolent and fraternal lodges in such great numbers in Tennessee and across the south. During Reconstruction, particularly in urban areas such as Nashville and Memphis, there were many African Americans working as manual laborers; they received subsistence wages and had higher unemployment rates than their white counterparts.[18] Women in particular, when they were able to find jobs, were typically hired for "unskilled" labor at the bottom of the wage scale; these jobs primarily consisted of domestic labor performed for nonfamily members at subsistence wages.[19] In such trying economic circumstances, African Americans realized the need to share resources in a variety of ways, which lead directly to the creation of a network of churches and benevolent and fraternal groups. After creating this network of organizations, designed to provide assistance, people then joined multiple lodges, looking to increase the size of their safety net.

However, membership in multiple organizations was not reserved only for those seeking to maximize their economic security. People joined multiple organizations for a variety of reasons, such as increased networking abilities, social opportunities, entertainment, or other personal reasons lost to history. Professor W. S. Thompson of Nashville, principal of the Meigs School in 1909, was a member of the Knights of Pythias, the Odd Fellows, the Masons, the Independent Order of Immaculates, and the Benevolent Society.[20] Undertaker G. W. Franklin of Chattanooga listed the different lodges to which he belonged in an advertisement for his business in 1910: the Good Samaritans, the Knights of Pythias, the Odd Fellows, and the Knights of the Wise Men.[21] Perhaps he hoped members of these different organizations would remember their shared membership and use his business in the future. Obituaries of African Americans in Tennessee often noted membership in multiple organizations for the deceased. Dr. Robert Fulton Boyd, a prominent African American doctor and businessperson in Nashville, died unexpectedly in July 1912. The *Nashville Globe*'s article about his death noted his role as the Supreme Grand Master of the Independent Order of Immaculates as well as his role as a Grand Worthy Counselor of the Court of Calanthe (the woman's auxiliary of the Knights of Pythias).[22] In Milan, in West Tennessee, when Washington Webb, a local community member died, it was noted that he was a member of both the Masons and the Victory Lodge No. 56 of the Knights of Pythias.[23]

FIGURE 3.1. Dr Robert F. Boyd was active in multiple lodges in Nashville, including the Immaculates and Knights of Africa. His grave is located in Mt. Ararat (Nashville).

Books and works written by African Americans also often highlighted members of the community who were highly active in the local lodge network. In 1929, the *Knoxville Negro*, written by Bartow G. Wilson, an African American writer for the *Knoxville Herald*, recounted biographies of multiple prominent African Americans living in Knoxville; the author pointed out several people who held membership in multiple fraternal and benevolent organizations. Wilson noted that Mr. William Ernest Brown, described as a rising businessperson with several businesses, was a member of the Knights of Pythias as well as the Elks.[24] Mr. Boyd Browder, a well-known photographer in Knoxville, was a member of both Masonic and Elk lodges.[25] Belonging to multiple organizations was not confined to businessmen, as others in different fields also joined multiple groups. Mr. Mitchell Burke, a teacher and letter carrier in Knoxville, was a member of the Odd Fellows and Knights of Pythias lodges.[26] In Memphis, William Porter is noted as being an officer in the United Brothers of Friendship as well as the Masons.[27] It was also not limited to men, as the *Knoxville Negro* noted that Mrs. Cora E. Burke, a former teacher and spouse of Mr. Mitchell Burke, was a member of the Court of Calanthe as well as of the Household of Ruth (the women's auxiliary for the Odd Fellows).[28]

As these sources show, people across the African American community joined multiple groups, perhaps showing that membership in one group did not automatically exclude you from membership in another group. It is evident from several lodge cemeteries in Tennessee that this acceptance extended to allowing people to be buried in a lodge cemetery while belonging to other lodge groups. Mt. Ararat (Nashville) is home to a number of burials of people who were members of several groups other than the Sons of Relief or the Benevolent Society, founders of the cemetery. There are several Masonic burials in the cemetery, including the grave of Rev. Nelson McGavock, whose monument notes him as the first Grand Master of the Prince Hall Masons of Tennessee. Other examples include two members of the Knights of Pythias, Albert Neely and Charley Winstead, who share a marker along with Kittie Maxwell and Mary Winstead, buried in the newer section of Mt. Ararat (Nashville). There are two grave markers for William H. McGavock, an undertaker in Nashville, one of which is a Mosaic Templar

FIGURE 3.2. The grave marker for Matildia Streeter shows a Mosaic Templar symbol at the top.

tombstone noting his membership in Jackson Chamber 2828 of Nashville. Mr. McGavock is an example of a person who belonged to multiple organizations, as noted in a 1908 article in the *Nashville Globe*. At that time, he was a member of the Independent Order of Immaculates, the Tyree Lodge of the Knights of Pythias, Benevolent Society No. 1, the United Brothers of Friendship, and the Sons and Daughters of Israel No. 4.[29] At Benevolent Society No. 11 Cemetery in Murfreesboro, there are several graves that show other lodge affiliations. The grave marker of George Scruggs, who died in 1915, shows a Masonic square and compass engraved on the top. There are at least two other members of the Masons buried at this cemetery, John Blackman and a member of the Shanes family. I also found a Mosaic Templar tombstone for Walter Osburn, a member of the Mountain Grove Chamber No. 3003 from Sewanee, Tennessee. Mount Ararat (Shelbyville), a cemetery established by the Ladies Benevolent Society, has a tombstone for Robert Dowell that has "K of P," which stands for the Knights of Pythias, carved on the stone above his name. Matildia Streeter, a Mosaic Templar member of Sunflower Chamber 2621 of Memphis, Tennessee, is also buried here. Although it is unclear if most of the people noted above were members of multiple lodge organizations in their towns, it does seem as if being a member of a different lodge did not necessarily deny one the opportunity to be buried in the local African American lodge cemetery. As with Mr. McGavock, who was a member of a number of organizations, it is possible that the people listed above were also members of more than one group.

Not only were people frequently members of multiple lodges, different lodges would also at times join together to share resources, such as halls or cemeteries. In Knoxville, for example, the Knights of the Wise Men, a fraternal group, met in Banner Lodge Hall in 1882, which belonged to the Banner Lodge of the Grand United Order of Odd Fellows.[30] The Odd Fellows, the Knights of Pythias, and the United Brothers of Friendship shared a lodge hall on North Liberty Street in Jackson in the early 1890s.[31] Several lodges of the Independent Order of Immaculates and the Grand United Order of Odd Fellows in Memphis met at a hall on Hernando Street in the late 1890s.[32] In Columbia, lodges of the Masons and the Odd Fellows shared a hall on Eighth

Street during at least a portion of the twentieth century.³³
Despite examples of lodges successfully sharing spaces and
working together, at times these partnerships turned bitter,
resulting in protracted lawsuits between the groups.

In Edgefield, two different benevolent groups, the
Edgefield Benevolent Society and the Ladies Benevolent
Society, established a shared cemetery, an action that led
to an acrimonious lawsuit between the groups that was
eventually heard by the Tennessee Supreme Court. The
Edgefield Benevolent Cemetery, located four miles outside
of Nashville on Brick Church Pike, was formally dedicated in
June 1872. The (male) Edgefield Benevolent Society invited
other groups to join the dedication service, and a procession
including members of the Sons of Relief, Benevolent Order
No. 1, the People's Aid Society, the Brothers of Charity of
Edgefield, the Mechanic's Society, and Benevolent Order
No. 2 of Edgefield marched down Main Street in Edgefield.
Various bands played and several ministers offered prayers
and sermons before a gathered crowd of more than six
thousand people.³⁴ Despite this happy and well-attended
event, within two years, the ownership of the cemetery was
contested, with the Edgefield Benevolent Society involved
in a lawsuit over cemetery's ownership.

The Edgefield Benevolent Society and the Ladies Benevolent Society were both established in Edgefield, a suburb of
Nashville located just across the Cumberland River from
the city, in the late 1860s. In 1869, these two groups met
separately at Paynes Chapel, a church first organized by
the AME church in 1866 that used a dirt cellar for worship
space.³⁵ The Ladies Benevolent Society met on the first
Monday night of the month and the Edgefield Benevolent

Society met on the second Monday night of the month. To save further on expenses, the two groups began meeting on the same night in the same location; however, the Ladies Benevolent Society explicitly stated that they wanted to keep their own organization and officers, separate from the Edgefield Benevolent Society and under their personal control.[36] Prior to purchasing the cemetery in 1872, the Ladies Benevolent Society agreed to the purchase of land for a cemetery jointly with the Edgefield Benevolent Society, with the Ladies Benevolent Society believing that each group would enjoy equal privileges and joint ownership of the property.[37]

Whatever decision the Edgefield Benevolent Society and the Ladies Benevolent Society made regarding ownership prior to the actual purchase, this decision was not reflected in the legal title to the property. The deed of purchase from Thomas Ballow, a white farmer, to the group listed the owners as the trustees of the Benevolent Society No. 2 of Edgefield (also referred to the as Edgefield Benevolent Society). There is no reference to the Ladies Benevolent Society anywhere in the deed. J. B. Williams, president of the Edgefield Benevolent Society, later asserted, "Benevolent Society No. 2 did purchase a tract of land as a cemetery . . . paid for said land out of money belonging to the Society." He went on to state, "There was no one else's money paid, the last dollar was paid by Society No. 2."[38] From the beginning of ownership, the male Edgefield Benevolent Society was determined to be regarded as the sole owner of the property. It is not clear if this attitude was challenged by the Ladies Benevolent Society at the time the deed to the property was prepared, or when the Ladies Benevolent

Society first became aware that they were not listed on the deed to the property.

The two groups continued to share a meeting space, although tensions between the groups began to increase. While the precise reasons for the split between the groups are unclear, a breach erupted between the two groups during a meeting in late January or early February 1874 (reports differ as to the date). Unsurprisingly, details vary between the different groups as to what exactly happened. Various people reported that the Edgefield Benevolent Society No. 2 tried to merge the two groups into one group, with the resulting group and its treasury under the control of the men. Green Bass, a member of the male group later expelled from Benevolent Society No. 2 because of his support of the Ladies Benevolent Society, claimed, "President J. B. Williams got up and said Ladies all that were in favor of being under this charter (holding it up) come over to the men's side. . . . He further said that all would come and live under the charter will get to bury at the cemetery."[39] In short, the president said any member of the Ladies Benevolent Society wishing to use the cemetery had to join the Edgefield Benevolent Society. Joseph McClain, a member of the Edgefield Benevolent Society, stated that some of the women did not take kindly to this proposed merger and loss of control of their organization, "They said they would give up part of the grave yard rather than go with the men."[40] Some supporters of the Ladies Benevolent Society claimed that the rupture occurred because the Benevolent Society No. 2 wanted access to the treasury of the women, not just to control the cemetery. George McFerrin claimed, "The cause of it [the split] was that after the purchase of the cemetery the brothers wanted to do away with the female treasury and merge them into one. The women were against this and this caused the split."[41]

Regardless of the reason for the split, the women of the Ladies Benevolent Society refused to concede their ownership interest in the cemetery, their right to organize separately from the men, or the right to control their own finances. Freed from the confines of slavery, these women were determined to control their own group and finances as they saw fit, refusing to yield any of their freedoms, even to other members of their community. The women sued the Edgefield Benevolent Society in Davidson County Chancery Court, and continued to fight their case all the way to the Tennessee Supreme Court. This is not surprising, as historian Laura Edwards has noted, African American women in the period following the Civil War "stepped up and claimed what they thought should be theirs."[42] Control of their own group was one of the few societally approved ways that women could participate in democratic traditions by electing their own officers, setting their agendas, and controlling their funds.[43] The very act of suing Edgefield Benevolent Society No. 2 shows the willingness of the members of the Ladies Benevolent Society to lay full claim to their recently established civil rights as new citizens of the United States. It is no wonder, then, that the Ladies Benevolent Society fought so hard to control their organization and that they used their newly gained rights to protect what they held dear.

In the end, the supreme court ruled that although the deed only listed the male Edgefield Benevolent Society as owner, the cemetery did belong equally to both groups. Additionally, the court ruled that the two groups were clearly distinct entities, ruling that "the Court is therefore of the opinion after scrutinizing all of the testimony in the cause, and doth so order & decree that the two Societies were and have continued to be, and still are separate and independent organizations, and entitled to the property in question in equal moieties."[44] Despite this auspicious resolution of the case in favor of the Ladies Benevolent Society, neither the lodges nor the cemetery ultimately survived. In 1997, a real estate developer purchased the cemetery property, described as "abandoned," and had the interred bodies moved and reinterred elsewhere to make room for an industrial park. At that time, archaeologists estimated that burials at the cemetery took place between 1872 and the 1930s, although some members of the community recounted that burials took place as late as the 1950s.[45] It was a sad end to the cemetery dedicated with such fanfare in 1872.

Other lodge cemeteries also became legal battlegrounds between different lodge groups. One example of this is Mt. Ararat Cemetery (Nashville). At the time of its establishment, the *Republican Banner*, a Nashville newspaper, reported that the ten-acre property cost the Sons of Relief and the Colored Benevolent Society $3,550 and noted arrangements would soon be made for "a substantial fence to be built and the grounds appropriately decorated."[46] For decades, the two groups managed the cemetery seemingly with no tensions. If there were any, they remained private, unknown to the city at large. Mt. Ararat (Nashville) was a popular cemetery for the African American community, and the care given to the cemetery was noted by many. Although it is unclear when the tradition began, Mt. Ararat celebrated an annual decoration day. In 1884, the Nashville *Daily American* reported on the May nineteenth decoration day, stating, "Nearly all day yesterday vehicles of all kinds loaded down with the best colored people in town could be seen leaving the city going toward the Mt. Ararat Cemetery. . . . The day was fine and Mt. Ararat Cemetery was beautifully decorated with flowers that covered nearly every grave before the many worshippers returned home."[47] However, beneath the surface, tensions percolated between members of the two groups over the cemetery's management.

By January 1900, whatever goodwill existed between the two groups evaporated when the Benevolent Society filed an injunction against the Sons of Relief over the management of the cemetery. The Benevolent Society alleged a number of ways they believed the Sons of Relief had mismanaged the cemetery, including the assertion that the Sons of Relief refused to file or register the deed to the cemetery, which the chancery court found to be untrue. The Benevolent Society alleged that the Sons of Relief allowed students of Meharry College, an African American medical school in Nashville, to rob graves of bodies for use in classes, an allegation that appears particularly macabre and startling. Regarding grave robbing, the Benevolent Society further alleged that the superintendent of the cemetery, Mr. Gannaway, conspired with the Sons of Relief to become superintendent to use the position to enable himself and others to rob graves. It is unclear if the Benevolent Society truly believed Mr. Gannaway assisted in grave robbing, or if they were using a particularly scurrilous rumor as an excuse to dismiss Mr. Gannaway and install someone different as superintendent. The court found all these allegations to be unfounded. To settle the suit between the groups, a compromise was reached in which Mr. Gannaway was dismissed as superintendent and an interim superintendent named while the two societies formed a new committee to oversee the cemetery.[48] The two groups remained in ownership together following the 1900 lawsuit. In 1911, the groups celebrated paying off a mortgage on the property by burning the mortgage at a meeting at Hightower Hall on Fourth Avenue South in Nashville.[49] If there were further tensions between the groups, they were apparently settled outside of the legal system.

Despite various lawsuits between groups, lodges were typically the most popular institution within the African American community prior to the Great Depression.[50] However, the importance of fraternalism and benevolent groups, along with the associated fraternal and benevolent lodges, began to decline in both the African American community and in American society in general by the middle of the twentieth century. Historians and sociologists disagree why this decline occurred, usually citing a myriad of possible reasons. As the twentieth century progressed, lodges were no longer the only entertainment option for people, with the rise of radio and movies.[51] Some societies, especially among immigrant groups and African American groups, dealt with accusations of mismanagement and corruption.

Additionally, the beginning of the twentieth century coincided with the implementation of legislation that limited some of the freedom to act that fraternal and benevolent groups had enjoyed. This law, known as the Mobile Law of 1905, defined fraternal groups as nonprofit organizations that contained a lodge system, ritual, tax exemption, and representational governance, possibly restricting the number of groups who could claim lodge status.

This law also required that lodges hold a certain amount of funds in reserve and show a gradual improvement in those reserves. This amount was sometimes more than smaller lodges could afford. If the lodge failed to show improvement in the amount of reserve cash on hand, the law empowered state insurance commissions to revoke the license of the group. Many African American groups in states such as Georgia, Kentucky, Mississippi, and other states were also required to also pay a deposit ranging from $5,000 to $10,000 to the state insurance commission, an almost impossible requirement for smaller groups.[52] Other financial reasons may have also contributed to the decline of fraternal groups. In 1944, Edward Palmer pointed out that many groups declined because they did not properly factor risk in their financial assessments. He noted that in the early years of an organization, while the growth rate is high and the death rate is low, fraternal and benevolent groups thrived. However, as members aged and the death rate increased, groups did not increase dues and assessments and they inevitably ran out of money and failed.[53] Legislation and the lack of proper risk assessment created cracks in the lodge system that threatened to destroy many groups.

Combined with the earlier financial pressures, the impact of the Great Depression proved to be the death blow to a number of organizations. Gunnar Myrdal in 1944 pointed out that the Depression left many groups unable to pay out their sickness and death benefits, and as a result, lodges declined in popularity and membership.[54] Other historians of African American groups suggest difficult economic times and bad management of money led to the decline of fraternal and benevolent groups by the 1930s and 1940s.[55]

While the Great Depression hurt almost all fraternal and benevolent groups, regardless of racial makeup, some argue that this hurt African American lodges more because they tended to be smaller and have poorer members than their white counterparts. The Great Migration of African Americans out of the South also dealt a financial blow to a number of groups, as it left fewer people to pay dues and keep the lodges functioning.[56] In short, the arguments that a number of financial issues proved overwhelming is a compelling one.

In addition to financial pressures, the ideals of fraternalism itself came under attack during the first decade of the twentieth century, while ideas of service came to be lauded. Isaac Rubinow, a theorist, economist, and author, questioned whether mutual aid and neighborhood cooperation actually solved issues such as poverty and dependence. People began to question groups that worked only for the betterment of members of that organization, rather than for the good of humanity in general. As a result, benevolent and fraternal organizations saw membership decline in some areas of the country. Service clubs, such as Rotary International, Lions International, and Kiwanis International, all established between 1905 and 1917, pledged to work for the betterment of their communities and the nation as a whole.[57] While it is unclear if the rise of service clubs negatively impacted Tennessee's lodge system, it is a possible explanation as to why lodges became less prominent. In short, there was probably no single reason for the decline of fraternalism in Tennessee. People stopped organizing new lodges and lodge cemeteries for any number of reasons. In addition to economic pressure and challenges to fraternal ideals, it can't be denied that culture and society itself changed in Tennessee in a number of ways over the course of the twentieth century. With the end of legalized segregation, there was no longer a need to establish segregated cemeteries or lodge networks. The creation of a governmental welfare system also lessened the need for the sickness and burial benefits offered by lodges. The way that people lived and worked changed, as did the needs that the lodge system addressed.

While the prevalence of lodge life has declined in the African American community both in Tennessee and in the United States over the course of the twentieth century, pockets of fraternalism and benevolence still exist across the state. Lodges of Masons, Elks, Shriners, and other groups continue to uphold the ideas of fraternalism and offer members a number of benefits. They also continue to give back to their communities in in a number of ways, such as providing scholarship opportunities for students. Although the lodge network changed, some groups left behind a tangible reminder of their former activity on the landscape: the lodge cemeteries. As will be discussed in detail later, these cemeteries not only continue to exist, many continue to be in use and persist in being central to their communities. So long as these cemeteries remain on the landscape in Tennessee, the ideals of fraternalism, helping others, friendship, and mutual aid will continue to persist.

CHAPTER 4

The Importance of Funerals and Cemeteries in Fraternalism

There are few greater events than the burial, and none which brings the community
together in more characteristic attitude.
The funeral is a social event, for which the
lodge appropriates the necessary expenses.

—HOWARD ODUM, 1910

In August 1878, the Nashville *Daily American* reported the death of a local resident, Johnson McGhee, from consumption, as tuberculosis was commonly referred to during that period. The death of a local resident from consumption was, on its face, not particularly newsworthy, particularly when the deceased was not a prominent politician, community leader, or former military leader. Other stories on the front page dealt with the increased number of yellow fever cases in Memphis and New Orleans, described President Hayes's tour of the northwestern United States, and covered a reciprocal treaty between the United States and Canada. What merited the placement of this story on the first page of the newspaper in 1878 was that the resident's real name was not actually Johnson McGhee, but Chang Ze Yow. According to the paper, Yow was the first Chinese resident of Nashville. He worked in a laundry business, and former partners reported he had lived in Nashville for approximately two years, following a time spent in New Orleans.

After Yow's death, his body was taken to the undertaker M. S. Combs, located at 74 N. Cherry Street, who had advertised in 1878 that his undertaking establishment had the "finest hearses and carriages in the city. Embalming bodies, and everything pertaining to a first class house, at lower charges than elsewhere."[1] A large number of persons came to pay their respects at the funeral. A problem arose, however, as to how to properly bury Yow. His cousin Shing Lee reportedly refused to assist in disposing of his relative's body. This created a predicament as Yow did not neatly fit into any of the available groups with cemeteries. He was not Jewish, so burial at Temple Cemetery, established in 1851, was not an option. He was not Catholic, so he could not be buried at Calvary Cemetery, established in 1868. Being Chinese, Yow was not considered white either, so there may have been some hesitation at interring him in the City Cemetery or Mount Olivet, two white cemeteries open for burials at the time. While Yow could have possibly been a member of the Young Men's Christian Association (YMCA), then located at Union and Cherry Streets, the YMCA did not offer burial benefits. Likewise, if Yow was a member of one of the several temperance groups flourishing in Nashville at the time, such as a lodge of the Grand Council United Friends of Temperance of Tennessee, none of them owned a cemetery or offer burial benefits to members.[2] Someone offered Yow's body a final resting place at Mt. Ararat Cemetery in Nashville, meaning that Yow would be interred with the city's African American population.[3]

The question of where to bury Yow is the same question that African Americans themselves faced during the late nineteenth and early twentieth centuries—where would one's body be interred after death? Who would ensure that a "proper burial" took place? Who would care for your dead body once you were gone? What would happen to you if you did not belong to a church with a cemetery, or if you were the member of a minority group? What if you or your family could not afford a burial plot in a cemetery, even if you were allowed to be buried there? Who would care for your grave? For many, the answer to these questions came from the various fraternal and benevolent groups located across the state. These groups provided peace of mind to their members about who would care for them when they became ill and also about what would happen to their bodies after death.

While there were no state laws in Tennessee during the nineteenth and twentieth centuries specifically requiring segregated burial practices, by the end of the 1880s, segregation had become entrenched in many different areas of life throughout the state.[4] As segregation practices grew, African Americans increasingly worked to care for their sick and to bury their dead. An idea repeated frequently in legal documents related to African American fraternal and benevolent groups is this duty of the African American community to care for their sick and to provide proper burial for the dead. The charter for the Colored Benevolent Society, as the Benevolent Society was alternately referred to, stated in section 2 "that said Society shall afford relief and assistance to its members, and of the needy of their race in the city of Nashville, in cases of sickness, death, or disability to work."[5] The constitution of the Sons of Relief stated that its purpose was "to provide for the widow and the fatherless in their afflictions; to bury the dead and elevate the living."[6] The charter for the Independent Order of Pole Bearers Number 9 stated their purpose was to "establish a means whereby we may secure for each other exemption from neglect in the exigencies of sickness, want and death; to secure for each other employment, and to hold social meetings for the purpose of the advancement of each other."[7] The Silver Moon Lodge of the Grand United Order of Odd Fellows stated in their articles of incorporation their purpose was for "aiding and assisting sick and distressed members, maintaining their widows and orphans, defraying the funeral expenses of deceased Brothers, administering all the relief in their power to members needing assistance consistent with the better welfare of the Order and upbuilding of society."[8] The Young Men's Aid Society of Wilson County stated their purpose was for "assisting the weak & distressed members, visiting & administering to the sick of the order, and burying the dead."[9] The nearly universal references to the need to bury their dead and care for the sick show how important these concepts were to the African American community at the time, as they felt the need they felt to codify them in legally binding documents.

Not only were African American lodges concerned with finding and creating places to bury their members, they were also concerned with providing a proper burial ritual. It was these strong feelings about the need for "proper" last rites that led to the formation of burial societies and benevolent groups in African American communities across the United States.[10] This is not surprising as it is believed that the African American community held a belief that the soul of the deceased would eventually return to Africa, if the deceased received a proper and respectful burial.[11] It is also believed that some African societies felt that death was not final; the dead simply went into other worlds, and without an elaborate funeral to help settle them in the worlds beyond, the dead would wander restlessly and cause trouble for those left behind. Prior to Emancipation, the enslaved living across the South were limited in the rituals they could perform for the dead; after Emancipation, these rituals became more complex.[12] Eventually, some groups put these rituals into writing.

Several groups active in Tennessee published their burial rituals in their constitution and bylaws. The Benevolent Society published their burial ritual in the 1890 edition of the *Constitution and General By-Laws of the Colored People's Benevolent Society of Tennessee*. The Burial Ritual takes up a full five pages in the *Constitution and General By-Laws*, compared to the one and half pages devoted to the installation of officers, the one page devoted to the reception of new members, and the two pages entitled "Rules of the Order." This alone highlights the concerns the members felt over ensuring a proper burial for the members of the organization. A closer examination of the ritual also shows the impact of Judeo-Christian beliefs on African American society in the nineteenth century as well as parallels to African traditions.

After the death of a lodge member, the living members of the Benevolent Society lodge met at their lodge hall in order to conduct a special service for the deceased. At this service, the president of the lodge announced the death of the member and stated, "We have been called to pay the last tribute of respect to one of our _____; whom death has claimed as his own." Lodge members responded to this opening with responses such as, "O Lord, incline our hearts to serve and fear Thee, and find favor in Thy sight, and may we meet Thee in peace." The lodge's chaplain then presided over the service, with singing and prayer. After the final prayer, the lodge members moved in a procession to the home of the recently deceased, the site of additional ceremony. There may be a parallel in lodges processing to the home of the deceased with Ozo and Igbo funerals in Africa. In Igbo burials, the tribe went first to the home of the deceased before carrying the body to the cemetery.[13] If true, it is interesting that this traditional African practice was maintained and made part of the lodge's burial ritual.

Upon arrival at the deceased member's home, the president stood at the head of the bed of the deceased and stated, "Thou hast left us. No more shall we hear thy voice in council here below, for God has called thee to himself." After this, members of the lodge answered with a responsive reading. The use of call and response in religious settings in the African American community is drawn from their African heritage, another example of an African influence in this ritual. The use of call and response in services was not confined to the African American community, but its meaning did differ between the white and African American communities. The white community typically used responsive answers to a sermon as a way to encourage the preacher or as a way to convey their emotion over the message. For the African American community, it was a necessary component of the service because it was felt that the service lacked a connection to God if call and response was not used.[14] After the responsive reading, the president moved to the foot of the bed of the deceased and the chaplain moved to the head of the bed. The chaplain then uttered the following statement:

Brethren, weep not for the dead, for we must all lay off this mortality, and put on immortality. Let me admonish you, as death is passing on every breeze, his power is felt everywhere, none are exempt, no mountain so high, no valley so low, that death hath found it not. The young, the old, the loved must die, and here we part with those near and dear; but we shall meet again in that land from whose bourne no traveler returns.[15]

The part of the ritual that took place at the decedent's home concluded with additional hymns and prayers. The ritual then specified "the Order shall then proceed with the corpse to the place where the funeral service is to be held, if relatives desire, and the following Scriptures shall be read by the Chaplain: Paul's Second Epistle to the Corinthians, fifth chapter, from 1st to 15th verse," which describes how believers will be given an eternal home in heaven following death. Following the funeral service, the Benevolent lodge had yet another part to play in the burial of the deceased member. The final part of the ritual occurs at the cemetery. Once at the cemetery, the president and chaplain spoke further words and prayers over the head and feet of the deceased member. Some argue that positioning mourners around the head and the feet of the deceased bears similarities to Igbo funerals, perhaps another remnant of African tradition.[16] Part of the chaplain's final words at the cemetery included the following entreaty to the living lodge members left behind:

> My brethren, the melancholy occasion that calls us to our brother's grave is fraught with rich instruction. Here, we are reminded that, like our brother, we shall soon be wrapped up in the winding sheet of death, and pass away to the spirit land from whose bourne no traveler returns. Life is but a bubble—every pulse one passes into eternity.[17]

After this uplifting reminder of the imminence of their own impending deaths, the Chaplain then pronounced a benediction, the burial concluded, and the members of the lodge marched solemnly back to the lodge for dismissal. It is unclear when this ritual began for the Benevolent Society, and how long or how often it was used by the lodges.

The Young Men's Aid Society in Laguardo, in Wilson County, also had a written burial ritual used at the death of a member of the society. In their ritual, members of the lodge held a service for the deceased at their lodge hall. The president announced the death of the member and stated, "we have been called to pay the last tribute of respect to one of our _____ whom death has claimed as his own. . . . Hence, it behooves us to be ready to meet this last great enemy of mortality." The membership responded with, "O, Lord, incline our hearts to serve and fear thee, and find favor in Thy sight, and may we meet Thee in peace." Following this, the lodge moved in procession to the home of the deceased, where more readings and responses occurred. The lodge then moved in procession with the deceased to the place of burial. If the relatives of the deceased did not object, the chaplain of the order would read II Corinthians 5: 1–15. Following a funeral sermon, the lodge would take charge of the remains and close out the ceremony and burial.[18] As with the Benevolent Society, all references in this ritual are Christian in nature.

The Independent Order of Good Samaritans and Daughters of Samaria had a written burial ritual, published in 1873.[19] Upon the death of a member, a special meeting of the lodge was called, and the members were asked to wear their official lodge regalia. After an opening song, the presiding officer offered a prayer and made the following statement: "The object of this meeting is to pay the last sad tribute of respect to the remains of our deceased brother (sister). Knowing that we shall in course of time number up our jewels on earth, bid farewell to friends, and acquaintances, and die our Fathers' God to meet. We shall now proceed with a portion of the funeral exercises." The presiding officer then read a passage from Job 19:25–27, which states that a redeemer lives and that believers will see the redeemer after death. The members responded by reading 1 Timothy 6:7 ("For we brought nothing into this world, and it is certain we can carry nothing out") and Job 1:21 ("Naked I came from my mother's womb, and naked I will depart. The Lord gave and the Lord has taken away; may the name of the Lord be praised.")[20]

Following the prayers and responsive readings, the lodge marched in procession to the home of the deceased in the following order:

1. Marshall (with scarf, and baton in hand covered in crepe.
2. Musicians.
3. Outside Sentinel, with sword.
4. Vice Chief, with supporters.
5. Members, two abreast.
6. Prelate, with Holy Bible.
7. Financial secretary and treasurer.
8. Recording secretary.
9. Worthy Chief, with supporters.
10. Past Officers.
11. Members of the Council.
12. Inside Sentinel, with sword.[21]

Once the lodge arrived at the house, the body of the deceased was placed in the procession, and the lodge marched to the graveyard, followed by the officiating clergymen, mourners, and friends of the deceased. The lodge members formed a circle around the grave and lowered the body of the deceased into the grave. The presiding officer, prelate, and officiating clergyman took positions at the head of the grave, and friends and mourners stood at the foot. A graveside service for the deceased then takes place.

During this graveside service, the prelate spoke about the lessons of death, advising the attendees that death is advancing on all. Following the prelate's speech about the inevitability of death, a lengthy call and response, led by the presiding officer and answered by the lodge members, commenced. Some of the call and response included the following language:

> P. O. [PRESIDING OFFICER].—"What man is he that liveth and shall not see death? Can he deliver his soul from the power of the grave?"
>
> RESPONSE.—"Dust thou art and unto dust shalt thou return."
>
> P. O.—"The Lord gave, and the Lord hath taken away."
>
> RESPONSE.—"Blessed be the name of the Lord"
>
> P. O.—"Shall my brother (sister) rise again?"
>
> RESPONSE.—"If the dead rise not, then is not Christ risen."[22]

After the call and response, if there was no officiating clergyman to make a closing statement at the service, the presiding officer would read the following: "Forasmuch as it hath pleased God, in his wise providence, to take out of this world the soul of our deceased brother (sister). We therefore commit his (her) body to the ground; earth to earth, ashes to ashes, dust to dust; looking for the general resurrection in the last day, and the life of the world to come, through Jesus Christ our Lord. Amen." A final song was offered as well as a final prayer. After this, the lodge members and presiding officers are instructed by the ritual to give the following signs, a string of numbers that had some meaning for the lodge members:

> 1st. 19-22-21-14-10 X 11-7-16-2 X 2-21-3-18-25 X 5-19-7-3 X 12-7-5-6 X 11-6-10-21-25-16 XX.

2nd. 10-9-16-10-8-18 x 16-2-10-20 x 18 inches, 17-3 x 13-6-7-3-16 x 15-17-16-2 x 19-21-22-20 x 18-7-15-3-15-21-6-18 xx.

3rd. 22-10-16 x 16-2-10-20 x 10-21-22-22 x 16-7 x 12-7-5-6 x 25-17-18-10 xx.

The text provides what it calls an "Explanation," although it does not provide any elucidation as to the meaning of the signs:

1st. 7-3-14-10 x 3-10-21-6 x 16-7 x 20-12 x 11-7-25-7-20 xx.

2nd. 11-5-16 x 3-7-15 x 2-10 x (25-2-10 x) 17-25 x 26-7-3-10 xx.

3rd. 10-8-10-3 x 25-7 x 13-21-6-10-15-10-22-22 xx.[23]

As with the other burial rituals associated with fraternal and benevolent groups, the ritual for the Good Samaritans uses explicitly Christian texts and symbolism, although there are some possible African traditions, as noted previously. Regarding the signs given at the grave of the deceased, the meaning behind this string of numbers is unclear. The Good Samaritans also used numbers to indicate signs that members would give each other "to enable us to discover in mixed company, members of our Order whether male or female."[24] In short, the ritual of the Good Samaritans is an intriguing mix of Christian text with some possible African traditions and an esoteric use of numerology. It is not clear how often this ritual was actually used by the Samaritans.

The United Brothers of Friendship and Sisters of the Mysterious Ten had a burial ritual, although it is not as esoteric as the ritual of the Good Samaritans or as lengthy as the Benevolent Society ritual. It is likely that some of those interred at Mysterious Ten Cemetery were buried with this ritual. Following the death of a lodge member, the lodge would hold a meeting of the membership, opened by the Worthy Master (W.M.). The W.M. then turned the ceremony over to the Senior Marshal, who directed the membership to create a line of procession. The line of procession was to be in the following order:

1. Two Sentinels with drawn swords.
2. Music.
3. First Degree Workmen.
4. Second Degree Workmen.
5. Third Degree Workmen.
6. Secretary and Treasurer.
7. Chaplain, with Holy Bible on cushion covered with black cloth.
8. Right and Left Supporters.
9. M. W. M. [Most Worthy Master] and D. M. [Deputy Master]
10. Fourth Degree Workmen.
11. Pallbearers. (Hearse.) Pallbearers.
12. Friends of the family, etc.[25]

Once the procession reached the church, the procession would part to allow the coffin to be carried through the group.

Following the funeral service and at the graveside, the Chaplain led the group in a call and response that had overtly Christian themes. Examples of the call and response include the following:

CHAPLAIN: If a man dieth, shall he live again?

RESPONSE: Yea, the day cometh and the hour draweth nigh when all that are in their graves shall hear the voice of the Son of God and come forth.[26]

After the call and response portion, a funeral hymn was sung. The song contained several lodge-related verses, such as the line, "O, meet me in the Lodge above, / Where all is peace and joy and love," and "We'll meet in that Grand Lodge above, / Where all is joy and God is love." After the hymn is sung by the lodge, the members were directed to give the following lodge signs:

> Clasp the hands in front of the body at arms' length and say "Unite;" raise hands up at full arms' length, cast eyes heavenward, and say, "Bless;" bring down hands, catching hold of arms half way between elbows and shoulders, and say, "And save us;" raise right hand, point up with forefinger, and say, "In Thy Kingdom," raise left hand also up at full arms' length, with hands open, and say, "O, Lord;" then let both hands fall to sides. Repeat three times.[27]

In addition to providing burial rituals, lodges also needed places to properly bury the dead. The fact that these cemeteries are located in both rural and urban areas, in multiple regions of the state, highlights the importance of creating burial spaces for these groups. African American lodge members across the state worried about what would happen to them or to a loved one after death. How would a proper burial be assured? The only reassurance that the proper rites and rituals as well as a proper interment would occur was to create their own cemeteries in which they had complete control.

In addition to properly burying the dead and providing a final resting place, people also worried about keeping graves safe and secure from danger. An ongoing concern at some of the lodge cemeteries was grave robbing, as events at Mt. Ararat (Nashville), where grave robbing had been an intermittent problem for decades, illustrate. An ad in the *Republican Banner* in 1873 referred to a horse and buggy left behind at the cemetery by two men attempting to disinter a dead body. They fled when discovered by the person who placed the ad.[28] The *Daily American* reported in 1879 that "snatchers" had been taking bodies from Mt. Ararat (Nashville) for several months. The sexton of the cemetery, Preston Norton, and a guard, Hampton Jones, resolved to begin watching the cemetery at night in hopes of apprehending the grave snatchers. On a Saturday night in November, four men (three African American and one white) entered the cemetery with the intent of taking a body, but were attacked and stopped by Norton and Jones. Two men escaped, and of the two captured, one was fined $25 and the other discharged. The paper further noted, "Bodies are said to be scarcer now than for some time past, and good 'cadavers' sell readily for about $6 each."[29] This is a reference to the practice of medical schools, of which Nashville had several, "finding" cadavers for student use at nearby cemeteries. The threat of grave robbing did not abate at the dawn of the twentieth century. In 1899, the *Nashville American* reported that the body of a young girl was found near a grave at Mt. Ararat, "from which it had evidently been exhumed by a grave robber who was frightened off."[30] Threats of grave robbing and the inability to stop it from occurring undermined the ability of the Benevolent Society and the Sons of Relief to provide a proper burial for their members. Odd Fellows Cemetery in Knoxville dealt with two grave robberies in 1909, and authorities searched both Knoxville College, an African American school, and Lincoln Memorial University Medical School for the stolen cadavers.[31] Cemeteries in rural areas probably did not face this threat.

The creation of burial rituals as well as the organization and protection of cemeteries for use by members show the importance of caring for the dead and ensuring proper burials to African American fraternal and benevolent groups. These cemeteries, whether or not they were established by a lodge, were special to the African American community, as they were seen as the realm of the deceased.[32] Additionally, cemeteries allowed African Americans to express their customs and beliefs in a material way, with grave objects and decorations and the way graveyards were spatially oriented. The lodge cemeteries are expressions, visual and spatial, that tell us not only about the dead but also about the people who created the cemetery.[33] The following chapters will examine the lodge cemeteries in more detail, looking at how individuals and the lodges themselves are commemorated in the cemeteries, as well as examining the geography and spatial orientation of the cemeteries.

CHAPTER 5

Remembering the Dead
Commemoration in Lodge Cemeteries

They are the proud possessors of a cemetery in which the remains of a king would
not be dishonored to lie.

—GREEN POLONIUS HAMILTON,
describing Zion Christian Cemetery,
Memphis (1908)

Perusing the *Memphis Daily Appeal* on October 27, 1877,
residents may have been surprised at this bleak announce-
ment: "Rev. Morris Henderson, a well-known colored minister, is quite ill, there being no hopes of his recovery."[1] Rever-
end Henderson, born into slavery in Amelia County, Virginia,
around 1802, migrated to Memphis in 1847.[2] He held church
services in the basement of the white First Baptist Church
from 1854 to February 1865; at that time, the congregation
abandoned the white church as a meeting place and moved

their worship services to a brush arbor. Leaving First Baptist allowed Henderson's congregation to escape the control of the white church and to plot their own separate and independent course.[3] This congregation became the Beale Street Baptist Church, and a revival at the church in 1866 led to more than one hundred new members joining the church. Shortly after this increase in membership, the congregation raised $5,000 to purchase a lot on Beale Street and began building the brick and stone building that still stands and is listed on the National Register of Historic Places.[4] Beyond serving the spiritual needs of its own members, Henderson's Beale Street Baptist also became the "mother church" of several African American Baptist congregations across Memphis, spreading his religious influence across the city.[5] When Henderson died on October 26, 1877, the *Public Ledger* described Henderson as "a colored preacher of age and note," and stated that Henderson's funeral "will be attended by almost the entire colored population of the city."[6] The local papers continued to remember Henderson in print for several days. On October 30, 1877, the *Memphis Daily Appeal* devoted an article to the funeral of Reverend Henderson, noting that

> Sunday the remains of Rev. Morris Henderson were buried in Zion cemetery. Rev. Morris Henderson was a colored minister, whose zeal and piety, to say nothing of his energy and active Christian life, endeared him to his race, and won for him the respect and confidence of the white people. Perhaps no colored man ever lived who held a higher position in the estimation of the people of Memphis.[7]

It was estimated that more than five thousand Memphians attended his funeral, and his cortege was made up of 172 vehicles.[8]

In addition to ministering for decades, Henderson had also been an active member of several benevolent groups during his lifetime. In that role, he organized a special railway excursion under the direction of the United Sons of Ham to attend the Nashville Industrial Exposition on September 21, 1874. The special fare of $5 covered a round trip to the exposition, and Rev. Henderson, along with L. C. Carter and Henry Boyd, were listed as superintendents of the excursion.[9] Henderson was also active in other community endeavors, such as serving on the board of directors for the Canfield Orphan Asylum, an orphanage for African Americans in Memphis.[10] In addition to his religious, fraternal, and community work, he was also politically active, and was arrested in 1876 for voting.[11] It is fair to say that Henderson was an influential man in the African American community in Reconstruction-era Memphis. Between his leadership of a prominent church, his participation in benevolent groups, his concern for the community, and his political involvement, Henderson was well known and respected by many of his fellow Memphians.

Many of Rev. Henderson's fellow Memphians wished to honor the memory of this man who had been so vital to the city's African American community in a tangible, permanent fashion. In 1881, the community decided to erect a lasting tribute to his memory, in the form of one of the largest and most elaborate monuments in the cemetery. This monument to Henderson, designed by J. White and Son Marble Monuments, was a four-foot-tall base supporting

FIGURE 5.1. The Rev. Morris Henderson grave marker as it appears in 2020. The statue of hope, not seen, is no longer on top the monument.

a five-foot figure representing Hope. Both the base and the figure were placed on three blocks of stone. The monument was approximately ten feet high in total. The front of this monument contained Henderson's epitaph with his name, death date, and age.[12] When it was unveiled at Zion Cemetery, a special train excursion was offered to those wanting to attend the ceremony on May 29, 1881. Trains would leave the Charleston depot (located on Charleston Avenue across from Old Madison) in Memphis at 12:30, 1:30, and 2:30 on that day, and a special fare of 25 cents for a round trip was announced. Additionally, and with a nod to the tightening strictures of Jim Crow segregation, the ad announced "A special car is provided for our white friends."[13] The placement of this monument on a small rise beside the main road, along with its height, gave the appearance of Rev. Henderson continuing to preside over his congregation and community. The area of the gravesite and memorial was designated as Morris Henderson Circle.[14] By placing a monument with Rev. Henderson's image in Zion Cemetery, Henderson's contemporaries could feel that they had done their best to honor and commemorate him. The monument would be a lasting testament to the works of Rev. Henderson, ensuring that Memphians would remember both the man and his many good works.

Despite the best intentions of creating a lasting monument to Rev. Henderson, both the monument and Zion Cemetery struggled to have people remember their existence, dealing with neglect as the twentieth century drew to a close. As of 2020, the statue of Hope that rested on top the Henderson monument no longer stands proudly but sits propped against the rear of the monument, its head missing. The waning popularity and use of the cemetery was gradual, beginning with a steady decline in burials. In 1907, the cemetery peaked at 1,060 burials. The number of burials dropped after that, until in 1925 only 437 were buried in the cemetery. The year 1926 saw the most precipitous reduction in burials, with only 44 interments occurring. After 1926, the decline in burials at the cemetery continued through 1974, and the exact cause is unclear.[15] By the 1930s, Memphis newspapers reported that African American churches were asking their congregations for donations to maintain and support the cemetery. Most of the shareholders of the Zion Cemetery Company, legal owners of the cemetery since the 1890s, had died by the 1960s, after which the cemetery fell into further disrepair.[16] In 1979, a local minister, Rev. Isaiah Rowser, began efforts to clean up the cemetery. He bulldozed the southwest corner of the cemetery in an effort to clear debris and inadvertently lost some gravestones in the process. After that work was stopped by court order, the cemetery continued to languish from neglect. In 1988, the General Board of Personnel Services of the CME Church, owner of the property since 1986, began work to restore the cemetery.[17] Sporadic restoration work continued at the cemetery until 2005, when a group of organizations and individuals created the Zion Community Project, Inc. This restoration effort continues, and the group works tirelessly to restore and celebrate the cemetery as an integral part of the community, as well as to remember those interred within.[18] Zion Community Project's efforts continue and highlight the ways commemoration has changed over time. The group has not erected new stone monuments or statues, but instead works through various media, such as newspapers, television, and a website, to tell the story of this place, to celebrate the cemetery, and to help people remember those who are buried here.

Lodge cemeteries provide a wealth of information on remembrance and the different types of commemoration within the African American community. Commemoration takes forms ranging from events designed to remember the dead, such as decoration days, to the types of grave markers found in cemeteries. One type of commemoration present in lodge cemeteries is a monument that has been erected in memory or honor of the lodge that established the cemetery. A surprising number of lodge cemeteries have this sort of commemorative marker located somewhere on the property. Another type of commemoration is individual in nature, represented by the wide variety of grave markers found at cemeteries. A third, more subtle type of commemoration and remembrance is botanical in nature, noted by a variety of plants (vinca, yucca, daffodils, and other plants) used to mark gravesites. A newer type of commemoration is found on the internet in the form of dedicated websites or aggregated websites containing burial locations, such as Find a Grave. These sites of virtual commemoration and remembrance allow people across the globe to post pictures and stories in an effort to remember the deceased. Historic markers, erected by the state historic commission or the local community, are also a type of commemoration, and several lodge cemeteries in Tennessee have historical markers present at their sites. All these differing forms of commemoration and remembrance in lodge cemeteries will be discussed in greater detail.

A popular form of remembrance in the South during the nineteenth and twentieth centuries centered around the celebration of decoration day. There were two types of decoration day in the South. The first is the Decoration Day that people traditionally think of, the one that initially focused on honoring the Civil War dead and was started primarily by white women in communities across the South; in fact, more than one community claims to be the site of the original Decoration Day. Although it may have started as a spiritual practice, historian David Blight has noted how the observance of this type of decoration day soon developed along partisan lines and gained a political meaning.[19] Over time, this celebration of Decoration Day included honoring those who died in other wars, such as World War I, and is now known as Memorial Day. There was also another type of decoration day that took part across the South that was not confined to remembering and honoring the Civil War dead. This decoration day tradition, also sometimes simply referred to as "decoration," still takes place in some parts of the South in both church and family cemeteries; in fact, I attended decoration day gatherings at a family cemetery in rural Wilson County, as well as at the small church cemetery in Moore County, Tennessee, where my grandparents are buried, well into the 1990s. This type of decoration day traditionally took place in either the late spring or early summer, with the date varying according to the needs of the community. The ones I attended usually occurred in May or June, before the heat of July and August made such gatherings unpleasant. In addition to decorating the graves of the departed, there were sermons or speeches, singing, and often "dinner on the ground"—a pot-luck-style picnic shared by all those in attendance. These decoration day events typically lasted all day, serving as a reunion of sorts for the community as well as a remembrance of the dead.[20]

This type of decoration day was celebrated in cemeteries, both white and African American, across Tennessee, as the historic record bears out. The *Savannah Courier* remarked on the decoration held at Wesley Chapel Cemetery in Nixon (Hardin County) in 1898, reporting, "The decoration day at Chapel Cemetery last Thursday was a grand success. The opening speech was made by Rev. J. M. Carter, followed by Rev. J. C. Roberts and Prof. J. M. Watson, after which we had recess and walked over to the cemetery and viewed the beautiful flowers and ornaments that decked the graves."[21] In 1898, more than five hundred people attended decoration day exercises at Lone Oak Cemetery in Lewisburg, Tennessee. The attendees were treated to a program that included songs, prayers, a sermon, and various addresses.[22] In 1910, the *Camden Chronicle* in Benton County reported on the upcoming decoration at Mount Carmel, stating, "Saturday, May 21, is the day set apart for the decoration at Mount Carmel. Dinner on the ground. There will be services in the forenoon and evening. All are invited."[23] Also in Lewisburg in May 1910, Head Springs Church held their decoration day, which began with friends and family of the deceased cleaning the graves. Following this, a dinner on the ground was held, followed by an address given by Rev. John Royal, after which the participants decorated the graves with flowers.[24]

Many African American lodge cemeteries in Tennessee also held annual decoration days to remember their departed. At Benevolent Society No. 79 Cemetery in Briersville, lodge members met at the lodge hall on July 28, 1912. They then marched together to the cemetery and held a short memorial service that included several popular hymns, such as "A Friend in Jesus" and "Blest Be the Tie That Binds." There were at least three different addresses or sermons given at various times during the day; one of these addresses was given by the editor of the *Nashville Globe*, Mr. D. A. Hart. Following the hymns and sermons, refreshments were served.[25] The Ladies Benevolent Society held an annual decoration day, usually in May, at their Mount Ararat (Shelbyville) cemetery beginning in 1894.[26] At the 1911 decoration, several addresses were given, and students from the local Turner Normal College, an African American school, presented a floral design for the grave of Dr. B. A. J. Nixon, who had been one of the pioneers of the school. Members of the college also performed several songs for the crowd.[27] At Mt. Ararat (Nashville) in 1908, the decoration day activities were scheduled for Sunday, May 31. The *Nashville Globe* reported, "The public is urged to attend, and all who have friends buried in the cemetery are requested to come prepared to decorate their graves with flowers and plants. All ministers of the city are most cordially invited to be present at 3 o'clock in the afternoon to take part in the exercises."[28] As this quote indicates, decoration day was an ecumenical affair, with ministers of different Christian denominations taking part. These decoration day activities were a form of commemoration, a way of remembering and honoring the dead of the community as well as being an opportunity for the living to fellowship with one another. It is very likely that the decoration day tradition continues at some of the lodge cemeteries in Tennessee.

I have found several African American lodge cemeteries in Tennessee with an interesting form of commemoration in the form of a monument dedicated to the lodge society that established the cemetery. Some of these monuments and

FIGURE 5.2. This obelisk in Mount Ararat Shelbyville is a marker for the Benevolent Society.

remembrances date to the period of cemetery foundation or immediately after; however, a few are of more recent origin. Interestingly, many of the monuments are larger and more elaborate than the individual tombstones in the cemetery, making them easy to find and recognize. All these monuments show a desire for the lodge to be remembered and honored for their care of their members. It is possible that more cemeteries contained this type of lodge marker, but those markers have not survived to the present day. It is also possible this type of marker was largely confined to the Benevolent Society, as most of the existing examples come from Benevolent Society cemeteries. Whatever the case, it is interesting to find these monuments, as they are often the only physical remnant left of that lodge.

Mount Ararat Cemetery (Shelbyville) contains a monument to the Benevolent Society that takes the form of an obelisk on a pedestal and is one of the more elaborate markers in the cemetery. It sits in the eastern portion of the cemetery. At first glance, I thought it was an elaborate individual tombstone. Only when I approached it and examined it more closely did I see that this was a marker to the Benevolent Society. The base of the marker in rough on all four sides, appearing hand carved or hand hewn. A smaller base sits on top of this base, with scrollwork on each side; the same scrollwork is repeated on each side of the obelisk. The pedestal contains an engraving to the Benevolent Society on one side. Sitting on top of the pedestal is the obelisk, and although somewhat defaced by time and climate, you can still make out the remnants of scrollwork carved on the sides of the obelisk. On one side of the pedestal is the inscription, "Erected to the Sacred Memory of the Honored Dead of the Benevolent Society. Their Works Do Follow Them." Interestingly, there are no names of any officers or members responsible for the erection of the monument engraved on the obelisk. This is not always the case with lodge markers. This is an entirely anonymous marker, seemingly only wanting to reflect and remember the lodge in a broad sense, with no focus on individual members or officers.

Benevolent 210 Cemetery in Port Royal contains several different commemorative markers and plaques for that lodge. During my initial visit to the site in 2013, a somewhat squat, medium-sized stone obelisk in the cemetery caught my attention, as it looked nothing like the other monuments or tombstones in the cemetery. This obelisk sat on top of a pedestal base. On the face of the base was a carving with what appeared to be the symbol of the Benevolent Society. This same symbol of a triangle with an anchor and heart in the center is found on the lodge sign located at entrance to the property. Beneath this symbol on the obelisk is engraved the number 42, an eroded word, and the number 49. The meaning of the carving is unclear as neither 42 nor 49 are associated with this particular lodge of the Benevolent Society. On the face of the obelisk is engraved "B. O.," similarly battered by time as are the rest of the carvings on this particular stone. When I visited the cemetery again in 2019, I noticed that this marker has fallen to the ground and has not been repaired. Although no longer erect, the marker is propped against its former base. Additionally, I noticed a newer commemorative sign to the order had been placed near the entrance to the property. It is a white wooden sign that contains a history of the order as well as a picture of the 1908 lodge hall that once stood on the property. This sign

FIGURE 5.3. This marker erected to commemorate the Benevolent Lodge
No. 210 hall as it appeared in 2013.

is weatherproofed and was erected in 2014 or 2015 as part
of an Eagle Scout project. The lodge hall also has an interesting set of commemorative markers located on the front.
The marker at the top is a reproduction of a photograph of
the original 1908 lodge hall, a two-story frame building that

burnt in 1994, the same image used on the sign. Beneath that is a marker stating the following:

BENEVOLENT LODGE
ORDER # 210
REBUILT
IN THE YEAR
OF OUR LORD
2001
BUILT IN APRIL 1908
BURNED AUG. 18, 1994

Beneath this inscription are listed the names of the president and trustees of the organization at the time of rebuilding. In this case, the lodge is remembering its long history, both good and bad. The continued existence of the lodge is remembered, as well as the devastating 1994 fire that destroyed their 1908 building. The officers, presumably those who had worked diligently for seven years to rebuild the lodge hall, are also remembered. This marker celebrates the lodge's presence in Port Royal and its triumph over those who sought to destroy its work.

Benevolent Society No. 11 Cemetery in Murfreesboro also has an elaborate monument to the lodge. As in Port Royal, it immediately grabbed my attention as different from all other monuments present in the cemetery, in this case because it is the tallest monument in the cemetery. This monument is a pedestal with an urn at the top. The urn at the top has a cross on one side. The words "Erected Dec. 11, 1902 Benevolent Society No. 11" are inscribed on the west side of the pedestal beneath a row of leaf and tree

FIGURE 5.4. The dedication markers for Benevolent Lodge No. 210 located on the side of the lodge hall call attention to the lodge's history.

FIGURE 5.5. This pedestal urn monument dedicated to the lodge is found at Benevolent Society No. 11 in Murfreesboro.

carvings. The east side of the pedestal has the names of the lodge's chaplains inscribed, also beneath the same pattern of leaf and tree carvings. These chaplains, Alex Simmons and William Jordan, were also listed as trustees on the deed when the property was purchased in 1897.[29] The monument is near a large tree but there are few marked graves in its immediate vicinity. Its placement in the cemetery also feels unique in that it is not near the geographical center of the property, nor is it near the entrance. It is located near an unpaved path through the cemetery, but not in an area that is a natural focal point of the cemetery. However, it is possible that at the time the monument was placed in 1902 this location was a focal point, or near the center of existing burials. As with the similar lodge monument at the Benevolent Society No. 210 cemetery and Mt. Ararat (Shelbyville), it is not clear why these monuments were erected by their lodges. Given their size, they must have been more expensive than the other monuments in the cemetery. Were the lodges flush with extra cash in the treasury and so they decided to erect a monument in their honor? Was a special collection taken up to erect these monuments? Did all Benevolent Society cemeteries in Middle Tennessee contain similar lodge monuments? We may never know why these particular monuments were erected, but they are interesting features of the cemeteries.

Odd Fellows Cemetery in Springfield has what may be a monument to the Grand United Order of Odd Fellows in the cemetery in the form of a pedestal tomb with a vaulted roof. The different sides of the monument contain carvings of several symbols associated with the GUOOF, such as the clasped hands, representing friendship. The phrase "Gone,

FIGURE 5.6. This intriguing marker at Odd Fellows Springfield contains a number of different carved figures but no names.

But Not Forgotten" is engraved above the hands. On the pedestal is an anchor crossed by another symbol that was important to the Odd Fellows, a chain whose links represented love, charity, and friendship or truth.[30] Anchors were a symbol of hope, based on Hebrews 6:19, "We have this hope as an anchor for the soul, firm and secure."[31] Above the anchor is a carving resembling draperies; on the opposite side of the pedestal there is a flower with the same drapery above it. A third side of the pedestal has what appears to be a sheaf of wheat with again the same drapery above it. Interestingly, some of these symbols are also often associated with Masons. Wheat may symbolize immortality and resurrection and was also a popular Masonic symbol.[32] On the final side of the pedestal is a cross with a crown on it, an image that symbolizes Christianity and the sovereignty of the Lord. It is also associated with Masons, symbolizing their power and authority to lead.[33] As with the other sides, there is carved drapery above the cross and crown. With no names engraved on the monument and several displays of symbols associated with both Masonry and Odd Fellows, I found it to be one of the most intriguing monuments in the cemetery.

It is interesting to note that a few of the cemeteries have signs or markers that are of more recent origin, showing that either the lodge continues in existence, or that the current cemetery owners wish to honor the historical antecedents of their cemetery. An example of this is found at the Benevolent Society No. 16 Cemetery in Goodlettsville, Tennessee. A large stone and concrete sign sits at the entrance of the cemetery. A stacked stone base, three stones high, forms the bottom of the sign. On top of the

FIGURE 5.7. The brick with wood inlay sign at the Sons of Ham Cemetery pays homage to the year the Sons of Ham were established.

base is a cement sign with the words "Benevolent Cemetery Lodge # 16 Est 1862" engraved on the face along with a dove. This cement sign is surrounded and topped by a single row of stones. It is unclear if the date refers to when the cemetery was purchased (or dedicated), of if the date refers to the year the Benevolent Society was organized. The sign appears to be relatively modern, perhaps erected within the last twenty years.

While not technically located in Southern Chain Cemetery in Knoxville, there is an interpretative sign at the adjoining Crestview Cemetery that tells the story of this African American cemetery complex in an effort to help visitors to the site appreciate its historical significance. At the Sons of Ham Cemetery in Madison, a large red brick monument in the shape of a headstone, with an oval top and a wooden inset, sits adjacent to the entrance of the cemetery. The brick is in a running bond, and appears to have been erected in the twentieth century. The wooden inset has "Dry Creek Cemetery Lodge Suns [*sic*] of Ham No 1 1869" engraved. Both of these commemorative monuments seek to honor the lodge that established the cemetery.

The remembrance and commemoration of individuals buried at lodge cemeteries varies widely, from elaborate obelisk monuments to more humble hand-carved concrete monuments. I use the words *tombstone, grave marker*, and *marker* interchangeably to refer to a permanent marker used to designate the grave of the deceased. Benevolent Society No. 11 Cemetery in Murfreesboro is an excellent example of the wide variety of commemorative markers present in these cemeteries. It must be noted that there are many more burials than grave markers in the cemetery, and that some of the markers have been moved or knocked over in the last few decades. Because of this, it is unclear if the unmarked graves are due to economic circumstances of the deceased, or if some of the stones that were there have been damaged or have disappeared over the years. One of the more elaborate tombstones in the cemetery belongs to George Scruggs; it is a handsome monument with a beveled (or angled) top. A Masonic symbol and his name are carved on the bevel. Another elaborate marker in this cemetery belongs to Nathan Turner. It is a die-on-base marker featuring an open gate and star carved at the top. Gates often represent the passage from one realm to another, and stars indicate divine guidance.[34] The tombstone for Annie McAlister has two carvings on its face—one of an angel kneeling, and one of a rose. Contrasted with these elaborate markers is the simple wooden cross with artificial flowers in the center that stands beside a metal funeral home marker for Josie Alexander. Metal funeral home markers are placed at burial sites by the funeral home at the time of burial. They are typically later removed when a permanent marker is placed at the grave site. An interesting "hybrid" tombstone found at this cemetery is a concrete marker with the metal funeral home marker encased in the center of the concrete. There are other concrete markers, likely handmade, in this cemetery, such as the one with rebar sticking out of the top and hand-carved name and birth and death dates of the deceased. Another concrete marker that captured my attention was one with a rounded top and reflective stickers, the type used on mailboxes, to spell out the name, birth date, and death date of the deceased. Over time, several of the stickers have peeled off, leaving it difficult to make out the identifying information about the deceased. In some places there are no markers but an outline with bricks on the ground of a burial plot. It is unclear if there was perhaps a tombstone, or multiple tombstones, within the burial plot that have been damaged or lost over time. All these markers speak to a desire to remember and honor the dead to ensure that they are not forgotten.

A particularly interesting tombstone in Benevolent Society No. 11 Cemetery is the tombstone of Jemima Raybun. This granite monument no longer stands, but has fallen and become sunken in the ground. Beneath her name and birth and death dates is an inscription reading, "Erected in loving memory of their Black Mammy," with the names of the white Hume family inscribed below. Raybun reportedly worked for the Hume family for years; this family included five white Hume brothers, including Alfred Hume, then

FIGURE 5.8. This marker for Jemima Raybun at Benevolent Society No. 11
Cemetery was installed by the white family for whom she worked.

president of the University of Mississippi, and Leland Hume,
a prominent Nashville educator. All the Hume brothers,
their spouses, and an uncle drove from Nashville to Murfreesboro for Raybun's memorial service in 1909, held at the
Benevolent No. 11 Cemetery. It was an interracial service,
which seems quite rare for the time, with an African American preacher officiating the funeral. Additionally, Mrs. J. B.
McClellan, Benevolent Society member and wife of a local
African American doctor, read a paper that paid tribute to

Raybun. Both Leland and Alfred Hume spoke with feeling at the service, as the *Nashville Globe* reported: "sometimes it seemed that they were so full [of emotion] they could scarcely speak."[35] The tombstone for Raybun, as well as the funeral service, highlight some of the tensions segregation placed on people. The Hume family apparently cared for Raybun, even after they became adults, and wanted to remember and honor her. They drove from Nashville in order to attend her funeral service, which was held in a segregated cemetery. It is unknown if the Hume family questioned why this loved one was buried in a separate, segregated cemetery, or if their presence in an African American space would create any uneasiness for the members of Raybun's African American community. If the situation had been reversed, it would have been more difficult for Raybun to attend a white funeral service for a member of the Hume family. Although the Hume family honored Raybun with a tombstone, this tombstone commemorated her role as mammy and caretaker, one who served them. Her tombstone lists her connection to this white family that she worked for and her service to them, but makes no mention of her actual family, such as her daughter, Annie Ransom, also present at the memorial service. This type of tombstone is found in African American cemeteries across the state, where the deceased is commemorated as a "good servant" to a white family. It reflects how whites could accept African Americans as servants but not as equals and is yet another visual reminder of the complicated and segregated society of the time. Raybun's marker also shows how complicated remembrance can be, as the marker remembers her service but erases any mention of who she was outside this work.

At Agnew Cemetery in Giles County, some of the tomb-stones from the period before 1960 have more decorative carvings and motifs than the later, more modern tomb-stones, which is often the case at cemeteries. A marker for four members of the Howard family from the mid-1950s is a double tombstone in the form of a die-on-base stone with an urn between the two separate markers. At the top, above the names of the deceased, are engraved a row of flowers and leaves. The tombstone for the infant of the Potter family, buried in 1946, has a dove sitting on a branch carved on the front of the die-on-base marker. The tombstone for Carrie Dobson, who died in 1947, has an evening primrose carved at each upper corner of the marker. The primrose typically represents eternal love, memory, youth, hope, and sadness.[36] Interestingly, a more recent burial, dating from 2016, con-tains a number of grave offerings; it is interesting because it is one of the only graves in the cemetery marked with grave offerings. In addition to the grave marker, the gravesite is outlined with pebbles and rocks. A small angel statue has been placed in front of the marker and a stone cross with a carving of an angel and an inscription about angels on its face is placed on the base of the stone. A handmade wooden cross with artificial flowers attached sits on the other side of the marker on the base. Much of the literature surround-ing African American graves discusses the wide array of offerings left on graves, ranging from household objects to shells and marbles; however, there are relatively few graves marked with offerings in the lodge cemeteries that I have visited in Tennessee.[37]

Benevolent Society No. 16 Cemetery in Davidson County has a number of more recent burials, and many of the marked burials contain modern grave markers. This cemetery also has at least two tombstones made of a black stone material. One of these monuments is a pentagon set on a base and has a picture of the deceased on the front in addition to the name and dates of life. There are at least two markers in the cemetery that are bench markers, presumably inviting a visitor to sit while visiting the deceased. Several of the gravesites have small angel statues placed either on the base of the tombstone or sitting propped beside or in front of the marker. As in other cemeteries, the older tombstones in this cemetery contain more elaborate carvings and engravings. The tombstone for Luke Crosswy, for example, has fallen off the base and now sits propped against it. On the face of the marker, above the name and life information for Mr. Crosswy, is engraved the phrase "Come Ye Blessed." Beneath this is an open gate with a star in the center. There are also two pillars on either side of the open gate. Another older marker has a similar open gate carving on its face, although the name and many of the details of the carving are eroded and are no longer legible. The remembrance of the dead in this case is reflected primarily in the use of modern tombstone types and small angel statues.

Benevolent Society No. 79 Cemetery in Davidson County contains a mixture of older and newer burials, and as such, there is a variety of different tombstones in this cemetery. Several of the newer burials do contain grave goods, such as pinwheels placed beside the tombstone of the deceased. As in other cemeteries, older tombstones appear to be more likely to contain more elaborate symbols and carvings, often with a message or verse beneath. An exception to this is a tombstone for Robert E. Love Jr., who died in 2014. This

FIGURE 5.9. This grave at Benevolent Society No. 84 Cemetery is outlined with both concrete blocks and bricks.

marker has two sets of praying hands carved at the top, with a Masonic symbol between the hands. Beneath the name of the deceased is engraved Psalm 1:1–2 ("Blessed is the man that walketh not in the counsel of the ungodly nor standeth in the way of sinners nor sitteth in the seat of the scornful but his delight is in the law of the Lord; and in His law doth he meditate day and night"). A few of the graves have bushes or trees that were planted at the grave of the deceased. While it is easy to overlook this small cemetery, the deceased within are remembered in a variety of ways.

Benevolent Society No. 84 Cemetery has few marked graves in the cemetery, and most of the tombstones that are present primarily date to the second half of the twentieth century. There is a pentagon-shaped cement stone from 1981 with the name and birth and death dates of the deceased hand carved in the marker. There are some graves that are marked with concrete blocks with no identifying information, showing a desire to mark the grave of the deceased, even if there were no funds for an elaborate marker. There are several military veteran burials in the cemetery, and these graves are marked by both a government-issued tombstone as well as a small American flag placed at the grave. In several places there is no permanent marker but the metal funeral home marker remains; this seems to indicate that this may have been a community that could not afford more elaborate and expensive tombstones. Several of these burials are decorated with some sort of artificial flowers or wreaths, again showing a desire by the community to remember and honor the dead by continuing to bring flowers to the gravesite.

Benevolent Society No. 210 Cemetery in Montgomery County contains a number of military veteran burials marked by both a government-issued marker and a small American flag at each grave. In addition to graves that remember and honor veterans, this cemetery also contains a number of older tombstones, from the earlier twentieth century. Although some of the older monuments have fallen, one can still make out the carvings present on the stones. A fallen tombstone for Louise Wilson, who died in 1934, has a gate that opens to a star in the center carved at the top, symbolizing passage to the next realm. Some of the older tombstones have carvings of two clasped hands, which may indicate membership in the GUOOF. A tombstone for Della Carney, who died in 1916, has a carving of a tree trunk lying on its side on top of the grave marker. It is possible that this is an American Woodmen marker; the American Woodmen were a fraternal organization for African Americans, parallel to the white Modern Woodmen of America. American Woodmen allowed both men and women to join.[38] One tombstone in this cemetery is a bench tombstone, similar to the ones found in Benevolent Society No. 16 Cemetery.

Mount Ararat Cemetery (Shelbyville) in Bedford County contains several interesting types of tombstones and grave markings, such as a box tomb made of bricks and topped by concrete. Several tombstones lie on the concrete top of the box grave, which is at least twelve bricks tall. There are a number of obelisk and pedestal tombstones also present in this cemetery, most of which date to the end of the nineteenth century or beginning of the twentieth century. Sallie Troxler Myers, who died in 1903, has a marker with a square base with two other squares stacked on it. The middle rectangular base has the last name Myers carved on it. A square base sits on top of the rectangular base and contains Sallie's information on the right. The left side is blank, and was perhaps intended for a spouse. Two columns sit atop that base and are topped with an arch. At the top of the arch is a small finial, and an urn sits between the two columns. The grave marker looks as if it were intended for two people, but only Sallie's information is carved on the stone. Another noteworthy grave is from the 1960s; it has a beveled plaque marker surrounded by large stone blocks that form a rectangular boundary filled with flowering plants around the grave. A grave for Emma White, who died in 1945 at age fifty-eight, has a small lamb affixed to the top of the die-on-base marker. This tombstone is curious because it is believed that lambs typically mark the graves of children and symbolize innocence; however, White was an adult at the time of death. There are other tombstones with small lambs affixed to the top, including one for Thaddeus Sims, who died in 1927 at the age of twenty-two. Perhaps lambs do not always represent the death of a child or innocence in African American communities, and it is time to explore the different meanings commemorative symbols may have in white and African American cemeteries.

Odd Fellows Cemetery in Springfield contains several interesting individual tombstones. One marker has a carving of a tree trunk, lying on its side, on top of a die-on-base marker with the decedent's name inscribed on the tree trunk, just like the marker in the Benevolent Society No. 210 Cemetery in Port Royal. As in Port Royal, it is very possible this is a marker for a member of the American Woodmen. It is also possible that both markers were carved by the same craftsperson, as the two cemeteries are not terribly far apart. More study is needed of stone masons and craftspeople who created tombstones for rural Tennessee communities. There are several government-issued tombstones for military veterans, but unlike in some of the other cemeteries, these graves are not also marked with small American flags. There are several small obelisks on base markers, and these tombstones are among the older ones in the cemetery, reflecting how that style of tombstone marker gradually fell out of favor. There is one marker made of cement with hand-carved lettering of the decedent's name and life information. A small hand with the index finger pointing upward, a symbol typically indicating the soul has risen to heaven,[39] is carved at the top of the marker.

Number Nine Hall Cemetery in Shelby County contains a number of concrete tombstones with hand-carved lettering

FIGURE 5.10. Example of a marker at Number Nine Hall Cemetery with a rounded top and hand-carved words.

and decorative motifs. Unlike some of the other lodge cemeteries, there do not appear to be large, rectangular family burial plots demarcated from the surrounding cemetery. Many of the tombstones in the cemetery are rounded at the top. Lines were drawn in the concrete, and information about the decedent, such as name and life information, is inscribed on the lines. A decorative element, such as a flower or circle, is often carved above the decedent's name. At least one of the graves is marked with fencing around

FIGURE 5.11. Example of a concrete marker with a metal funeral home marker stuck in the top at Young Men's Aid Society Cemetery

its borders with artificial flowers placed atop the burial site inside the enclosure.

The Young Men's Aid Society Cemetery in Wilson County contains several examples of an interesting type of personal commemoration which is a metal funeral home marker that has been driven into a concrete slab. The slab contains no carvings or information and appears to exist primarily to be the home for the small metal marker. There are multiple tombstones made in this fashion present in the cemetery. Several of them have the same last name, so it is possible that this family particularly favored this

FIGURE 5.12. The marker at Zion Christian Cemetery for Rev. Africa Bailey was erected by the Sisters of Monumental Club No. 1.

type of commemorative marker for the deceased. An older tombstone dating from 1893 has an open Bible carved at the top of the stone. Beneath the name of the deceased is the inscription, "Her happy soul has winged its way, / To one pure, bright, eternal day." This phrase was popular on tombstones—a quick web search for the phrase uncovered pictures of many tombstones across the United States, from New York to Texas, with the same inscription. There are a number of government-issued markers for military veterans, but none of those graves appeared to be additionally marked with a small American flag.

Zion Christian Cemetery tombstones largely reflect the older, more decorative type of tombstones found in lodge cemeteries, which supports the idea that the cemetery fell out of popularity beginning in the 1920s. The tombstone for Rev. Morris Henderson, described earlier, was possibly the most ornate tombstone present in the cemetery at one time. The tombstone for another prominent Reconstruction minister, Rev. Africa Bailey, has also fallen. While this tombstone appears to have been a die on base or die in socket, the front of the tombstone is engraved with his name, date of death, a quotation that has eroded, and the engraved name of the group, the Sisters of Monumental Club No. 1, that erected the tombstone. It is unclear what type of club this was. There appear to be no grave goods marking graves at Zion Christian Cemetery, at least at this time. A number of those buried here do not have permanent markers at their graves, and with the loss of some of the burial registers, it is difficult to commemorate fully all the deceased buried at this site.

There are two unusual and handmade markers at the Odd Fellows Cemetery complex in Knoxville that may speak to a common African practice. These stones contain pieces of broken glass and ceramic, like a plate, embedded into the concrete of the marker. In *The Afro-American Tradition in Decorative Arts*, John Michael Vlach commented on the practice of leaving grave offerings of pottery or pressed glass containers on African American graves. He noted the purpose of these goods was to keep the interred soul at rest as well as pay homage to the dead; in that light, these objects were seen as sanctified.[40] He also noted a modern practice he had observed of grave monuments with shells, glass, coins, ceramic, and other items pressed into the monument.[41] Charlotte King also documented the use of glass fragments embedded into burial monuments in her study of the African American cemetery of New Philadelphia, Illinois. She likens it to the same tradition Vlach

FIGURE 5.13. Interesting marker embedded with broken glassware at Odd Fellows complex, in Knoxville.

noted of leaving broken glass and ceramic vessels on burial sites.[42] These grave markers at Odd Fellows Cemetery are the only ones I've found in my research, and are possibly truly unique examples of an African tradition lingering in East Tennessee.

Both the Southern Chain Cemetery in Knoxville and the Colored Masonic Cemetery in Morristown contain examples of grave scraping, a practice not widely seen in Tennessee. Scraping is the removal of all grass from a grave or cemetery. D. Gregory Jeane noted the practice as a feature of what he termed the Upland Folk Cemetery of the South, identifying it as one of the most distinctive traits. He described entire cemeteries scraped clean of all grass, although he pointed out that in some places, newer burial areas were left grassed, while individual graves were scraped clean. Jeane contended that the practice may have European origins.[43] Terry Jordan also noted the presence of scraped graves in Texas and traced its origins to the West African slave coast. Jordan indicated that removing the grass was part of a cultural tradition of removing grass from yards, fields, and burial grounds, as it was an unwelcome intruder.[44] At Southern Chain Cemetery, there is only one grave area that has been entirely scraped of grass. This area is surrounded by tombstones on three sides, indicating that possibly more than one person is buried at that site. Colored Masonic Cemetery in Morristown also contains several scraped graves. At both Southern Chain and Colored Masonic, the scraped graves are very much a minority.

In many instances, the individual graves and tombstones in the lodge cemeteries are not dissimilar from the tombstones found in white cemeteries, which was initially

FIGURE 5.14. An example of a scraped grave at Southern Chain Cemetery.

surprising. Several authors have described differences between white and African American cemeteries. John Michael Vlach writes, "Black graves are made distinct by the placement of a wide variety of offerings on top of the burial mound."[45] Carroll Van West noted the easiest way to distinguish a rural white cemetery from a rural African American cemetery was grave goods, stating, "What they lack in large, ornate headstones—the easiest way to distinguish a rural white cemetery from a rural black cemetery— they compensate for with clear African American patterns, from the older black tradition of burying a loved one with broken pottery and other items on the grave to a more modern treatment of low concrete vaults over the graves."[46] While some of the cemeteries had graves with grave goods, many of the African American lodge cemeteries were virtually indistinguishable from their white counterparts. This raises the question whether personal commemoration in African American cemeteries has changed over the years and is a topic ripe for additional exploration.

The lodge cemeteries reflect the ways commemoration and remembrance has changed over the last century. Cemeteries such as Sons of Ham in Nashville, which has burials dating back to the nineteenth century and continues in use as an active cemetery, is an excellent place to see these changes. The south side of the cemetery, particularly on the hill, is the oldest section of the cemetery, and in this area, the older markers are simpler, usually a die on base or die in socket. The only information on the tombstone is a name of the deceased and death year, although sometimes a birth year is also added. Grave markers dating from the first twenty years of the twentieth century are more elaborate in design. These markers are still die-on-base type, but often contain an engraving or carving of some sort in addition to the names and birth and death dates. The more recent burials, in the western section of the cemetery, have personal items, such as flags, pinwheels, angel statues, and solar landscape lights like the ones used to mark pathways, at grave sites. Tombstones in this section are also more likely to be more modern, made of granite or concrete. There are also a number of graves in this section marked by small metal signs erected by funeral homes. Although not intended to be used for permanent commemoration, several of these signs show that they have been in place for a number of years. One such grave at Sons of Ham contains the metal funeral home sign surrounded by a flower pinwheel, four small bouquets of artificial flowers, and at least four solar outdoor lights. Sons of Ham Cemetery shows how grave markers became more elaborate during the course of the twentieth century. More recent graves are also more likely to contain personal items, which is likely due to there still being people alive who visit the cemetery to decorate the graves of the recently deceased.

An interesting type of familial or kinship commemoration observed at several of the lodge cemeteries is a large square or rectangular area separated from the other graves with bricks or some other type of building material such as concrete blocks laid on the ground. Inside these areas are typically several grave sites, sometimes marked by a gravestone but not always. Benevolent Society No. 84 Cemetery in Davidson County contains two such burial areas. The border consists of both bricks and concrete blocks, which are not placed in any discernible pattern. Some of the bricks are placed at an angle in the ground, and others have been driven into the ground at a 90-degree angle. A flat lawn marker sits in the middle of one of the four sides of the square grave area. Inside the area are four cut-off PVC pipes, each with a plant inside, and it seems possible this must be a kinship or familial burial plot. A second rectangular burial area of this sort is located on the west side of the cemetery, with a border constructed entirely of bricks. At least two graves, both marked with government-issued lawn markers, are inside the area.

Odd Fellow Cemetery in Springfield also contains one of these rectangular grave areas. The borders are constructed of long, mainly unbroken courses of concrete. Two slightly raised flat markers, of Laura and Junious Smith, a married couple, are located on the west side of one of the markers. There are no other marked graves inside the rectangular

FIGURE 5.15. This rectangular plot at Mount Ararat (Shelbyville) may contain kinship or familial burials.

area. Benevolent Society No. 11 Cemetery in Murfreesboro also contains several of these types of burial areas; however, due to the condition of this cemetery, some of the areas have lost one or more sides of the rectangular bounded area. It is not clear in any of the cases of this grave type if the people buried inside the rectangular area form a kinship grouping, but it seems apparent that those interred within wished to be buried with particular others. Another cemetery with rectangular familial or kinship plots include Mount Ararat (Shelbyville). In one plot there, the burial area is marked by a concrete block fence, four blocks tall. An opening is located on one side to allow access to the burial area. Tombstones are placed beside the interior wall, lining the rectangle. The cemetery also contains other rectangular familial plots demarcated in other ways beside concrete block fencing. These are typically marked by some sort of concrete or stones set into the ground. This type of plot is not confined to the lodge cemeteries of Middle Tennessee, as evidence of these types of burials is also found at Zion Christian Cemetery in Memphis.

Similar to the kinship burial areas described above, Mt. Ararat Cemetery (Nashville) contains several family grave markers, something that is not apparent at other lodge cemeteries across the state. There is one grave marker per family, and they vary in shape and size and display the name of the family buried together. This practice does not appear to be confined to one section of the cemetery, or to one period; these single-family markers are found in both the older and newer sections of the cemetery. Recent examples include a beveled slanted monument for "Pleas Gooch, Sr. & Family" (undated); a maker inscribed "F. L. JOHИSOИ Family Lot" (undated); and a square lot paved in concrete with a marker inscribed "J. P. Carney's Family" (undated). There are sometimes no indications of the names of the individuals buried together in these familial plots. The older section of the cemetery has several examples of a single stone with multiple names inscribed. One example is an obelisk marker with the names and dates of Winston T. McGhee (Feb. 21, 1894–Jan. 1, 1911), Samella McGhee Paskett (May 13, 1896–May 21, 1920), W. T. Paskett (Mar. 13, 1917–Mar. 19, 1917), and Thelmond Paskett (Feb. 20, 1918–May 19, 1918) inscribed on the marker. The use of marked family plots is not common in the lodge cemeteries of Tennessee, although historians and researchers have noted this practice in other areas. Lynn Rainville's study of African American cemeteries in Central Virginia noted these types of markers in her research, indicating that they became popular there in the

FIGURE 5.16. The F. L. Johnson plot at Mt. Ararat (Nashville) is an example of a familial burial plot. It is not clear how many of the family are buried at this site.

late nineteenth century.[47] D. Gregory Jeane's work on folk cemeteries in the upland South also noticed the emergence of demarcated family plots in cemeteries established in the late nineteenth century.[48]

Many of the lodge cemeteries in Tennessee contain grave sites that appear at first glance to be unmarked. However, upon further examination, it becomes clear that these graves are marked with various plants and trees. This appears to be true at all of the lodge cemeteries in Tennessee, regardless of which lodge established the cemetery initially. Benevolent Society No. 210 Cemetery at Port Royal contains an area of apparently unmarked graves, evidenced by grave depressions. However, next to several of these depressions are yucca bushes, a traditional plant associated with African American graves, showing the grave is marked, although not by a traditional

FIGURE 5.17. Example of graves marked by botanicals at Benevolent Society No. 11 Cemetery.

stone marker. More than half the graves in Benevolent Society No. 11 Cemetery in Murfreesboro are unmarked by traditional stones, but a number of those have a yucca bush or a cedar tree planted at the grave depression to mark the burial site. The marking of graves with plants, including yuccas, daylilies, periwinkles, and cedar trees, is a not uncommon feature of African American cemeteries.[49] You see graves marked by yuccas, cedars, and other plants in cemeteries across the state, including Benevolent Society No. 79 Cemetery in Madison, Mt. Ararat (Nashville), Odd Fellows Cemetery in Springfield, and the Young Men's Aid Society Cemetery in Laguardo. The use of plants to mark graves is seen in both rural and urban cemeteries and seems prevalent across the state. It has been noted that during the eighteenth and nineteenth centuries only a minority of the African American population across the United States could afford a stone marker that preserved biographical information.[50]

A fourth type of commemoration and remembrance of the dead is not unique to lodge cemeteries, but it is a modern manifestation of remembrance. Virtual commemoration takes several forms. One example is a website dedicated solely to an individual cemetery, such as Zion Christian Cemetery in Memphis. The Zion Community Project, whose purpose is to preserve the cemetery, has a website dedicated solely to the cemetery (www.zioncommunityproject.org) that contains a short history of the establishment of the cemetery as well as information on some of its well-known burials. There is a section, "News & Press," with links to different news stories about the cemetery. One section, "About Us," documents the work of the Zion Community Project to protect, restore, and preserve the cemetery. A photo gallery not only documents some of the preservation work performed at the cemetery but also shows some of the individual gravestones. The website also offers a search engine to enable users to search a database of Zion Cemetery burial records. It is an excellent example of a virtual commemoration that lets people from across the world see the cemetery and learn if their relatives are interred there. A similar endeavor for the Odd Fellows / Daughters of Zion / Good Samaritan Cemetery in Knoxville is located on the website of the University of Tennessee's College of Architecture and Design (archdesign.utk.edu/projects/odd-fellows-cemetery). Members of this department have been working with community members in Knoxville to restore that cemetery, and the department's webpages have information on the project and the history of the cemetery. These websites allow a larger community to access the cemetery and makes the history of the site more accessible to a larger public.

While not unique to lodge cemeteries in Tennessee, websites that contain cemetery transcriptions, such as Find a Grave (www.findagrave.com) and Billion Graves (billiongraves.com), are another type of virtual commemoration. Using these sites, people can search for a cemetery by name and/or location. Users can submit images, both of the gravestone or the people interred, as well as obituaries and biographical information. When it is known, the location of the cemetery is provided, as well as a map and GPS coordinates. Some cemeteries listed on these sites also contain a brief description of the cemetery as a whole. For example, the Find a Grave page for Mount Ararat Cemetery (Shelbyville) includes images for nearly one thousand memorials at the time of this writing.[51] Many of the individual memorials contain a picture of the deceased and biographical information. In some cases, there is no photo of the deceased, but there is a photo of the tombstone, and known familial relationships are also listed. This type of commemoration allows individuals to share information about the deceased, and these sites are of great benefit to those interested in genealogical research. This type of virtual commemoration, however, is typically focused entirely on the deceased individuals, with little to no information about the lodge or other organization that created the cemetery.

A final type of commemoration is the presence of historical markers at lodge cemeteries, typically erected by a state or local historical commission. These markers typically commemorate either the lodge or the cemetery, although at least one of the newer historical markers commemorates the victims of lynching. At present, these historical markers are

FIGURE 5.18. The state historic marker at Mt Ararat (Nashville) lists only a few of the many notable people buried at this cemetery.

confined to larger cemeteries located in the major cities of the state. The Tennessee Historical Commission installed a historical marker at Odd Fellows Cemetery in Knox County; it notes that the cemetery was established in 1880 by the Banner Lodge of the Grand United Order of Odd Fellows and lists the expansion of the cemetery by the Daughters of Zion, the Good Samaritans, and Silver Moon Lodge of the Grand United Order of Odd Fellows. It points out that the cemetery is the resting place of a number of Knoxville's leaders of the African American community, particularly in the areas of religion, politics, education, and business. However, it lists none of the names of these prominent leaders. It also provides no information about anything related to these lodges other than the fact they established a cemetery.

A state historical marker is also located at Mt. Ararat Cemetery (Nashville) in Davidson County. It states that the cemetery was the first African American cemetery in Nashville and was established by the Colored Sons of Relief and Colored Benevolent Society. It lists a few of the notable persons buried in the cemetery, such as Rev. Nelson Merry, sculptor William Edmondson, and several members of the Fisk Jubilee Singers, although none of the names of the Fisk Jubilee Singers are noted. It also notes how the cemetery became part of Greenwood Cemetery in 1983, although it does not specify that Greenwood Cemetery is also a historic African American cemetery founded by prominent African American businessman Preston Taylor. Given the word count limitations for historical markers, this one does a fair job of conveying why the site is historically significant.

Zion Christian Cemetery is also the site of a state historical marker that notes the establishment of the cemetery in 1876 by the United Sons of Zion Association. The marker describes the organization as "a group of former slaves who responded to the need for a respectable burial site." It lists the burials of a few prominent local African Americans, such as Georgia Patton Washington, one of the first female African American doctors in Memphis, and Thomas Cassels, believed to be the first African American lawyer in Memphis and a member of the Tennessee General Assembly, elected to a single term in 1880.[52] This marker is

FIGURE 5.19. The lynching marker at Zion Cemetery was erected in 2017 as part of an effort to recall and commemorate the victims of the Peoples Grocery lynching of 1892.

located adjacent to South Parkway East and is visible from the road. Zion Christian Cemetery also contains a historical marker for Thomas Moss, Calvin McDowell, and William Henry Stewart. They were falsely accused of raping a white woman in 1892 and lynched by an angry mob, an incident known as the People's Grocery Lynching. This marker is interesting in that it was funded by the US National Park Service and was requested by a professor at the University of Memphis.[53] It is another step in a series of events that began in 2017 designed to recall and commemorate the victims of the People's Grocery Lynching on its 125th anniversary. Also of note is the location of this marker. It is not visible from South Parkway East but is placed at the burial site for Thomas Moss. The only way to see it is to enter the cemetery and walk up to the section where Moss is buried. While it is an admirable idea to remember these lynching victims, the marker is not placed where many will see it and learn about this tragic event.

It is noteworthy how few lodge cemeteries have a historical marker of any sort to commemorate the lodge or those buried within. While some of the cemeteries may not have statewide historical significance, many of these sites, such as Benevolent Society No. 210, Sons of Ham, and Agnew Benevolent Cemeteries, are significant to their communities and demonstrate the presence of a separate African American population. The lack of historic markers or displays about African American communities has been an issue discussed by public historians for several decades. In the 1990s, while conducting a cross-country survey of markers, monuments, and historic sites, author James Loewen found that women and African Americans were significantly underrepresented in these places of remembrance.[54] What is being conveyed by not commemorating places that have significance to local African American communities? Is it reinforcing a narrative that some histories are less valid and less worthy of commemoration than others? How do these "commemorative silences," as they are described by geographer Derek Alderman, continue to perpetuate inequitable power balances?[55] These are interesting questions, particularly at a time when across the nation people are questioning why statues and memorials for segregationists, slave traders, and Confederates continue to hold places of prominence in towns when the contributions and sacrifices made by minority individuals remain ignored and uncommemorated. Should lodge cemeteries and/or the communities in which they reside be the subject of commemoration in the form of historic markers? It is a question that will undoubtedly be raised in the coming decades as the stories of the contributions of fraternalism and benevolence to the larger African American community becomes better understood.

As has been shown in this chapter, commemoration and remembrance vary in lodge cemeteries. Commemoration ranges from decoration day events to corporate remembrance in the shape of lodge monuments, which shows an effort to remind future generations of the work undertaken by the lodge on behalf of the community. Commemoration and remembrance is also personal, and the lodge cemeteries reflect a number of different types of grave markers and show the ways practices have shifted over time. In addition to the permanent types of markers represented by stone and concrete, botanical markers in the form of flowers, plants, and trees are also present in these cemeteries and should not be overlooked. Although these botanical markers do not give us the names of the deceased, they do show care and a desire to mark the final resting place of a loved one. Commemoration and remembrance have also changed in recent years with the advent of websites that reach a larger, more far-flung society. Finally, the presence of historical markers also highlights the attempts made by the larger historical community to recognize significant sites of African American history throughout the state, and the ways this recognition still falls short. Rev. Henderson's monument may no longer loom large over Zion Christian Cemetery, but it is still there, and there are people working to preserve the cemetery. He is still remembered, and at the end, that is the point of commemoration: to remember the dead after they are gone.

CHAPTER 6

Segregated Landscapes

But the longer I remain in the South, the
more clearly I come to understand how
wide and deep, in other, less easily discernible ways, the chasm between races is
becoming.

—RAY STANNARD BAKER, 1908

Two cemeteries sit adjacent to each other in the small town
of Shelbyville in Bedford County, Tennessee. Willow Mount
Cemetery is the older of the two, dating to the middle of the
1840s. The cemetery's main entrance has a rock fence with
a large iron arch with the words "Willow Mount" above the
entryway. The cemetery contains both newer gravestones
as well as the types of monuments typically associated with
the Victorian era. There are weeping angels huddled over
the graves of those "gone too soon." There are monuments
featuring elaborate scrollwork, angel motifs, draped urns,
and other symbolism of the type Victorians were so fond of
using to express their grief in stone. A monument dedicated

FIGURE 6.1. These fences between Willow Mount and Mount Ararat (Shelbyville) Cemeteries bear mute testimony to the realities of segregation.

"In Memory of Our Confederate Dead" is topped by an unsmiling soldier standing guard over the nearly six hundred unnamed combatants that rest in the cemetery. In short, it is the type of cemetery found in nearly every Tennessee town that predates the Civil War. And like many of those cemeteries, space for the burial of one's loved ones was, for most of the cemetery's existence, only available to the white inhabitants of Shelbyville.

A second cemetery is separated from Willow Mount by a road lined with two fences—stacked stone on one side, chain-link on the other. There are marked graves in the second cemetery, but far fewer weeping angels or elaborate scroll work on tombs. No monuments exist to remember the soldiers of the Civil War, although there is a government-issued marker for a United States Colored Troop (USCT) veteran of the Civil War. There is a stone to commemorate the Benevolent Society. This handsome obelisk, some of its carvings eroded by time, reads, "Erected to the sacred memory of the honored dead of the Benevolent Society. Their works do follow them. August 1897." A number of large, old trees keep watch over those interred within this space. If anything is to be remembered in this cemetery, it is the organization that ensured the proper burial of its members. This cemetery is newer than Willow Mount and is called Mount Ararat; it was established by the Ladies Benevolent Society in the late nineteenth century.

The two cemeteries highlight the role of geography in the lodge cemeteries of Tennessee, and also the ways segregation played itself out on the landscape of Tennessee during the decades following the Civil War. At the time of its creation, Willow Mount's policy of not interring the enslaved permitted them to avoid serving African American communities; this practice did not change after the coming of freedom. To deal with the realities of segregation, members of the Ladies Benevolent Society purchased property directly adjacent to an older, established white cemetery and created their own burial grounds for the honorable disposition of deceased members. It is a story that plays out all over the state. Separate lodges, schools, churches, cemeteries, and sometimes even separate communities sprang up across the state, sometimes literally separated by a fence.

Geography is an important component of African American lodge cemeteries, both in the context of their placement within local African American cemeteries, themselves segregated from the white community, and in the context of the larger, segregated landscapes. The placement of these cemeteries is no accident, but it is important to understand the context of their establishment rather than their locations in current times. An excellent example of this is the Benevolent Society No. 11 Cemetery in Murfreesboro, Tennessee. Today the cemetery sits in the middle of an industrial and commercial area. Warehouses, some empty, sit nearby. To access the cemetery, one must either park at a dead end, behind a self-storage facility, and walk beneath a busy overpass of a state highway to access the cemetery, or park at an adjacent business and attempt to step over the fence. Accessing the cemetery today, one might assume that the cemetery has always been located in an undesirable spot, a place not associated with images of peaceful slumber. However, at the time the cemetery was established, the area was not as heavily industrialized as it is today. The cemetery was located near the Prewitt Spurr & Co. Stave Company, which contained several dry kilns, an iron-clad warehouse, several sheds, and other buildings according to the 1897 Sanborn Fire Insurance Map of Murfreesboro.[1] However, other than the stave company, there were not many other factories or industries located nearby, ensuring a reasonably quiet final resting place. The founders of the cemetery could not have predicted the explosive growth Murfreesboro would go through during the late twentieth and early twenty-first centuries that would encroach on a number of cemeteries in the city. This is why it is important to consider what an area looked like at the time the cemetery was established, as the landscape of many Tennessee towns changed dramatically beginning in the mid-twentieth century. These changes were caused by urban renewal, the creation of an interstate road system that displaced many communities, and increased populations that changed the landscape from rural to urban or suburban. It is important

FIGURE 6.2. This overgrown burial area at Agnew Benevolent Cemetery is an example of burials located outside the acknowledged boundaries of the cemetery.

to know the ways that geography and development have impacted these cemeteries.

A curious geographic feature at a few of the lodge cemeteries in Tennessee relates to the cemetery boundaries. At some cemeteries, there appear to be graves outside the area maintained and demarcated as the cemetery. Agnew Benevolent Cemetery is one such example. The main part of the cemetery is well maintained and square in shape. However, there is an overgrown area at the western edge of the cemetery that contains multiple burials. It is unclear why this part of the cemetery is overgrown and not maintained like the rest of the cemetery. Benevolent Society No. 79 Cemetery in Madison also has at least one burial in an overgrown area at the southern border of the cemetery, between the maintained portion of the cemetery and an adjoining house. The grave clearly belongs with the cemetery but appears forgotten. At Benevolent Society No. 84 Cemetery, the northern, rear boundary of the cemetery is also uncertain. There are several burials in this area, which is not maintained and is full of bushes and other brush. It is unknown why some of the lodge cemeteries appear to have unclear boundaries, or areas with burials that are not maintained. For Benevolent Society No. 84 and Benevolent Society No. 79 Cemeteries, it could be that the creation of suburban neighborhoods around the cemetery has made the property boundaries ambiguous, and if the lodge is no longer active, there may no longer be people who know the precise boundaries of the cemetery.

In several instances, lodges purchased a single piece of property and built both a lodge hall and a cemetery. The best current example of this in Tennessee is the Benevolent Society No. 210 Cemetery in Port Royal, in Montgomery County. Port Royal is one of the older towns in Middle Tennessee, and the first white permanent settlers arrived in the area in 1784. Located on the Red River, Port Royal was a busy river town during the early nineteenth century, and a broom factory operated there in the later half of the nineteenth century.[2] By the 1870s, however, Port Royal was described as a small village with three general stores and a grocer.[3] In 1877, there was a white Masonic lodge on the main street in town, adjacent to the store and post office, as shown on the D.G. Beers 1877 map of Montgomery County, Tennessee.[4] The map does not indicate, however, the location of the Benevolent Lodge.

The Benevolent Lodge in Port Royal traces its origins to 1872, when the group organized in a log cabin school room.[5]

In 1890, the Benevolent Lodge purchased a lot in town, on the primary street, and built a small lodge hall. After inhabiting this space in town for less than twenty years, the lodge purchased three acres on the north side of Port Royal and sold the lot in town. It is not known why the Benevolent Society lodge in Port Royal sold their location on the main street of the town to move north of town. Whatever the reason, this move out of town gave the lodge cemetery room for expansion and soon both a burial ground and a hall were part of a complex for the lodge, which also included a barbecue pavilion, providing for the various burial, association, and social needs of the community. The building stayed in use by the lodge until white supremacists burned it in 1994. After years of fundraising, the lodge built and dedicated a new building in 2001.[6] The site currently consists of a brick, one-story lodge building flanked by the cemetery on one side and the pavilion on the other. The lodge cemetery is clearly an integral part of the site, but it is recessed from the lodge building and separated by a simple fence consisting of small wooden poles and a single chain.

There are other examples of lodge cemeteries adjacent to lodge buildings, such as the Benevolent Society No. 84 Cemetery in the Hamilton Church Pike area of Antioch in Davidson County. At the time of my initial site survey in December 2012, the cemetery, which was well maintained but had no signage, contained a one-story lodge building that appeared to no longer be in use. It was built out of concrete blocks and had a set of two stone steps leading into the building. Peeking inside I saw a light switch, indicating the building was once electrified. A few benches remained in the building, but a chunk of the rear corner of the building

FIGURE 6.3. The Independent Pole Bearers No. 9 Lodge Hall as it appeared in 2013. It burned down in 2018.

was missing. By the winter of 2015, the building no longer existed, having collapsed. The debris from the building remains on the site. The exact age of the lodge is unknown, although there are references to the lodge by 1909, when the *Nashville Globe* reported, "Several members of Benevolent Society Number 107 participated in the election of officers of B.O. Number 84 on Saturday night last at Hamilton Hill."[7] As with the Port Royal Benevolent Society No. 210 lodge and cemetery complex, the lodge hall is closer to the road and the burials were recessed to the left of the building. It appears that the tombstones may extend into the suburban backyards that surround the cemetery, reflecting that the cemetery's surroundings today are quite different than they were one hundred years ago.

The Independent Pole Bearers Number Nine lodge also created a complex with a building adjacent to the cemetery. The site, located in rural Shelby County, south of Memphis and close to the Mississippi border, is also adjacent to a church. When I first visited the site in 2013, the lodge building, built out of concrete blocks, was obviously still in use. The building burned down on Christmas Day in 2018. At the time of the destruction, a chairman of the group related in an interview that the society was still active and had 150 members.[8] Rather than rebuild a lodge hall, the society built a covered pavilion on the location of the former lodge building, and the society continues to assist with the burial and funeral plans of its members.[9]

The Sons of Ham organization in Briersville, in Davidson County, also had a building located near to the lodge cemetery at some point, although the lodge building does not appear to exist any longer. In 1908, it was reported in the *Nashville Tennessean* that the group "was founded in 1870 and owns an acre and half of land on Dry Creek and a hall that is used for lodge and church buildings."[10] Two years later, it was reported that the lodge members met in their hall and marched over to their cemetery to hold a short memorial service for the oldest member of the group, Mr. Luke Gee.[11] The Davidson County property assessor shows that the lodge's property was adjacent to the building, and that there has not been a building on the property since at least 1999.[12] When I have visited the site, I have been unable to discern the remnants of the lodge or to gather a clear idea of its location on the property.

The idea that the lodge was an important part of the community is also borne out by the placement of the lodge cemeteries within African American communities. Several cemeteries are located adjacent to historically African American churches or schools, and some are placed in historic African American neighborhoods. The Agnew Benevolent Cemetery in Giles County is directly adjacent to St. Paul-Agnew AME Church and until the somewhat recent placement of a sign at the cemetery, it appeared to be the cemetery for the church. Benevolent Society No. 16 Cemetery in Goodlettsville is located across the street from First Baptist Church, an African American congregation established in 1923.[13] In Wilson County, the Benevolent Cemetery in Mays Chapel, named for the African American church in the community, is located "below the church," less than a mile from the church property. Also in Wilson County, the Greenlawn Cemetery, established by the Benevolent Society, is located approximately one-third of a mile north of Williamson Chapel CME Church. In addition to the church, Needmore Elementary School, a Rosenwald School built in 1936 for the African American students of the community, continues to stand. The community contained a lodge hall, built circa 1920, that was shared by the Knights of Pythias and the Benevolent Society and also served as a school building prior to the 1936 construction of Needmore School.[14] The Mysterious Ten Cemetery is situated across the street from a historic African American congregation in Knoxville, and the Colored Masonic Cemetery in Morristown is directly adjacent to the Rock of Ages Baptist Church. In that instance, however, the cemetery predates the church, as the Rock of Ages congregation moved to its current location in 1940, after their original property was purchased by the TVA.[15] These examples all show how these lodges were located within the heart of their communities, and these communities typically contained segregated schools, churches, and lodge halls that met the educational, spiritual, and social needs of the community. Remnants of the larger segregated landscape are present in some of the lodge cemeteries located across the state of Tennessee. During the time of tightening Jim Crow segregation, cemeteries were not the only separate institutions African Americans established for their society. These segregated places were well-known to their communities and did not always have signs, as both races commonly recognized and accepted certain areas, such as hotels and libraries, as white spaces. At other times, racial space was defined by boundaries not clearly visible to community outsiders.[16] Charles S. Johnson noted in his work *Patterns of Negro Segregation* that "very rigid segregation exists in taking care of the dead; there are parallel funeral establishments and cemeteries in all parts of the South."[17] In Tennessee, many towns had separate African American funeral homes. In at least two instances, in Brownsville and Dyersburg, the funeral home and a Masonic lodge shared the same building.[18] Lodge buildings are part of the segregated landscape in Tennessee.

Segregation persisted even into death, but unlike municipalities of Atlanta, Georgia, that adopted ordinances prohibiting African Americans from being interred in white cemeteries, segregated cemeteries in Tennessee were a matter of custom and practice, not legislation.[19] In Tennessee, as in other places in the South, African Americans were typically allowed to purchase land to establish their own cemeteries in communities across the state.[20] Although there is no exact count of the number of separate African

American cemeteries located throughout the United States, commentators such as W. E. B. Du Bois noted that almost every town in the South had a cemetery owned and operated by African Americans. In his 1907 work *Economic Co-Operation among Negro Americans,* he stated, "there must be at least 500 such cemeteries in the United States, and perhaps twice that number."[21] This segregation often played out on the landscape itself, with fences or other physical barriers sometimes separating the white from the African American cemetery, as in Columbia, Tennessee. The white (and older) Rose Hill Cemetery is physically separated from the African American Rosemount Cemetery by a chain link fence. This stark reality of segregation as evidenced on the physical landscape, where it could not be escaped, was a daily reminder to the members of the African American community of the injustices, both petty and large, that were daily endured. In his work *The Souls of Black Folk,* Du Bois noted, "It is usually possible to draw in every Southern community a physical color-line on the map, on the one side of which whites dwell and on the other Negroes."[22] It is important to note that Du Bois used his experiences as a schoolteacher in Tennessee in the late nineteenth century to write that book, and it is reasonable to surmise that some of his observations of segregation come from Tennessee. Others beside Du Bois noted the spoken and unspoken ways segregation pervaded daily life. Lillian Smith, a white Southern activist, described the spatial boundaries of segregation that everyone in the community knew but no one discussed:

There are the signs without words: big white church on Main Street, little unpainted colored church on the rim of town; big white school, little ramshackly colored school;

big white house, little unpainted cabins; white graveyard with marble shafts, colored graveyard with mounds of dirt. And there are the invisible lines that turn and bend and cut the town into segments. Invisible, but electrically charged with taboo.[23]

Several of the lodge cemeteries surveyed in Tennessee are located immediately adjacent to a white cemetery. As described earlier, Mount Ararat Cemetery (Shelbyville), in Bedford County, is separated from the larger, older, white Willow Mount Cemetery by a road and two sets of fences. Willow Mount, established in 1844 when the older Old City Cemetery in Shelbyville reached capacity, did not allow African American burials.[24] Mount Ararat is not as old, established some time after the Civil War but before the beginning of the twentieth century. The two cemeteries are separated by the remnants of a rock wall, physically separating the white burial ground from the African American burial ground.

While the line of demarcation is quite clear between Mount Ararat Cemetery (Shelbyville) and Willow Mount Cemetery, sometimes the line of segregation is not as obvious to the modern observer of the cemetery. An excellent example of this is the Benevolent Society No. 16 Cemetery in Goodlettsville in Davidson County, which sits directly adjacent to the white Cole Cemetery. The age of Cole Cemetery is unclear, although published cemetery transcriptions list a burial in the cemetery as early as 1860.[25] There are no physical fences or lines on the landscape that denote the boundaries of the two clearly separate cemeteries. Apart from the monuments, the only items on the landscape between the two are two stacked-stone posts on a hillside leading to the

FIGURE 6.4. The boundary between the white Cole Cemetery and Benevolent Society No. 16 Cemetery is not apparent to modern eyes.

white cemetery. The whites are buried in Cole Cemetery on the hillside, while the Benevolent Society No. 16 Cemetery is located on the lower, flatter ground. Although a current observer of the cemetery would find it difficult to locate the boundary between the two, the members of this community were likely aware of exactly where that line was located. It is interesting to note, however, that the Benevolent Society No. 16 Cemetery lies across the road from an African American church, the First Baptist Church, indicating that the cemetery and the church were part of the same African American community. It also shows how segregated landscapes and boundaries were fluid. Both whites and African Americans lived in the same community but they could not be buried together. They created two cemeteries, both of which are within eyesight of an African American church.

It may be interesting to note that several African American lodge cemeteries are situated near Jewish or Catholic cemeteries in their local communities, possibly marking the uneasy ways that different ethnic, racial, and religious communities shared space on the landscape in Tennessee during the nineteenth century. Mt. Ararat Cemetery (Nashville) is located one mile from the Catholic Calvary Cemetery, established in 1868, a year before Mt. Ararat. Mt. Ararat is also located approximately one and a half miles from Mount Olivet Cemetery, established in 1856 for the white community, with its "Confederate Circle," home to approximately 1,500 Confederate veterans. This area is interesting in that it contains cemeteries for three different groups, and one wonders if the members of the groups were as separated in life as they are in death.

The Odd Fellows Cemetery complex in Knoxville is adjacent or near to Calvary Cemetery (Catholic, established 1869) and Bethel Cemetery (Confederate, established 1873). When the Catholic community in Knoxville established Calvary in 1869, the property was described as "so rough it was feared by many people it would prove a failure; but by hard work it has been so far beautified that it is now in good condition and in time will be very beautiful."[26] Bethel Cemetery, also known as Confederate Cemetery, is the final resting place for more than 1,600 Confederate soldiers. It was a private cemetery, in the ownership of and under the care of the Winstead family, until 1989, at which point the final member of the Winstead family willed the cemetery to the Hazen Historical Museum Foundation.[27] The segregated society that dictated people of different races could not eat in the same places or sit beside each in school but allowed for these same persons to lie in separate yet adjacent final resting places is mind-boggling, and shows the difficulty later generations face when trying to understand the underlying principles of segregation.

In Memphis, this spatial segregation between the races is visible on the landscape as well. As discussed in Chapter 2, there were several African American communities located in Memphis.[28] However, even with its segregated neighborhoods, Memphis has an area in which three cemeteries, white and African American, are located near each other. Zion Christian Cemetery in Memphis is located not quite a mile from the Temple Israel Cemetery (Jewish, established 1846) and approximately three-fourths of a mile from Calvary Cemetery (Catholic, established 1867), all three located south of the Memphis city center.

Either born out of legalized prejudice and segregation, or out of a desire to create community, there are a large number of African American enclaves and neighborhoods in Tennessee that were established in the years immediately following the Civil War. The urge to create separate black enclaves was not always driven by segregation; in the years immediately following Emancipation in Tennessee, African Americans worked purposefully to create an independent black society and to "divorce themselves in every respect from whites and to fructify the nascent black communities that had germinated in the days of slavery."[29] Examples abound, and some continue their existence upon the Tennessee landscape. Promise Land, an eloquently named community, was established by freedmen in Dickson County during the Reconstruction period. Many of the initial settlers originally came to the area as enslaved laborers to work in the iron works or on farms in the county. By 1881, the community had organized and boasted a church and a school, both of which still stand. The school serves the community as a museum and community meeting place,[30] and the church sits one hundred yards away, on an adjacent parcel. Free

FIGURE 6.5. Fort Cooper School in Hickman County was a part of that African American enclave for decades. The school also contained a burial ground, shown to the right of the building.

Hill, located on the Cumberland Plateau in Clay County, was established by the formerly enslaved people of Virginia Hill. She purchased two thousand acres of land, freed them and gave them the property, and then left the area. At its high point, Free Hill consisted of two grocery stores, two churches, a school, three clubs, and two restaurants.[31] The Fort Cooper community in Hickman County was established by the formerly enslaved Nathan George following the Civil War. The community was home to a church and a school, as well as a community cemetery.[32] Although the school is no longer open, the church continues in existence. Like lodge cemeteries, these separate black communities were created intentionally as places where African Americans could live without white oversight or interference, and many of them still exist, although they are not as large as they once were.

Numerous lodge cemeteries in Tennessee are placed in what were African American enclaves, and the remnants of the built environment of those enclaves remain on the landscape. One example is the Odd Fellows / Daughters of Zion / Good Samaritan Cemetery in Knoxville, Tennessee. It is located directly across from Eastport Elementary, originally organized as an African American school. Although the cemeteries predate the school, which was established in 1905, they were clearly part of a larger African American enclave.[33] Also located in the Eastport community were African American churches such as the Eastport AME Zion Church and Seney's Chapel, both located on Nelson Avenue near the school.[34] The Mabry Street ME Church, an African American congregation, inhabited a building one street west of Nelson Avenue, on East Vine Street.[35] An African American undertaker, C. S. Jarnigan, was located nearby at 505 Nelson Avenue. There were several grocery stores in the neighborhood as well, such as Johnson & Amerine, owned by an African American and located on Patton Street, and establishments belonging to A. C. Cook and Alexander Davis, both located on East Vine Street.[36] With several churches, a school, a cemetery complex, grocery stores, and an undertaker, African American residents of this section of Knoxville clearly had their own society that met many of their needs.

The Sons of Ham Cemetery in Davidson County was also located in and part of an African American enclave. In 1908, the *Nashville Tennessean* noted that the Sons of Ham had a hall on Dry Creek used for church and lodge meetings.[37] In 1909, the Davidson County Board of Education voted to allot $1,000 to build a new school in the Dry Creek community for African American children. One of eight new schools the board voted to build, it was noted that not one of these communities currently had a separate school building. Schools operated in churches with no desks and were all badly crowded.[38] It is unknown which church in Dry Creek housed the school, although it may also have been held in the Sons of Ham lodge. The one-room school built by the county, along with two others, was replaced in 1958 with an African American school on Brick Church Pike.[39] As with many communities, the church was at the heart of the community, with the *Nashville Globe* describing a number of revivals, Sunday School exhibitions, rallies, and special church services held in the years between 1907 and 1918. The Sons of Ham lodge was a part of this vibrant and separate African American community, and the cemetery is one of the last community spaces remaining.

Studying the location of lodge cemeteries in relation to their communities and to their landscapes, one cannot help noticing the role of both segregation and geography in the placement of the cemeteries. In larger towns and cities, the placement of the cemeteries bears out what geographers and historians have noted about residential segregation in Southern cities. By the mid-nineteenth century, African American sections of towns were typically divided from white sections of town by a railway.[40] This is seen with the location of Benevolent Society No. 11 Cemetery in Murfreesboro, Union Forever Cemetery in Memphis, and the Mt. Ararat and Sons of Ham Cemeteries in Nashville, all located near railroads. Railways often formed a convenient and clear distinction between the white section of town and the section of town that housed the "other," whether African Americans or other ethnic groups.[41] In urban places across the South, African Americans were allowed space in the least desirable areas, such as near the railroad tracks, near

FIGURE 6.6. This steep slope at Mt. Ararat (Nashville) Cemetery may indicate that the land was not desired by white residents, which is why African Americans were able to establish their cemetery at this location.

city dumps, on land with steep slopes, or any area that had low residential appeal for white residents.[42]

In several ways, geography played a crucial role in the placement and establishment of African American lodge cemeteries. In some cases, the cemeteries are a part of a larger neighborhood or community established in the post-Civil War era as African Americans created their own spaces across the state. While some of these communities still exist, in other instances one of the last remnants of these separate African American communities is the lodge cemetery, highlighting the ways these geographic landscapes were segregated, and the ways that segregation can still be seen on the landscape in the twenty-first century. Understanding the role of geography in the creation of African American cemeteries and community institutions provides more context for these cemeteries.

CHAPTER 7

The Silences of the Lodge Cemeteries

"Unmarked" Graves and Hiding in Plain Sight

History isn't what happened but what gets
written down, and the various sources that
make up the archival record generally overlooked the lives of poor black southerners.

—CASEY CEP

A cemetery sits at the edge of a dead-end street in a suburban neighborhood in Davidson County. Remnants of
a stacked stone fence, four to five stones high, are present at the eastern boundary of the property. Several old,
large trees are scattered throughout the cemetery, offering shaded resting places for those interred at this space.
The trees are a mix of cedar and deciduous, ensuring that

there is always something green in the cemetery, even on a chilly November day. Lines of bushes form the southern, western, and northern boundaries of the property. If a person closes their eyes, they could almost imagine they were standing in a semi-rural setting. The cemetery is in good maintenance, with few broken monuments; some of the monuments, however, have begun to bury themselves deeply into the dirt. A cross street, adjacent to the cemetery, separates the cemetery on one side from an office park. A dialysis clinic is located diagonally across the street. A suburban home is located on the south side of the cemetery. The cemetery has no signage and is almost unnoticeable in its location. There is no hint that this is Benevolent Society No. 79 Cemetery, and that this suburban area was once a small farming community.

Benevolent Society No. 79 Cemetery resides in what was formerly known as the Briarville (or Brierville) community; in fact, the street address for the cemetery is Briarville Road. In 1907, the *Nashville Tennessean* referenced the area as "the neighborhood of Brierville, in the old Nineteenth District, composed principally of Afro-American citizens."[1] While the exact population of the community is unknown, it was large enough to warrant local government building a new school for the community in 1909 at the cost of $1,000.[2] There was also a local baseball team, the Brierville Roosters, who played nearby teams such as the Neeley Bend Unions and Goodlettsville Blue.[3] So while not a large community, it was large enough to be home to a school for African Americans, a baseball team, a cemetery (Benevolent Society No. 79 Cemetery), two churches (Mt. Calvary Baptist Church and Brierville AME church), at least two benevolent organizations (the Benevolent Society and the Royal

Sons and Daughters of the Temple No. 1), and at least one social club (the Carnation Social Club).[4]

Today, there are few physical remnants of this once bustling community. Briarville School is long gone, likely closed during school desegregation. Briarville Road itself has been changed, now terminating at the cemetery and then continuing after a break of ninety feet.[5] The cemetery remains, but it is unmarked and almost hidden in plain sight. Despite this, it is in good condition and continues to be used, with recent burials. It is a silent reminder of the Benevolent Society and its former importance in the heart of the community. It is also a demonstration of the ways lodges continue to be useful to their communities even after ceasing operations. The Benevolent Society No. 79 may no longer be as active and vibrant as it once was, but its cemetery remains for the community to continue to give their loved ones proper burials, fulfilling one of the original purposes of the Benevolent Society.

Benevolent Society No. 79 Cemetery also symbolizes some of the different types of silences that surround lodge cemeteries in Tennessee. There is the silence of cemeteries with no signage, that seek to hide in plain sight, a silence that obscures the ties of the cemetery to fraternalism and benevolence. There are the silences of the graves of those that came to violent and brutal ends in a racist society, such as the unmarked grave of George Johnson, a young man lynched by a mob of at least seventy-five men in Murfreesboro in 1908 after being arrested for "attempted rape" for grabbing the arm of a white teenage girl. A funeral procession accompanied him to his final, unmarked resting spot in Benevolent Society No. 11 Cemetery in Murfreesboro.[6]

There is the silence of the large numbers of unmarked graves found in these cemeteries, where gravesites outnumber tomb markers and speak volumes with their very silence. However, these silences can be deceptive in some ways. While the cemeteries themselves may sometimes lack signage, they continue to exist and they often continue to be actively used by their local communities. Cemeteries may appear to have large numbers of unmarked graves until they are examined more closely, revealing that there are ways other than using concrete or marble monuments that African Americans mark and remember the graves of their loved ones.

In site visits to several lodge cemeteries in Tennessee, I was struck by the number of "unmarked" graves in proportion to total number of burials. Several of those who study African American cemeteries have commented on the lack of formal markers and presence of unmarked graves in the burial grounds of the marginalized. Sherene Baugher and Richard Veit noted in their work *The Archaeology of American Cemeteries and Gravemarkers* that "the burial grounds of the poor, marginalized, and minority groups are particularly at risk, as they may lack formal markers and clear titles."[7] Others, such as Christina Brooks, have considered whether the lack of grave markers results from the socioeconomic status of a group or if it reflects cultural patterns.[8] Emmeline Morris, in her thesis on an African American cemetery, noted that African American burial grounds are often misunderstood, as people mistake their appearance for an abandoned site.[9]

In addition to the lack of formal markers, researchers have historically used their own cultural and racial biases to condemn the ways African American cemeteries differ from traditional Anglo- and Euro-American cemeteries in terms of upkeep and design. Harold Williams, who wrote a thesis on landscaping in African American communities in 1944, noted, "Negro cemeteries are usually the most unsightly area of the community. Of seventeen cemeteries visited, only two were in even acceptable condition. While this does not reflect directly the lack of interest and respect of the communities for the cemetery, it does show the absence of any effective effort to correct the problems in providing for its care." He went on to criticize the lack of formal plan in African American cemeteries, noting, "generally no thought had been given to the design and layout of the grounds, resulting in an unsightly development at its best."[10] More recent scholars have not condemned African American cemeteries for their differences but have simply pointed out the ways they do not conform to more traditional expectations of cemeteries. John Michael Vlach, for example, notes, "the common expectation for a cemetery is neat rows of stones and markers on a well-mowed green lawn. Afro-American graves in rural areas do not conform to this norm."[11] Several lodge cemeteries in Tennessee are similar to the type of African American cemetery describe by Vlach with their "haphazard" arrangement of burial sites not laid out in orderly rows.

It is important to note that several of the African American lodge cemeteries in Tennessee continue numerous "unmarked" graves. Unmarked graves typically describe those that do not have a permanent marker of some sort, either of stone or metal. Yet these graves are marked in other, less permanent ways. As discussed in a previous chapter, several lodge cemeteries in Tennessee have clearly outlined burial spaces marked by plants, such as yucca, buttercups, vinca, cedar trees, and others. However, there is a cultural bias in believing that graves in African American cemeteries without tombstones are unmarked. Archaeologists studying African American cemeteries in South Carolina noted that some graves were marked with plants, typically cedars or yuccas, and this may relate to the African tradition of the living spirit, an idea that death is not the end. Anthropologists have also noted that yuccas may have been used by African Americans to "keep the spirits out" of a cemetery.[12] It has also been suggested that plant markers were used because, while marking graves mattered to the current generation, it was less important to the community that future generations know burial locations of the dead. Additionally, by using temporary markers, the community ensures that the cemetery is available to those that wish to bury their dead in that it signifies there is room for "one more person."[13]

Benevolent Society No. 11 Cemetery in Murfreesboro is one that when examined superficially appears to have many more unmarked graves than marked ones. Rev. Melvin Hughes, in his 1996 work *A History of Rutherford County's African American Community*, noted that the cemetery was the resting place of approximately 320 people and transcribed their names and burial dates.[14] However, John Lodl, Rutherford County archivist, and his staff searched death certificates, obituaries, and other written sources, and they documented at least 689 burials at the cemetery.[15] Visits to the Benevolent Society No. 11 Cemetery initially confirmed that most of the burials were simply not marked. Field work was complicated by the fact that the cemetery has frequently been overgrown with weeds, grass, and trees, making it difficult to visually assess it. Continued efforts by community members, however, have resulted in a cemetery in which most of the weeds and overgrowth has been removed, making assessments easier. My visit to the cemetery in November 2019 revealed that there are many depressions on the northern half of the cemetery, indicating unmarked burials. Many of these depressions, however, feature the presence of yucca plants, indicating that the grave has been marked in the past. Other plant indicators, such as cedar trees, were also visible around grave depressions. In some areas there were borders of brick or stone outlining rectangular burial plots, clearly showing that gravesites have been marked.

Benevolent Society No. 84 Cemetery in Davidson County also has a similar pattern in containing more unmarked than marked graves. The Davidson County Cemetery Survey Project listed thirteen tombstone inscriptions and twenty-plus fieldstones present during their 2003 site survey.[16] However, as with Benevolent Society No. 11 Cemetery, there are sections of plots that are marked with plants or other types of markers. One had a border of red bricks, arranged in a square, with four plants inside the square. Unlike some of the other lodge cemeteries, there are no yucca plants marking burials at this cemetery.

Another type of silence found in African American lodge cemeteries is a lack of signage, allowing them to hide in plain sight. This is more common in cemeteries that are not located in the major cities. Zion Christian Cemetery in Memphis is difficult to miss, with its thirty thousand burials, large iron sign, state historical marker, and location on a busy road. The same is true of Mt. Ararat (Nashville), which is also marked by a large and ornate gate as well as with a state historical marker. Other cemeteries are clearly burial places and are well-maintained; however, they have no cemetery marker or sign denoting the name of the cemetery, as with the Colored Masonic Cemetery in Morristown. Many of the lodge cemeteries of Tennessee are unmarked and often hidden from plain sight. This is true at Benevolent Society No. 84 Cemetery, Mays Chapel Benevolent Cemetery, King David No. 187 Cemetery, Colored Mutual Cemetery, and Union Forever Cemetery. Benevolent Society No. 11 Cemetery in Murfreesboro, for example, has no direct access to the cemetery from any roadway. It sits beneath an overpass of a busy highway. While there was once a sign at the cemetery, only the posts remain. Thousands of people drive over the bridge above the cemetery daily with no idea that more than six hundred African Americans are buried below. The cemetery described in the introduction to this book, Benevolent Society No. 79 Cemetery in Madison, contains no signage and is nestled in what is now a suburb of Nashville. Also in Davidson County is the unmarked and unsigned Benevolent Society No. 84 Cemetery. It too is located in a suburban neighborhood of Nashville, and there are no visible hints that this cemetery was established by the Benevolent Society. Mays Chapel Cemetery is similarly unmarked, with few markers visible from the road; most passersby would assume after a cursory glance that it is an empty field. Colored Mutual Cemetery in Rutherford County not only has no signage, but it is also extraordinarily difficult to find, located between an apartment complex and a busy highway. It is difficult to determine whether these cemeteries are unsigned due to age—perhaps previous signs have deteriorated or been destroyed—or if they are purposefully unsigned so as to not attract the notice of those who might wish to harm the cemetery.

Conversely, several lodge cemeteries have received signs within the last five to ten years. When I first visited Agnew Benevolent Cemetery in 2013, there was no signage at the cemetery. With its location immediately adjacent to St. Paul-Agnew AME Church, it appeared to be a church cemetery. A visit to the site in 2020 revealed a sign placed at the entrance to the cemetery, on the southern edge of the property, reading, "Agnew Cemetery Est. 1904 by Benevolent Society." Benevolent Society No. 91 Cemetery has a similar story. At my initial site visit in 2012, the cemetery was not marked by any sign. A return visit in 2020 revealed a sign proclaiming this as the Benevolent Lodge No. 91 Cemetery. In these cases, it appears the community wishes to remember and honor the origins of these cemeteries.

A question to consider is what do these silences mean for African American lodge cemeteries? Are they an intentional move by the local community meant to protect the cemeteries from those that would bring harm in the form of vandalism and destruction? The threat to African American resources of any type in the South has not abated since the enactment of the Civil Rights Act of 1964; indeed, within this generation African American churches across the South, including Tennessee, have been burned by those wishing to inflict harm upon the community. Perhaps the silences only pertain to outsiders, those not part of the local community. For those who live in these communities and continue to use the cemeteries, the idea that these cemeteries are hidden is preposterous. They know that the cemetery is there; they know its history and meaning for the community. Why

FIGURE 7.1. The sign at Agnew Benevolent Cemetery was erected between 2013 and 2020, showing how a community remembers its history.

does it need to be marked with a sign for benefit of outsiders? Both of these questions then raise a larger question: should these silences be disturbed? Should the location of these sacred places be disclosed so that outsiders can visit? Who benefits by making these places more widely known?

The danger to allowing these places to remain silent is the very real risk of destruction in the name of development or progress. It has been noted that the voices of the descendants of those buried at historic African American cemeteries are ignored if the burial ground is in the way of new construction or economic development.[17] Earlier I noted the case of Edgefield Benevolent Society Cemetery, which was the subject of a lawsuit in the 1870s between the separate male and female societies over who owned the property. Although the lawsuit was resolved, the cemetery fell victim to development in the twentieth century.

There have been numerous stories of "forgotten" African American cemeteries being "discovered" within the last few decades across the United States. While constructing a General Administration Services building for the federal government in Manhattan in 1991, graves were discovered twenty-four feet below ground. It was determined that this was the site of the "Negros Burial Ground" depicted on a 1755 map of New York. Since then, an African Burial Ground Visitor Center has been erected to interpret the story of slavery in New York.[18] In June 2020, it was confirmed that a historic African American cemetery was beneath a parking lot in Clearwater, Florida; within the year prior to the discovery, at least four other historic African American cemeteries were identified in the Tampa Bay area.[19] In October 2020, it was reported that Clemson University in South Carolina was working to identify the identities of the 604 unmarked graves found in Woodland Cemetery, located on the university's campus. It is believed that the graves likely belonged to enslaved people, domestic workers, convict laborers, and sharecroppers who lived on the land in the nineteenth century.[20] Cemeteries belonging to African Americans have been found closer to home as well, such as the Eastport Cemetery in Knoxville. According to a news article published in 2018, the site is so overgrown with brush and scrub that neighbors do not realize that it is the site of between five and six thousand African American burials. The site has been neglected for more than sixty years, and although there are some who wish to save and preserve the site, it does not appear that this has happened as of this writing.[21] As these cases illustrate, there are countless African American cemeteries that have been overlooked and at times developed over, through the last decades. When we allow these overlooked places to remain silent, we run the risk of suppressing an important part of our collective history. As Tennesseans, knowing the story of these places will provide a fuller and richer history of our past.

CONCLUSION

The Persistence of Lodges and Lodge Cemeteries

We want to get them to understand that
a cemetery is not just a place for dead
people. It can be a place to sit and relax,
meditate . . .

—STEVEN SCRUGGS, organizer, Odd
Fellows Cemetery and Potters Field
Rehabilitation Project

In August 2016, an Illumination Tribute was held at the
Odd Fellows Cemetery complex in Knoxville, Tennessee.
The tribute took place in August as part of the city's Emancipation Day ceremonies. African Americans in Knoxville
and East Tennessee began observing Emancipation Day
in the early 1870s; it commemorates the occasion when
the then military governor of Tennessee, Andrew Johnson,
freed his personal slaves on August 8, 1863, in Greeneville.
These festivities continued in East Tennessee well into the

early twentieth century.[1] Although largely confined to East
Tennessee, August 8 was celebrated as Emancipation Day
in Nashville in 1908. That day saw the formal dedication
of Greenwood Park, an African American park created by
businessman and pastor Preston Taylor. He advertised the
event as "Emancipation Day" in the *Nashville Globe* and
promised a grand parade, program, baseball game, con-
cert, sham battle, and fireworks.[2] In 2016, a coalition of
the Knoxville ReAnimation Coalition and members of the
University of Tennessee's College of Architecture decided
to mark Emancipation Day with a candle lighting at the
cemetery. The event included singing, a reading of names
of those buried at the site, and the lighting of hundreds of
candles throughout the cemetery complex. It also marked
new walkways through the cemetery built by their joint
efforts.[3] This event highlighted the persistence of the Odd
Fellows Cemetery complex, long neglected by Knoxville,
but whose fortunes began to change in the first decade of
the twenty-first century. Although a candlelight illumination of graves was not likely a commemorative event envi-
sioned by the founding groups of the cemetery, the story
of the Odd Fellows Cemetery complex is one that shows
the remarkable and sometimes unusual ways lodge cemeteries in Tennessee continue to persist and thrive into the
twenty-first century.

As described earlier, the Odd Fellows Cemetery complex
was created when four different lodge groups established
cemeteries adjacent to each other in the early 1880s in what
is now East Knoxville. It is estimated that there are more than
six thousand interments in this cemetery complex, many of
them unmarked by traditional stone tombstones. By 2003,
when Robert McGinnis was transcribing and marking the

cemeteries of Knox County, he noted that the cemeteries were "overgrown with brush and small trees. Several attempts have been made over the years to clean the area, but the block continues to be a community dumping ground."[4] In 2008, a professor at the University of Tennessee's College of Architecture, Katherine Ambroziak, began working with a small grassroots organization in East Knoxville, the Knoxville ReAnimation Coalition (KRC), to restore the cemetery. In addition to reclaiming the cemetery, Ambroziak, KRC, and others have worked to create an interactive memorial landscape for the community. Students in several architecture classes designed "rituals" to support community celebration and often invited community members to take part in these rituals. Incoming freshman at the University of Tennessee have participated in a service program at the cemetery that is actively involved in staking out and constructing paths into the cemetery from the adjoining neighborhood to allow safe passage and access to the cemetery.[5]

Although historians point out that fraternalism is on the wane, particularly when compared to early twentieth-century membership highs, not all the lodges associated with cemeteries in Tennessee are dead. Several lodges continue to exist and are active participants in their communities. Independent Order of Pole Bearers Lodge Number 9 in rural Shelby County continues with active members and events. The group, also known as the International Pallbearers Association, is one of the last remaining lodges left of the Pole Bearers, and there were 150 members in the group as of December 2018, when their lodge building, located beside the active cemetery, burned on Christmas morning.[6] The society continues to meet in a new pavilion and to assist its members with funeral arrangements.[7]

Another lodge that remains active is Benevolent Society No. 210 in Port Royal, in Montgomery County. As discussed earlier, the lodge hall for the group was burned by white supremacists in 1994, and a new lodge hall erected in 2001. The group continues to work in its community, giving scholarships to students and monetary gifts to widows, providing health screenings for the community, and mentoring youth in the community.[8] The group also hosts an annual picnic each year in August.

While a few benevolent lodges and more fraternal groups continue to exist in the state, it is clear that historians are not mistaken in believing that the heyday of fraternalism has passed. The Improved Benevolent and Protective Order of Elks of the World continues to exist, as do the Prince Hall Masons. The Grand United Order of Odd Follows is in the process of rebuilding the lodge in Tennessee, as they have previously done in other states such as South Carolina and Alabama.[9] One interesting note, however, is that fewer members of fraternal organizations are very poor. Because the government, in the form of unemployment benefits, Social Security, and Medicare, now provides a social safety net for Americans, fraternal lodges no longer offer extensive mutual aid as they did to their members one hundred years ago.[10]

Just as the needs regarding mutual aid and having a place for burial has changed for African American society in Tennessee, so have some of the lodge cemeteries transformed, becoming true community burial spaces that continue to evolve to fit the needs of the community. While the Sons of Ham lodge organization appears to no longer exist, their cemetery is now known as the Dry Creek Cemetery, named for the community it is a part of as well as the creek that borders the cemetery. Burials continue to occur, and a new, paved driveway and a sign have been added to the property within the last two years. The Ladies Benevolent Society No. 44 may no longer exist in Shelbyville, but their cemetery, Mount Ararat, continues in constant use by the community. The Young Men's Aid Society in Laguardo has seen a new sign installed and renewed interest in the cemetery in the last five years although the society is defunct. The Odd Fellows Cemetery complex in Knoxville is the site of numerous activities hosted by both the community and the University of Tennessee as a local grassroots organization works to discover and remember those buried there. The Zion Christian Cemetery in Memphis is also the focus of restoration efforts by a grassroots organization trying to tell the story of how important this cemetery is to the history of Memphis itself.

For all these success stories, other lodge cemeteries have declined in use and become neglected during the late twentieth century. Benevolent Society No. 11 Cemetery in Murfreesboro goes through cycles of neglect and maintenance as the local African American community struggles to restore the cemetery and rescue it from becoming a homeless encampment. The Union Forever Cemetery in Memphis is overgrown and classified as "residential" property by the property assessor's office, not "religious," as most cemeteries in Tennessee are. The lodge hall located on the property of the Benevolent Society No. 84 Cemetery in Antioch collapsed in the winter of 2014-2015, and five years later, the debris remained on the property. Some of the lodge cemeteries in the state face the same risk as other small or African American cemeteries across the state—falling into neglect and being redeveloped by property owners in rapidly growing areas.

While the number of identified and visited African American cemeteries remaining on the landscape of the state may be small, they tell a large story. The history of the lodge cemeteries in Tennessee is the history of both fraternalism and the African American community in this state following the Civil War. During a time when the formerly enslaved were making new lives and creating communities, they faced difficulties. What would happen if they became sick and were unable to work? Who would ensure that they received a proper burial when they died? Who would care for a widow or a child? Fraternal and benevolent groups sprang into existence to meet these needs, and in doing so, met a variety of other needs. They provided places for African Americans to practice leadership skills, to socialize, to entertain themselves, and to network and meet others. When faced with few places that would allow them to bury their dead due to their race, fraternal and benevolent groups pooled their resources to purchase property and establish cemeteries.

Studying these cemeteries reveals information about the African American community in Tennessee. The gravestones left behind give us clues about the lodges themselves as well as the individuals who could afford stone markers. Conversely, the unmarked graves of the cemeteries reveal other ways graves were commemorated, such as with various plants. The placement of cemeteries on the landscape often reveals the segregated landscape on which they were constructed. Seeing two cemeteries, one white and one African American, separated by a fence reveals how segregation touched all aspects of Southern life, even into death. The continued use of the cemeteries, even after the demise of the lodges responsible for organizing them, shows the persistence of cemeteries in community life. At some point, these places ceased to belong solely to the lodges and instead began to belong to the surrounding communities. In doing so, the cemeteries fulfilled the promise of fraternalism and benevolence. They became part of the glue that bound disparate peoples into one group, a unified whole. Even though many of the lodges described here no longer officially exist, their spirit lives on in the communities that surround the lodge cemeteries of Tennessee.

GLOSSARY OF TERMS

There is an amazing variety of tombstones and grave markers found in cemeteries. What follows is a brief description of some of the markers I have found in African American lodge cemeteries across the state. This is not intended as a full description, nor does it encompass all the different types of grave markers found in the lodge cemeteries in the state.[1]

ALTAR TOMB: A solid gravestone that resembles a religious altar.

BEDSTEAD: A grave marker that is in the shape of a bed. There will be a marker where the headboard of a bed is typically found.

BENCH MARKER: A grave marker in the shape of a bench which can be used for sitting.

BEVEL MARKER: A gravestone that is rectangular and set low to the ground. It has straight sides and the top is set at an angle.

BOX TOMB: A tomb that is in the shape of the box and is above ground. Some will have a grave marker on top of the box with identifying information for those interred within the box tomb.

DIE ON BASE: A headstone grave marker that has been placed on a base, usually granite, concrete, or the same material as the headstone.

DRESSED: Describes a stone that is completely smoothed

FINIAL: An ornament, sometimes spherical in shape, on the post of a fence or a grave marker.

FOOTSTONE: A flat grave marker, usually of stone, placed at the foot of a grave. It is typically flush with the earth, although it can be raised.

FUNERAL HOME MARKER: A small, usually rectangular marker issued by a funeral home that displays the name of the deceased and the name of the funeral home; occasionally, the birth and/or death years of the deceased are also listed. The marker has a small stake the end that is placed in the ground. It is inexpensive and sometimes used to mark a grave before a more permanent gravestone can be placed at the site.

GOVERNMENT ISSUE: A grave marker issued by the United States government and used to mark the grave of a military veteran. These markers are usually a headstone or a lawn-marker type of monument. In addition to the name of the deceased, the marker will list the unit and branch of military in which the deceased served.

GRAVE DEPRESSION: A hollow, or sunken, spot in the earth over a grave. It is usually caused by the collapse of the coffin.

GRAVE OFFERING: Item(s) left at a grave that typically hold some religious or other meaning to the deceased or to those left behind. Grave offerings can include shells, jewelry, coins, small statutes, flowers, clocks, or any item that has meaning for the community.

HEADSTONE: A flat grave marker, usually of stone, placed at the head of a grave. It can be placed alone or in conjunction with a footstone. It stands at a right angle to the grave.

LAWN MARKER: A flat type of grave marker that is flush with the earth. Some have a spot in which a vase may be placed.

LEDGER STONE: A grave marker that lies horizontal and is flush with the ground.

OBELISK: A grave marker that is tall and slim, usually square, with a pointed top. They can range in height.

ORIENTATION: The cardinal direction the graves are laid out in.

PEDESTAL TOMB: A grave marker, usually square in shape, that is placed on a pedestal of the same material. The pedestal is topped in some way. A pedestal with an urn at the top is referred to as a *pedestal with urn*. A pedestal that has the top carved in a manner reminiscent of a vaulted ceiling is referred to as a *pedestal tomb—vaulted roof.*

UNDRESSED: A grave marker that has not been made completely smooth so that it looks unfinished.

URN: Tall, rounded vase with a base.

NOTES

INTRODUCTION

Epigraph. W. E. B. Du Bois, *Black Reconstruction in America 1860–1880* (New York: Harcourt, Brace, 1935; New York: Free Press, 1998), 694–95. Citations refer to the Free Press edition.

1. Robert Tracy McKenzie, "Reconstruction," *Tennessee Encyclopedia*, last updated March 1, 2018, https://tennesseeencyclopedia.net/entries/reconstruction.
2. McKenzie, "Reconstruction."
3. Caneta Skelley Hankins and Michael Thomas Gavin, *Plowshares and Swords: Tennessee Farm Families Tell Civil War Stories* (Murfreesboro: Center for Historic Preservation at Middle Tennessee State University, 2013), 130.
4. McKenzie, "Reconstruction."
5. Paul H. Bergeron, Stephen V. Ash, and Jeanette Keith, *Tennesseans and Their History* (Knoxville: University of Tennessee Press, 1999), 167.
6. Stephen V. Ash, *Middle Tennessee Society Transformed 1860–1870: War and Peace in the Upper South* (Baton Rouge: Louisiana State University Press, 1988), 209.
7. Alrutheus Ambush Taylor, *The Negro in Tennessee, 1865–1880* (Washington, DC: Associated Publishers, 1941), 34.
8. Ash, *Middle Tennessee Society Transformed*, 197.
9. Mark V. Wetherington, "Ku Klux Klan," *Tennessee Encyclopedia*, last updated March 1, 2018, https://tennesseeencyclopedia.net/entries/ku-klux-klan.
10. Ash, *Middle Tennessee Society Transformed*, 203–4.
11. Wetherington, "Ku Klux Klan."
12. Eric Foner, *Reconstruction: America's Unfinished Revolution 1863–1877*, rev. ed. (New York: Harper Collins, 1988; New York: Perennial Classics, 2002), 89. Citations refer to the Perennial Classics edition.

13. Carroll Van West, "Historic Rural African-American Churches in Tennessee, 1850–1970," NPS form 10-900, reference # 64500618. National Register of Historic Places, Digital Archive on NPGallery. National Park Service, Washington, DC. https://npgallery.nps.gov/NRHP. Sect. E, p. 9.

14. Foner, *Reconstruction*, 95.

15. Edward L. Ayers, *The Promise of the New South: Life after Reconstruction* (2007, rprt. Oxford, UK: Oxford University Press, 1992), 39.

16. Bergeron, Ash, and Keith, *Tennesseans and Their History*, 171.

17. Judy Bussell LeForge, "State Colored Conventions of Tennessee, 1865–1866," *Tennessee Historical Quarterly* 65, no. 3 (Fall 2006), 236.

18. Bergeron, Ash, and Keith, *Tennesseans and Their History*, 171.

19. "Biographies of 19th Century Legislators," *"This Honorable Body": African American Legislators in 19th Century Tennessee*, Tennessee State Library and Archives, 2013, accessed July 5, 2020, https://sharetngov.tnsosfiles.com/tsla/exhibits/blackhistory/bios.htm.

20. Kathleen R. Zebley, "Freedmen's Bureau," *Tennessee Encyclopedia*, last updated March 1, 2018, https://tennesseeencyclopedia.net/entries/freedmens-bureau.

21. Bobby L. Lovett, *The African-American History of Nashville, Tennessee, 1780–1930: Elites and Dilemmas* (Fayetteville: University of Arkansas Press, 1999), 112–13.

22. Joseph H. Cartwright, *The Triumph of Jim Crow: Tennessee Race Relations in the 1880s* (Knoxville: University of Tennessee Press, 1976), 161, 169–70.

23. Cartwright, *The Triumph of Jim Crow*, 175.

24. Howard N. Rabinowitz, *Race Relations in the Urban South 1865–1890*, rev. ed. (New York: Oxford University Press, 1978; Athens: University of Georgia Press, 1996), 127. Citations refer to the 1996 edition.

25. Cartwright, *The Triumph of Jim Crow*, 183.

26. Kenneth W. Goings and Gerald L. Smith, "'Unhidden' Transcripts: Memphis and African American Agency, 1862–1920," *Journal of Urban History* 21, no. 3 (March 1995), 385.

27. Ayers, *The Promise of the New South*, 9.

28. Ayers, *The Promise of the New South*, 22.

29. James E. Fickle, "Industry," *Tennessee Encyclopedia*, last updated March 1, 2018, https://tennesseeencyclopedia.net/entries/industry.

30. Rabinowitz, *Race Relations in the Urban South*, 63, 66.

31. Brian D. Page, "Sutton E. Griggs," *Tennessee Encyclopedia*, last updated March 1, 2018, https://tennesseeencyclopedia.net/entries/sutton-e-griggs.

32. Sutton E. Griggs, *The One Great Question: A Study of Southern Conditions at Close Range* (Nashville, TN: Orion Publishing, 1907), 13.

33. Griggs, *The One Great Question*, 19.
34. Griggs, *The One Great Question*, 31.
35. Michael McGerr, *A Fierce Discontent: The Rise and Fall of the Progressive Movement in America 1870–1920* (New York: Free Press, 2003), 216.
36. Bergeron, *Tennesseans and Their History*, 212.
37. Carole Stanford Bucey, "Tennessee in the Twentieth Century," *Tennessee Historical Quarterly* 69, no. 3 (Fall 2010), 263.
38. Lester C. Lamon, *Black Tennesseans 1900–1930* (Knoxville: University of Tennessee Press, 1977), 6, 19.
39. Lamon, *Black Tennesseans*, 2.
40. Bobby L. Lovett, "Benjamin 'Pap' Singleton," *Tennessee Encyclopedia*, last updated March 1, 2018, https://tennesseeencyclopedia.net/entries/benjamin-singleton.
41. Lamon, *Black Tennesseans*, 126–27.
42. Margaret Ripley Wolfe, "World War I," *Tennessee Encyclopedia*, last updated March 1, 2018, https://tennesseeencyclopedia.net/entries/world-war-i.
43. Lamon, *Black Tennesseans*, 232–34.
44. Enkeshi Thom El-Amin, "Chocolate City Way Up South in Appalachia: Black Knoxville at the Intersection of Race, Place, and Region" (Ph.D. diss., University of Tennessee, 2019), 53.
45. Dan Pierce, "Austin Peay," *Tennessee Encyclopedia*, last updated March 1, 2018, https://tennesseeencyclopedia.net/entries/austin-peay.
46. Bergeron, Ash, and Keith, *Tennesseans and Their History*, 235.
47. Bergeron, Ash, and Keith, *Tennesseans and Their History*, 247–48.
48. Wetherington, "Ku Klux Klan."

CHAPTER 1

Epigraph. Albert C. Stevens, *The Cyclopaedia of Fraternities* (New York: E. B. Treat and Company, 1907), v.

1. Property listing for 0 Mitchell Road, Crye-Leike Real Estate Services, accessed July 26, 2020, https://www.crye-leike.com/0-mitchell-rd/memphis/ms/tid-memphis-mlsnum-10072225.
2. "Cemeteries," Shelby County Register of Deeds, accessed July 26, 2020, https://register.shelby.tn.us/cemeteries.php; property details for parcel 075074 00083C, Shelby County Register of Deeds, accessed July 26, 2020, https://gis.register.shelby.tn.us/?task=parcelQuery&cemetery=Y&parcelid=075074%20%2000083C.

3. Alan Downer, "Native Americans and Historic Preservation," in *A Richer Heritage: Historic Preservation in the Twenty-First Century*, ed. Robert E. Stipe (Chapel Hill: University of North Carolina Press, 2003), 419.

4. Sherene Baugher and Richard F. Veit, *The Archaeology of American Cemeteries and Gravemarkers* (Gainesville: University of Florida Press, 2014), 29.

5. "Human Remains and Burials," Tennessee Department of Environment and Conservation, accessed August 1, 2020, https://www.tn.gov/ environment/program-areas/arch-archaeology/services-and-resources/ human-remains-and-burials.html.

6. "Laws Regarding Cemeteries in Tennessee," Tennessee Department of Environment and Conservation, accessed August 1, 2020, https:// www.tn.gov/content/dam/tn/environment/archaeology/documents/ TCA_Cemeteries.pdf.

7. Alexis de Tocqueville, *Democracy in America*, trans. Henry Reeve (New York: George Dearborn, 1838), 171.

8. Foner, *Reconstruction*, 95.

9. Rabinowitz, *Race Relations in the Urban South*, 140.

10. Taylor, *The Negro in Tennessee*, 235.

11. Foner, *Reconstruction*, 95.

12. Theda Skocpol, Ariane Liazos, and Marshall Ganz, *What A Mighty Power We Can Be: African American Fraternal Groups and the Struggle for Racial Equality* (Princeton, NJ: Princeton University Press, 2006), 70.

13. The Knoxville Hebrew Benevolent Society met monthly. *Helms' Knoxville City Directory* (Knoxville: T. Haws, 1869), 57. The Chattanooga Turn Verein met weekly and in addition to officers had a teacher of gymnastics. *Parham's First Annual Directory to the City of Chattanooga* (Chattanooga: Lou. L. Parham, 1871), 33.

14. "Friendly Sons of Saint Patrick," accessed August 10, 2020, www. friendlysons.com; *Edwards' Memphis Directory* (Memphis, TN: Southern Publishing, 1868), 31.

15. The Tenth Legion Division, No. 10 met weekly on Tuesday nights at St. Cloud's Hill. The Temple Division, No. 22 met weekly on Friday nights at Temperance Hall, located on College Street. The Elysian Grove Division, No. 195, met weekly on Wednesday nights at a different Temperance Hall, this one located on Market Street. *Nashville City and Business Directory for 1860–1861* (Nashville, TN: L. P. Williams, 1860), 81.

16. C. G. Woodson, "Insurance Business among Negroes," *Journal of Negro History* 14, no. 2 (April 1929): 211.

17. Skocpol, Liazos, and Ganz, *What a Mighty Power*, 52.
18. Lamon, *Black Tennesseans 1900–1930*, 200, 204.
19. Skocpol, Liazos, and Ganz, *What a Mighty Power*, 34; Joanna Brooks, "Prince Hall, Freemasonry, and Genealogy," *African American Review* 34, no. 2 (Summer 2000): 198.
20. Skocpol, Liazos, and Ganz, *What a Mighty Power*, 34.
21. David T. Beito, *From Mutual Aid to the Welfare State: Fraternal Societies and Social Services, 1890–1967* (Chapel Hill: University of North Carolina Press, 2000), 11.
22. Skocpol, Liazos, and Ganz, *What a Mighty Power*, 38.
23. Skocpol, Liazos, and Ganz, *What a Mighty Power*, 37.
24. The title page of the Constitution of the Colored Benevolent Society published in 1890 states the group was organized on August 15, 1853.
25. Elsa Barkley Brown, "To Catch the Vision of Freedom: Reconstructing Southern Black Women's Political History, 1865–1880," in *African American Women and the Vote, 1837–1965*, ed. Ann D. Gordon and Bettye Collier-Thomas (Cambridge: University of Massachusetts Press, 1997), 67–68.
26. Jacqueline Jones, *Labor of Love, Labor of Sorrow: Black Women, Work and Family, from Slavery to the Present* (New York: Vintage Books, 1985), 126–27.
27. Foner, *Reconstruction*, 95–96.
28. W. P. Burrell and D. E. Johnson, *Twenty-Five Years History of the Grand Fountain of the United Order of True Reformers 1881–1905* (Richmond, VA: Grand Fountain, United Order of True Reformers, 1909), 75, 77.
29. *Constitution of the Working People's Labor and Art Association*, "Preface." (Nashville, TN: Walden University Press, 1901). Found in the *Working Peoples Association v. Sons & Daughters of Cyrene*, Rutherford County Chancery Court file, Rutherford County Archives, Murfreesboro, Tennessee. File referred to hereinafter as *Working Peoples Association v. Sons & Daughters of Cyrene.*
30. Articles of Incorporation, Independent Order of Pole Bearers No. 9, RG 42, Secretary of State Charters of Incorporation, series IV, vol. O-O, p. 178. Tennessee State Library and Archives, Nashville, TN.
31. "Negro Masons," *Memphis Daily Appeal*, June 28, 1871, 4.
32. "Masons and Immaculates Insulted," *Nashville Globe*, May 29, 1908, 4.
33. "Masons Buy First Liberty Bonds," *Nashville Globe*, April 12, 1918, 1.
34. "Prince Hall Masons Urge Members to Vote, Register," *Memphis World*, July 27, 1957, 1.
35. Bobby L. Lovett, *The Civil Rights Movement in Tennessee: A Narrative History* (Knoxville: University of Tennessee Press, 2005), 260.

36. Skocpol, Liazos, and Ganz, *What a Mighty Power*, 38.
37. Gloria Brown Melton, "Blacks in Memphis, Tennessee, 1920–1955: A Historical Study" (PhD diss., Washington State University, 1982), 15–16.
38. Melton, "Blacks in Memphis," 16.
39. "Brief History," Improved Benevolent and Protective Order of Elks of the World, accessed August 10, 2020, https://www.ibpoew.org/history.
40. Charles H. Brooks, *The Official History and Manual of the Grand United Order of Odd Fellows* (Philadelphia, PA: Odd Fellows' Journal Print, 1902), 117.
41. Skocpol, Liazos, and Ganz, *What a Mighty Power*, 37.
42. "Ten Thousand Odd Fellows, The Slogan," *Nashville*, September 30, 1910, 3.
43. National historian of the GUOOF, email to author, May 14, 2020.
44. Skocpol, Liazos, and Ganz, *What a Mighty Power*, 46–47.
45. Edward Nelson Palmer, "Negro Secret Societies," *Social Forces* 23 no. 2 (December 1944): 209.
46. "The City; Local News in Brief," *Nashville Union and American*, August 18, 1870, 1.
47. "Festive Colored People," *Nashville Union and American*, June 19, 1874, 4.
48. "Good Samaritan Lodge Anniversary," *Knoxville Daily Chronicle*, June 17, 1882, 1.
49. Skocpol, Liazos, and Ganz, *What a Mighty Power*, 38.
50. Green Polonius Hamilton, *The Bright Side of Memphis* (Memphis: G. P. Hamilton, 1908), 208.
51. "Courts," *The Crisis* 3, no. 5 (March 1912), 189
52. "Pythians Win Point," *Nashville Globe*, May 3, 1912, 1.
53. "Fraternities," *The Crisis* 19, no. 5 (March 1920): 280.
54. Stevens, *The Cyclopaedia of Fraternities*, 198.
55. Hamilton, *The Bright Side of Memphis*, 208.
56. *Directory of Jackson, Tennessee* (Jackson, TN: Jackson City Directory Co., 1891), 16. *Marshall-Bruce-Polk Co's Nashville City Directory* (Nashville, TN: Marshall-Bruce-Polk, 1924), 502.
57. "Franklin Notes," *Nashville Globe*, August 29, 1913, 6.
58. Stevens, *The Cyclopaedia of Fraternities*, 198.
59. Beito, *From Mutual Aid to the Welfare State*, 181–85.
60. "What We Do," Knights and Daughters of Tabor, accessed May 31, 2020, http://www.knightsanddaughtersoftabor.com/what-we-do.
61. Skocpol, Liazos, and Ganz, *What a Mighty Power*, 54.
62. John M. Giggie, "Mosaic Templars of America," in *Organizing Black America: An Encyclopedia of African American Associations*, ed. Nina Mjagkij (New York: Garland Publishing, 2001), 301.

63. Bryan McDade, Curator of Collections, Mosaic Templars Cultural Center, Little Rock, Arkansas, email to author, February 26, 2013.

64. Taylor, *The Negro in Tennessee*, 156.

65. *Constitution and General By-Laws of the Colored People's Benevolent Society of Tennessee* (Nashville, TN: Chas. LeRoi, 1890), cover page.

66. Edgefield Benevolent Society, *Constitution and By-laws of the Edgefield Benevolent Society* (Nashville, TN: Union and American Book and Job Print, 1870), 3; from *Ladies Benevolent Society No. 2 of Edgefield v. Benevolent Society No. 2 of Edgefield*, Davidson County Chancery Court, case no. 7962, Metro Archives, Nashville, TN.

67. "The Origination of Benevolent Lodge Order #210," Benevolent Lodge Order #210, accessed August 1, 2020, http://benevolentlodge210.org.

68. Stevens, *The Cyclopaedia of Fraternities*, 141.

69. "Order of Immaculates in Session," *Nashville Globe*, August 16, 1907, 7.

70. "I.O.I.," *Pulaski Citizen*, July 11, 1878, 3.

71. "One Thousand Dollars Well Applied," *Milan Exchange*, April 22, 1882, 8.

72. "Immaculates," *Memphis Daily Appeal*, July 3, 1884, 1.

73. Hamilton, *The Bright Side of Memphis*, 207.

74. *Marshall-Bruce-Polk Co's Nashville City Directory* (1924), 30.

75. Commissioner of Insurance, *Annual Report of the Commissioner of Insurance of the State of Alabama for the Year Ending December 31, 1920* (Montgomery, AL: Brown Printing, 1921), 58.

76. "Negro Lodge in Session," *Daily Arkansas Gazette*, September 17, 1920, 13.

77. "Gallatin," *Chicago Defender*, April 14, 1945, 9A.

78. "Immaculates Close Grand Lodge Session," *Huntsville Mirror*, August 9, 1952, 1.

79. "Local News," *Memphis Daily Appeal*, August 25, 1870, 4.

80. "Brevities," *Public Ledger*, May 30, 1871, 3.

81. "Ledger Lines," *Public Ledger*, June 5, 1874, 3.

82. "Ledger Lines," *Public Ledger*, June 28, 1875, 3.

83. "Local Paragraphs," *Memphis Daily Appeal*, July 3, 1875, 4.

84. "The Fourth," *Memphis Daily Appeal*, July 6, 1875, 1.

85. "The Fourth," *Memphis Daily Appeal*, July 6, 1875, 1.

86. Brian S. Wills, "Nathan Bedford Forrest," *Tennessee Encyclopedia*, last updated March 1, 2018, https://tennesseeencyclopedia.net/entries/nathan-bedford-forrest.

87. Hamilton, *The Bright Side of Memphis*, 207

88. Articles of Incorporation, Independent Order of Pole Bearers Association No. 2, p. 212.

89. *Boyle & Chapman's Memphis City Directory* (Memphis, TN: Boyle and Chapman, 1872), 471.

90. "Celebration," *Public Ledger*, December 31, 1873, 2.

91. Hamilton, *The Bright Side of Memphis*, 208.

92. Shay Arthur, "Building with Historical Connections Destroyed in Christmas Morning Fire," News Channel 3, December 25, 2018, https://wreg.com/2018/12/25/building-with-historical-connections-destroyed-in-christmas-morning-fire.

93. "A Most Worthy Example," *Nashville Union & Dispatch*, January 7, 1868, 2.

94. Articles of Incorporation, Daughters of Zion No. 1, RG 42, Secretary of State Charters of Incorporation, series IV, vol. A, p. 209. Tennessee State Library and Archives, Nashville, TN.

95. "The Fourth," *Memphis Daily Appeal*, July 6, 1867, 3.

96. Daughters of Zion No. 3, Freedmen's Savings & Trust Register, Signatures of Depositors, Nashville and Memphis, Tennessee, Norfolk, Richmond, Virginia, 1871–74. Microfilm collection, Tennessee State Library and Archives, Nashville, TN.

97. *Boyle & Chapman's Memphis City Directory* (Memphis: Boyle & Chapman, 1874), 478.

98. *Boyle & Chapman's* (1874), 478.

99. Brian D. Page, "'Stand By the Flag': Nationalism and African-American Celebrations of the Fourth of July in Memphis, 1866–1887," *Tennessee Historical Quarterly* 58, no. 4 (Winter 1999): 290.

100. Hamilton, *The Bright Side of Memphis*, 200.

101. *Boyle & Chapman's* (1874), 478.

102. Milbrey Heard and Zhukov Camphor, "Zion Cemetery," NPS form 10-900, reference # 90000301. National Register of Historic Places, Digital Archive on NPGallery. National Park Service, Washington, DC. https://npgallery.nps.gov/NRHP, Sect. 8.

103. "The New Officers," *Daily American*, August 9, 1890, 4.

104. "Supreme Grand Lodge Meets," *Nashville American*, July 26, 1910, 10.

105. "A.U.K. & D. of A.," *Daily American*, August 29, 1890, 5.

106. "Well Known Colored Physician Dies Here," *Nashville Tennessean and the Nashville American*, August 15, 1920, B8.

107. R. F. Boyd, "What Are the Causes of the Great Mortality among the Negroes in the Cities of the South, and How Is That Mortality to be Lessened?," in *Twentieth Century Negro Literature*, ed. D.W. Culp (Napierville, IL: J. L. Nichols, 1902), 214.

108. "A.U.K. & D. of A.," *Daily American*, August 29, 1890, 5.

109. Page, "Stand by the Flag," 289.

110. "Broken Out Again," *Memphis Commercial*, May 14, 1891, 5; "Celebration by Sons of Ham," *Daily Union and American*, June 9, 1866, 4.

111. "'The Sons of Ham' in Memphis—the West India Emancipation and a Convention at Nashville," *Daily Union and American*, August 5, 1866, 1.

112. Tony Martin, "The Banneker Literary Institute of Philadelphia: African American Intellectual Activism before the War of the Slaveholders' Rebellion," *Journal of African American History* 87, no. 3 (Summer 2002): 311.

113. "The Fourth," *Memphis Daily Appeal*, July 6, 1875, 1. Information on the location of Alexander Park from *Sholes' Memphis Directory for 1881* (Memphis, TN: Sholes, 1881), 35.

114. *Public Ledger*, April 12, 1880, 1.

115. "Broken Out Again," *Memphis Commercial*, May 14, 1891, 5. The news article concerns problems at Beale Street Baptist Church and mentions a meeting held at the Sons of Ham Hall on the corner of Beale and Hernando Streets.

116. *Acts of the State of Tennessee, Passed by the First Session of the Thirty-Sixth General Assembly for the Years 1869–1870* (Nashville, TN: Jones, Purvis, 1870), 567.

117. "The Sons of Ham," *Nashville Union and American*, September 22, 1872, 4.

118. *Nashville Daily Union*, March 21, 1865, 3.

119. "The Sons of Relief An Order with a History," *Nashville Globe*, November 14, 1913, 8.

120. Lovett, *The African-American History of Nashville*, 108

121. Articles of Incorporation, Sons of Relief, RG 42, Secretary of State Charters of Incorporation, series IV, vol. B, p. 169. Tennessee State Library and Archives, Nashville, TN.

122. Articles of Incorporation, Sons of Relief, p. 387.

123. "Day of Jubilee," *Nashville Union and American*, April 27, 1870, 1.

124. "Sand Hill Notes," *Nashville Globe*, September 12, 1913, 3.

125. David M. Fahey, "United Brothers of Friendship and Sisters of the Mysterious Ten," in Mjagkij, ed., *Organizing Black America*, 577.

126. William J. Simmons, *Men of Mark: Eminent, Progressive and Rising* (Cleveland, OH: Geo. M. Rewell, 1887), 545–47.

127. Stevens, *Cyclopaedia of Fraternities*, 288.

128. Stevens, *Cyclopaedia of Fraternities*, 288.

129. W. H. Gibson, *History of the United Brothers of Friendship and Sisters of the Mysterious Ten* (Louisville, KY: Bradley & Gilbert, 1897), 111.

130. "U.B.F., S.M.T. Meet in Twentieth Annual Session," *Nashville Globe*, August 26, 1910, 1.

131. "Personal," *Nashville Globe*, June 20, 1913, 4.

132. Skocpol, Liazos, and Ganz, *What a Mighty Power*, 50.

133. *Constitution of the Working People's Labor and Art Association* (Nashville, TN: Walden University Press, 1901), Introduction and Preface, *Working Peoples Association v. Sons & Daughters of Cyrene*, Rutherford County Archives.

134. *Constitution of the Working People's Labor and Art Association*, 37–38, 50.

135. *Constitution of the Working People's Labor and Art Association*, 37.

136. *Constitution of the Working People's Labor and Art Association*, Introduction.

137. *Nashville City Directory 1890* (Nashville, TN: Martin and Bruce, 1890), 99, 568.

138. *Constitution of the Working People's Labor and Art Association*, 40.

139. "Nineteenth Annual Convention," *Nashville Globe*, August 20, 1909, 1.

140. Deposition of John Watkins, dated November 17, 1915. *Working Peoples Association v. Sons and Daughters of Cyrene*, Rutherford County Archives, Murfreesboro, Tennessee.

141. *Proceedings from the Twenty-Fourth Annual Convention*, *Working Peoples Association v. Sons & Daughters of Cyrene*, Rutherford County Archives.

142. Deposition of James Bumpass, dated December 9, 1915. *Working Peoples Association v. Sons & Daughters of Cyrene*, Rutherford County Archives.

143. Briersville is spelled a number of different ways in different sources. Alternate spellings include Briarsville, Brierville, and Briarville; "Briersville Notes," *Nashville Globe*, September 13, 1912, 3.

144. Carroll Van West, "United Sons and Daughters of Charity Lodge Hall," *Tennessee Encyclopedia*, last updated March 1, 2018, https://tennesseeencyclopedia.net/entries/united-sons-and-daughters-of-charity-lodge-hall.

145. Beginning in 2012, the author began a systematic attempt to document the different African American fraternal and benevolent groups in Tennessee. Sources used included Sanborn Insurance Maps, deeds, published cemetery records (focusing on identified African American cemeteries), published African American histories of communities and counties of Tennessee, digitized newspapers, and digital property assessor records. From this, a list was created, and the author began visiting and documenting verified lodge cemetery and lodge building sites. At each location, GPS coordinates were collected as well as documentation of the features of the sites.

146. John Michael Vlach, *By the Work of Their Hands: Studies in Afro-American Folklife* (Ann Arbor, MI: UMI Research Press, 1991), 109.

Vlach also discusses the importance of cemeteries in African American life in his work *The Afro-American Tradition in Decorative Arts* (Cleveland, OH: Cleveland Museum of Art, 1978).

147. Lynn Rainville, "Protecting Our Shared Heritage in African-American Cemeteries," *Journal of Field Archaeology* 34, no. 2 (Summer 2009): 196.

148. Otey M. Scruggs, "The Economic and Racial Components of Jim Crow," in *Key Issues in the Afro-American Experience*, ed. Nathan I. Huggins, Martin Kilson, and Daniel M. Fox (New York: Harcourt Brace Jovanovich, 1971), 83

149. Population figures taken from "All United States Data," *Social Explorer*, accessed March 14, 2020, https://www.socialexplorer.com/a9676d974c/explore.

150. Rainville, "Protecting Our Shared Heritage," 197.

CHAPTER 2

Epigraph. Vlach, *The Afro-American Tradition*, 139.

1. "Identified as Man Sought For," *Nashville Tennessean*, April 29, 1908, 1.

2. John Leiper, "Negro Hanged in Outskirts of Murfreesboro," *Nashville American*, August 29, 1908, 1.

3. "Body of Lynched Negro Interred," *Nashville Tennessean*, August 30, 1908, 8.

4. The population of Murfreesboro in 1910 was 4,679, and the population in 1900 was 3,999. Department of Commerce and Labor, Bureau of the Census, *Thirteenth Census of the United States Taken in the Year 1910; Vol. 3. Population Reports by States* (Washington, DC: Government Printing Office, 1913), 733, https://www2.census.gov/library/publications/decennial/1910/volume-3/volume-3-p6.pdf.

5. "Body of Lynched Negro Interred," 8.

6. J. B. Killebrew, *West Tennessee: Its Resources and Advantages* (Nashville, TN: Tavel, Eastman and Howell, 1879), 35.

7. John E. Harkins, "Memphis," *Tennessee Encyclopedia*, last updated March 1, 2018, http://tennesseeencyclopedia.net/entries/memphis.

8. William D. Miller, "Rural Ideals in Memphis Life at the Turn of the Century," *West Tennessee Historical Society Papers* 4 (1950): 41, 42.

9. Roger Biles, "'Cotton Fields or Skyscrapers?' The Case of Memphis, Tennessee," *Historian* 50, no. 2 (February 1988): 224.

10. Christopher Silver and John V. Moeser, *The Separate City: Black Communities in the Urban South 1940–1960* (Lexington: University of Kentucky Press, 2015), 33.

11. W. L. Miller, "Progressive Dyersburg," *Nashville Globe*, July 22, 1910, 3.
12. "Jackson, the Fifth City in the State," *Nashville Globe*, January 27, 1911, 2.
13. "Somerville Notes," *Nashville Globe*, November 11, 1910, 7.
14. Heard and Camphor, "Zion Cemetery," sect. 7.
15. Sanborn Fire Insurance Map from Memphis, Shelby County, Tennessee (Sanborn Map Company, 1888). Sheet 21B. https://www.loc.gov/item/sanborn08348_001; Hamilton, *The Bright Side of Memphis*, 223.
16. Heard and Camphor, "Zion Cemetery," sect. 7.
17. Heard and Camphor, "Zion Cemetery," sect. 8.
18. "Historical Marker Unveiling at Zion Christian Cemetery," Lynching Sites Project, March 23, 2019, https://lynchingsitesmem.org/event/historical-marker-unveiling-zion-christian-cemetery.
19. Heard and Camphor, "Zion Cemetery," sect. 7, p. 2.
20. "Articles of Incorporation," Independent Order of Pole Bearers No. 9, p. 178.
21. 1900 US Census, Shelby County, Tennessee, population schedule, Joe Burns, Twelfth Civil District, sheet 5, dwelling 85, family 94, Joe Burns household; digital image, Ancestry, accessed July 20, 2020, www.ancestry.com.
22. 1910 US Census, Shelby County, Tennessee, population schedule, Pierce Homes, Twelfth Civil District, sheet 3, dwelling 38, family 37, Pierce Holmes household; digital image, Ancestry, accessed July 20, 2020, www.ancestry.com.
23. Brian Daniel Page, "Local Matters: Race, Place, and Community Politics after the Civil War" (PhD diss., Ohio State University, 2009), 13.
24. Armstead L. Robinson, "Plans Dat Comed from God: Institution Building and the Emergence of Black Leadership in Reconstruction Memphis," in *Church and Community among Black Southerners, 1865–1900*, ed. Donald G. Nieman (New York: Garland Publishing, 1994), 101.
25. "Sumner," *Memphis Daily Appeal*, March 23, 1874, 4.
26. *1911 Memphis City Directory* (Memphis, TN: R. L. Polk, 1911), 68.
27. "Union Forever Cemetery," Find a Grave, accessed July 26, 2020, https://www.findagrave.com/cemetery/2441993/union-forever-cemetery.
28. Frederick B. Goddard, *Where to Emigrate and Why* (New York: Frederick B. Goddard, Publisher, 1869), 468.
29. J. B. Killebrew, *Introduction to the Resources of Tennessee*, vol. 2 (Nashville, TN: Tavel, Eastman and Howell, 1874), 619.
30. Lamon, *Black Tennesseans*, 2-3.

31. W. L. Miller, "Winchester and Franklin County," *Nashville Globe*, August 26, 1910, 3; W. L. Miller, "Tullahoma and Coffee County," *Nashville Globe*, August 26, 1910, 3.

32. "Murfreesboro: Her Hustling Negro Citizens," *Nashville Globe*, May 13, 1910, 6.

33. Deed from W. D. Reynolds to Trustees of Agnew Benevolent Society, Giles County Deed Book 60, p. 496. Giles County Microfilm records, Tennessee State Library and Archives, Nashville, Tennessee; 1900 US Census, Giles County, Tennessee, population schedule, 22 District, sheet 10, dwelling 171, family 172, William D. Reynolds household; digital image, Ancestry, accessed May 3, 2020, www.ancestry.com.

34. James L. Wood, *The Historical Development of the Negro in Giles County* (Pulaski: J. L. Wood, 2000), 160.

35. "Benevolent Order No. 210," in *Montgomery County, Tennessee Family History Book 2000* (Paducah, KY: Turner Publishing Company, 2000), 47.

36. John F. Baker Jr., *The Washingtons of Wessyngton Plantation* (New York: Atria Books, 2009), 283, 284.

37. Beth Null Dorris, "VU Children's Hospital Gives Thousands of Families Hope," *Nashville Tennessean*, March 19, 1986, 6.

38. Jean M. Durrett, Diane Williams, and Yolanda G. Reid, *Robertson County Tennessee Cemetery Records* (Springfield, TN: Y. G. Reid, 1987), 80.

39. Durrett, Williams, and Reid, *Robertson County Tennessee Cemetery Records*, 79.

40. Deed from E. A. Hicks, Clerk and Master, to Grand United Order of Odd Fellows No. 2806, November 6, 1916, Robertson County Deed Book 112, pp. 572–73. Robertson County Microfilm Records, Tennessee State Library and Archives, Nashville, Tennessee.

41. W. L. Miller, "Springfield and Robertson County," *Nashville Globe*, September 9, 1910, 3; Sanborn Fire Insurance Map from Springfield, Robertson County. Sanborn Map Company, April 1913. Sheet 6. Proquest Digital Sanborn Maps, 1867–1970 database.

42. "Cemeteries," City of Springfield website, accessed November 29, 2019, https://www.springfield-tn.org/167/Cemeteries.

43. Deed from J. B. Mathes to Trustees of the Colored Benevolent Society, November 20, 1885, Davidson County Deed Book 93, pp. 510–11; "General Property Information: 0 Cafe Rd," Davidson County Assessor of Property, accessed October 17, 2020, https://www.padctn.org/prc/property/3579/card/1.

44. *Proceedings of the Fifty-Eighth Delegated Assembly of the Benevolent Orders of the State of Tennessee* (Nashville, TN: J. Ralston Kenan, 1926), 53.

45. "Tennessee Legislature," *Nashville Union and American*, December 2, 1868, 1.
46. "The Sons of Ham," *Daily American*, May 2, 1878, 4.
47. See "Madison Station Notes," *Nashville Globe*, February 7, 1913, 3; "Madison St. Notes," *Nashville Globe*, June 27, 1913, 3.
48. "Suit for $20,000 Damages Filed," *Nashville Tennessean*, April 24, 1908, 3.
49. Deed from Alex Pettis and Parillee Pettis to Ed Yeatman and Earl Stall, Trustees, July 16, 1904, Davidson County Deed Book 523, pp. 341–42. Davidson County Microfilm Records, Tennessee State Library and Archives, Nashville, Tennessee.
50. "Another Landmark Removed," *Nashville Globe*, July 25, 1913, 1.
51. *Benevolent Proceedings*, 53.
52. Lovett, *The African American History of Nashville*, 108.
53. "Mt. Ararat Cemetery," *Republican Banner*, October 6, 1869, 4.
54. "The State Prison Inspectors," *Daily American*, February 19, 1885, 5.
55. "The Penitentiary," *Daily American*, February 21, 1885, 5.
56. Frank Cason, "Once Proud Cemetery Now Just an Eyesore," *Nashville Tennessean*, March 5, 1973, 15.
57. "Ownership of Cemetery Transferred," *Nashville Tennessean*, August 16, 1982, 13.
58. Greenwood Cemetery itself is a historic African American cemetery, established in 1889 by African American undertaker Preston Taylor; Lovett, *The African American History of Nashville*, 109.
59. "Una Notes," *Nashville Globe*, March 19, 1909, 6.
60. *Benevolent Proceedings*, 49, 53.
61. "Late News from Capitol Hill," *Nashville American*, November 29, 1902, 5.
62. 1910 US Census, Rutherford County, Tennessee, population schedule, Third Civil District, sheet 15A, dwelling 287, family 296, Nathan Matthews household; digital image, Ancestry, accessed April 2, 2020, www.ancestry.com; 1910 US Census, Rutherford County, Tennessee, population schedule, Third Civil District, sheet 12A, dwelling 224, family 231, Dock Brown household; digital image, Ancestry, accessed April 2, 2020, www.ancestry.com; 1900 US Census, Rutherford County, Tennessee, population schedule, Third Civil District, sheet 5, dwelling 90, family 90, Abe Drennon household; digital image, Ancestry, accessed April 2, 2020, www.ancestry.com; 1900 US Census, Rutherford County, Tennessee, population schedule, Third Civil District, sheet 8, dwelling 141, family 142, Stewart Ridley household; digital image, Ancestry, accessed April 2, 2020, www.ancestry.com.

63. Deed from John F. Tucker and Linnie C. Tucker to Colored Mutual Aid Society No. One (1), July 1, 1905, Rutherford County Deed Book 56, p. 524. Rutherford County Register of Deeds, Murfreesboro, Tennessee.

64. Michelle Willard, "Historic Preservation," *Daily News Journal*, January 22, 2014, 1.

65. John Lodl, Rutherford County Archivist, email to author, June 3, 2020.

66. "RC Archives Cemetery Lookup App: 'Colored Mutual Cemetery,'" accessed October 17, 2020, http://rcgis.maps.arcgis.com/apps/webappviewer/index.html?id=e055c9ad47564cb5a33538346648bb1e.

67. Deed from Alfred Miller and wife to Alexander Simmons, William Jordan and other Trustees of Benevolent Lodge No. 11, January 7, 1897, Rutherford County Deed Book 38, pp. 338–39. Rutherford County Register of Deeds, Murfreesboro, Tennessee.

68. *Benevolent Proceedings*, 48, 53.

69. There are two different Mount Ararat Cemeteries discussed within, and both appear to use the abbreviation Mt. Ararat. I will differentiate them in the text by using Mt. Ararat (Nashville) and Mount Ararat (Shelbyville).

70. "Shelbyville Notes," *Nashville Globe*, May 26, 1911, 6.

71. "Shelbyville Notes," *Nashville Globe*, May 6, 1910, 6.

72. *Benevolent Proceedings*, 53.

73. Deed from Emanuel Lester and Louella Lester to Benevolent Order No. 91, October 10, 1936, Wilson County Deed Book 104, p. 164. Wilson County Microfilm Collection, Tennessee State Library and Archives, Nashville, Tennessee.

74. *Benevolent Proceedings*, 49, 53.

75. Patricia Ward Lockett, Mattie McHollin and Wilson County Black History Committee, *In Their Own Voices: An Account of the Presence of African Americans in Wilson County* (Wilson County, TN: Lebanon Democrat, 1999), 132–33.

76. Lockett, McHollin, and Wilson County Black History Committee, *In Their Own Voices*, 217.

77. Articles of Incorporation, Young Men's Aid Society, RG 42, Secretary of State Charters of Incorporation, series IV, vol. A, p. 602. Tennessee State Library and Archives, Nashville, TN.

78. Lockett, McHollin, and Wilson County Black History Committee, *In Their Own Voices*, 204.

79. Deed from W. L. Bradshaw to Andy Davis, Green Bandy, Amen Tipton, James Bloodworth and Jack Bandy, Trustees of the Laguardo Young Mens Aid Society, February 17, 1885, Wilson County Deed Book S-2, pp. 452–53. Wilson County Microfilm Records, Tennessee

State Library and Archives, Nashville, Tennessee; 1880 US Census, Wilson County, Tennessee, population schedule, District 4, sheet 27A, household 235, W. L. Bradshaw household; digital image, Ancestry, accessed May 10, 2020, www.ancestry.com.

80. J. B. Killebrew, *Tennessee: Its Agricultural and Mineral Wealth* (Nashville, TN: Tavel, Eastman and Howell, 1876), 37.
81. Lamon, *Black Tennesseans*, 3.
82. Michael Aaron Blum, "'An Island of Peace in a Sea of Racial Strife': The Civil Rights Movement in Knoxville, Tennessee" (PhD dissertation, University of Memphis, 2014), 22.
83. Blum, "'An Island of Peace,'" 23.
84. Blum, "'An Island of Peace,'" 27, 43.
85. Brooks, *Official History and Manual*, 211.
86. *City Directory of Chattanooga and Suburbs* (Chattanooga: G. M. Connelly, 1902), 17, 19.
87. "Harriman: The Beautiful City," *Nashville Globe*, June 17, 1910, 3.
88. 1880 US Census, Knox County, Tennessee, population schedule, Shieldstown, Sheet 5A, dwelling 44, household 49, Preston L. Blang household; digital image, Ancestry, accessed May 10, 2020, www.ancestry.com.
89. Robert Booker, *The History of Blacks in Knoxville, Tennessee: The First One Hundred Years, 1791–1891* (Knoxville, TN: Beck Cultural Center, 1990), 62.
90. "Cemetery Dedication by the Colored Odd Fellows," *Knoxville Daily Chronicle*, June 24, 1882, 1.
91. Deed from Preston L. Blang and Sarah A. Blang to Martha Bridges, et al., Trustees of the Daughters of Zion, March 23, 1881, Knox County Deed Book U-3, p. 546. Knox County Microfilm Records, Tennessee State Library and Archives, Nashville, Tennessee.
92. "Daughters of Zion," *Knoxville Daily Chronicle*, April 24, 1881, 4.
93. "Dedication of a Colored Cemetery," *Knoxville Daily Chronicle*, November 4, 1881, 1.
94. "Card of Thanks," *Knoxville Daily Chronicle*, April 30, 1882, 4.
95. "Daughters of Zion Hold Annual Meeting at Bethel," *Knoxville Journal*, June 5, 1927, 26.
96. "Real Estate Transfers," *Knoxville Daily Chronicle*, May 1, 1881, 1.
97. Robert A. McGinnis, *In Everlasting Remembrance, The Cemeteries of the Old 1st and 2nd Districts of Knox County, Tennessee* (Knoxville, TN: R. A. McGinnis, 2003), 127.
98. "Good Samaritan Lodge Anniversary," *Knoxville Daily Chronicle*, June 17, 1882, 1.
99. *Knoxville Directory 1882* (Nashville, TN: Standard Directory Co., 1882), 36.

100. "To Give Weiner Roast," *Knoxville News-Sentinel*, June 12, 1934, 7.

101. Brooker, *The History of Blacks in Knoxville*, 63.

102. "Colored Odd Fellows' Demonstration," *Knoxville Daily Chronicle*, May 9, 1880, 4. The article references the celebration being the third anniversary of the Silver Moon Lodge.

103. "Colored Odd Fellows' Celebration," *Knoxville Daily Chronicle*, May 28, 1881, 4.

104. *Knoxville Directory 1882*, 36

105. "Odd Fellows Cemetery," University of Tennessee Knoxville. College of Architecture and Design, accessed November 20, 2019, https://archdesign.utk.edu/projects/odd-fellows-cemetery.

106. McGinnis, *In Everlasting Remembrance*, 75.

107. McGinnis, *In Everlasting Remembrance*, 75.

108. Bartow G. Wilson, *The Knoxville Negro* (Knoxville, TN: Trent Printing, 1929), 66. The Sisters of the Mysterious Ten are also mentioned in J. H. Daves, *A Social Study of the Colored Population of Knoxville, Tennessee* (Knoxville, TN: Free Colored Library, 1926), 15; accessed from the Calvin M. McClung Historical Collection, https://cmdc.knoxlib.org/digital/collection/p15136coll4/id/1357.

109. Bert Vincent, "Strolling with Bert Vincent," *Knoxville News-Sentinel*, June 3, 1956, 33.

110. "County Schools Open Today," *Journal and Tribune* (Knoxville), August 12, 1907, 10.

111. "School at Oakwood Rated 'Perfect,'" *Knoxville Journal*, May 26, 1939, 21.

112. *Knoxville City Directory 1935* (Knoxville, TN: City Directory Co. of Knoxville, 1935), 349.

113. Robert A. McGinnis, *Gone and All but Forgotten: The African-American Cemeteries of Knox County, Tennessee* (Knoxville, TN: Robert A. McGinnis, 2006), 161.

114. "West View Historic Cemetery District," Knox Heritage, accessed February 9, 2021, http://knoxheritage.org/our-work/west-view-historic-cemetery-district.

115. "Colored Odd Fellows Will Celebrate Their Anniversary the First Sunday in May," *Knoxville Sentinel*, April 26, 1897, 3.

116. *Knoxville Sentinel*, July 8, 1897, 8; *Knoxville Sentinel*, June 23, 1897, 7.

117. "First Annual Reception," *Journal and Tribune* (Knoxville), January 4, 1903, 5.

118. "West View Historic Cemetery District."

119. Robert A. McGinnis, *Loves Lives On: African/American Cemeteries of East Tennessee* (Knoxville, TN: Robert A. McGinnis, 2017), 130.

120. Marguerite W. Williams, *Cemeteries of Hamblen County, Tennessee*, vol. 3 (Morristown, TN: Hamblen County Genealogical Society, 1996), 125.

121. Department of Commerce, *Thirteenth Census*, 600.
122. Kevin Cason, "Morristown College," *Tennessee Encyclopedia*, last updated March 1, 2018, https://tennesseeencyclopedia.net/entries/morristown-college.
123. Willie P. Osborne, Clara L. Osborne, and Luie Hargraves, eds. *Contributions of Blacks to Hamblen County 1796 to 1996* (Morristown, TN: Progressive Business Association, 1995), 293.
124. "Colored Masons Build," *Morristown Gazette*, January 23, 1907, 3.
125. "Uncle John Prince Dies," *Morristown Gazette Mail*, February 19, 1934, 3.
126. "Chas. Dockery Services Sunday," *Morristown Gazette Mail*, March 23, 1962, 8.

CHAPTER 3

Epigraph. W. E. B. Du Bois, *Economic Co-operation among Negro-Americans* (Atlanta, GA: Atlanta University Press, 1907), 92.

1. "Annual Pythian Celebration," *Nashville Globe*, April 2, 1909, 1.
2. Department of Commerce, *Thirteenth Census*, 616.
3. Howard Odum, "Social and Mental Traits of the Negro: Research into the Conditions of the Negro Race in Southern Towns," (PhD diss., Columbia University, 1910), 134.
4. Hortense Powdermaker, *After Freedom: A Cultural Study in the Deep South* (New York: Viking Press, 1939; Madison: University of Wisconsin Press, 1993), 122. Citations refer to 1993 edition.
5. Paul Lawrence Dunbar, "Hidden in Plain Sight: African American Secret Societies and Black Freemasonry," *Journal of African American Studies* 16, no. 4 (December 2012): 623.
6. Dunbar, "Hidden in Plain Sight," 623.
7. Dunbar, "Hidden in Plain Sight," 629.
8. Foner, *Reconstruction*, 95.
9. Elsa Barkley Brown, "Negotiating and Transforming the Public Sphere: African American Political Life in the Transition from Slavery to Freedom," *Public Culture* 7, no. 1 (Winter 1994): 117.
10. "Meeting of the Colored Relief Association—Twelve Dollars and Forty-Five Cents Collected for the Benefit of Yellow Fever Sufferers," *Bolivar Bulletin*, September 26, 1878, 1.
11. "City Notices," *Nashville Union and American*, April 14, 1874, 4.
12. "Shelbyville Notes," *Nashville Globe*, May 24, 1907, 9.
13. "Great Gathering of Pythians," *Nashville Globe*, July 12, 1907, 1.

14. "A.M.E. Zion Conference," *Memphis Daily Appeal*, March 24, 1870, 4.
15. "Laying a Cornerstone," *Knoxville Whig and Chronicle*, September 1, 1875, 8.
16. "The G.U.O.O.F.," *Daily American*, May 3, 1876, 3.
17. Skocpol, Liazos, and Ganz, *What a Mighty Power*, 47.
18. Foner, *Reconstruction*, 396.
19. Jones, *Labor of Love, Labor of Sorrow*, 74.
20. "Prof. W. S. Thompson A Benedict," *Nashville Globe*, November 26, 1909, 4.
21. Advertisement for G. W. Franklin Jr., found in the *Nashville Globe*, June 24, 1910, 10.
22. "Dr. Robert Fulton Boyd Crosses the Bar," *Nashville Globe,* July 26, 1912, 1.
23. "Milan," *Nashville Globe*, February 15, 1918, 3.
24. Wilson, *The Knoxville Negro*, 10.
25. Wilson, *The Knoxville Negro*, 11.
26. Wilson, *The Knoxville Negro*, 12.
27. Hamilton, *The Bright Side of Memphis*, 208, 210.
28. Wilson, *The Knoxville Negro*, 12.
29. "A New Undertaking Company," *Nashville Globe*, July 10, 1908, 7.
30. *Knoxville Directory* (1882), 36–37.
31. *Directory of Jackson, Tennessee* (1891), 16.
32. *Memphis City Directory 1898* (Memphis, TN: R. L. Polk, 1898), 82, 83.
33. Gail Williams O'Brien, *The Color of Law: Race, Violence, and Justice in the Post–World War II South* (Chapel Hill: University of North Carolina Press, 1999), 64. *Century Review 1805–1905 Maury County, Tennessee,* published in 1905, lists the Morning Star Lodge 11 of the Masons and the Tennessee Lodge 1701 of the GUOOF as both meeting at Gholston Hall. D. P. Robbins, *Century Review 1805–1905 Maury County, Tennessee* (Columbia, TN: Maury County Historical Society, 1905),181. https://books.google.com/books?id=9dQBAAAAMAAJ.
34. "Dedication of a Cemetery," *Nashville Union and American*, June 11, 1872, 4.
35. Lovett, *The African-American History of Nashville*, 176.
36. Deposition of Joseph McClain, Davidson County Chancery Court Case No. 7962, Metro Archives, Nashville, Tennessee.
37. Original Bill, *Ladies Benevolent Society No. 2 of Edgefield v. Benevolent Society No. 2 of Edgefield*, Tennessee Supreme Court, 1876, box 39(a), Tennessee State Library and Archives, Nashville, Tennessee.
38. Deposition of J. B. Williams, Davidson County Chancery Court Case No. 7962, Metro Archives, Nashville, TN.

39. Deposition of Green Bass, Davidson County Chancery Court Case No. 7962, Metro Archives, Nashville, TN.

40. Deposition of Joseph McClain, Davidson County Chancery Court Case No. 7962, Metro Archives, Nashville, TN.

41. Deposition of George McFerrin, Davidson County Chancery Court Case No. 7962, Metro Archives, Nashville, TN.

42. Laura F. Edwards, *Scarlett Doesn't Live Here Anymore: Southern Women in the Civil War Era* (Urbana: University of Illinois Press, 2000), 142.

43. Brown, "To Catch the Vision of Freedom," 72.

44. Final Decree, November 9. 1875, *Ladies Benevolent Society No. 2 of Edgefield v. Benevolent Society No. 2 of Edgefield*, Tennessee Supreme Court, Middle Tennessee Division, 1876, Box 39(1), Tennessee State Library and Archives.

45. Carrie Ferguson, "Bordeaux Graveyard Yields Civil War-Era History Lesson," *Nashville Tennessean*, April 5, 1997, 3B.

46. "Purchase of a Colored Cemetery," *Republican Banner*, March 27, 1869, 4.

47. "The Mt. Ararat Decoration," *Daily American*, May 19, 1884, 4.

48. Final Decree, *Benevolent Society No. 1 of Nashville v. The Sons of Relief of Nashville No. 1 et al.*, Davidson County Chancery Court, book 56, p. 470. Metro Archives, Nashville, TN.

49. "Burning of Mortgages," *Nashville Tennessean and the Nashville American*, May 2, 1911, 7.

50. Dunbar, "Hidden in Plain Sight," 630.

51. Beito, *From Mutual Aid to Welfare State*, 204–5.

52. Beito, *From Mutual Aid to Welfare State*, 140, 206–7.

53. Palmer, "Negro Secret Societies," 211.

54. Gunnar Myrdal, *An American Dilemma: The Negro Problem and American Democracy* (New York: Harper and Brothers, 1944), 955.

55. J. S. Butler, *Entrepreneurship and Self-Help among African Americans* (Albany : State University of New York Press, 1991), 105

56. Skocpol, Liazos, and Ganz, *What a Mighty Power*, 259.

57. Beito, *From Mutual Aid to Welfare State*, 215–17.

CHAPTER 4

1. *Nashville and Edgefield City Directory for 1878* (Nashville, TN: Tavel, Eastman and Howell, 1878), 98.

2. *The Nashville and Edgefield City Directory for 1878*, 42, 65.

3. "A Chinaman Passes Away," *Daily American*, August 27, 1878, 1.

4. Cartwright, *The Triumph of Jim Crow*, 173.

5. "Charter," in *Constitution and General By-Laws of the Colored People's Benevolent Society of Tennessee* (Nashville, TN: Chas. LeRoi, 1890), 3.

6. *Incorporation, Constitution, By-Laws and Resolutions of the Nashville Order Sons of Relief, No. 1* (Nashville: A.M.E. Sunday School Union, 1889), 3. *Sons of Relief et al. v. George W. Travis et al.*, RG 170: Supreme Court Case Files, Middle Division, box MT 912, Tennessee State Library and Archives, Nashville, TN. Hereinafter referred to as "*Sons of Relief et al. v. George W. Travis et al.* files."

7. Articles of Incorporation, Independent Order of Pole Bearers No. 9, p. 178.

8. Articles of Incorporation, Silver Moon Lodge No. 1803, Grand United Order of Odd Fellows, RG 42, Secretary of State Charters of Incorporation, series IV, vol. O, p. 297. Tennessee State Library and Archives, Nashville, TN.

9. Articles of Incorporation, Young Men's Aid Society, RG 42, Secretary of State Charters of Incorporation, series IV, vol. A, p. 602. Tennessee State Library and Archives, Nashville, TN.

10. Vlach, *The Afro-American Tradition*, 139.

11. Roberta Hughes Wright and Wilbur B. Hughes, *Lay Down Body: Living History in African American Cemeteries* (Detroit, MI: Visible Ink Press, 1996), 268.

12. Betty M. Kuyk, "The African Derivation of Black Fraternal Orders in the United States," *Comparative Studies in Society and History* 25, no. 4 (October 1983): 577.

13. Kuyk, "The African Derivation," 577.

14. Eugene D. Genovese, *Roll, Jordan, Roll: The World the Slaves Made* (New York: Vintage Books, 1976), 240.

15. "Burial Ritual," 25–26, *Sons of Relief et al. v. George W. Travis et al.* files.

16. Kuyk, "The African Derivation," 578.

17. "Burial Ritual," 27–28, *Sons of Relief et al. v. George W. Travis et al.* files.

18. Lockett, McHollin, and Wilson County Black History Committee, *In Their Own Voices*, 205–6.

19. *Burial Service of the Independent Order of Good Samaritans and Daughters of Samaria in America* (Washington, DC: W. Koch, 1873), 3–12. https://archive.org/details/burialserviceofi00inde.

20. All Biblical quotations are from the New International Version (NIV).

21. *Burial Service of the Independent Order of Good Samaritans*, 5.

22. *Burial Service of the Independent Order of Good Samaritans*, 7.

23. *Burial Service of the Independent Order of Good Samaritans*, 12.

24. *Ritual of Subordinate Lodge of the Independent Order of Good Samaritans and Daughters of Samaria in America* (Washington, DC: W. Koch, 1872), 11. https://archive.org/details/ritualofsubordi00inde.

25. Willis N. Brent, Morgan T. White, and W. H. Leonard, *Ritual and Degree Book of the United Brothers of Friendship, Containing Forms and Ceremonies of the First, Second, Third, and Fourth Degrees* (Louisville, KY: United Brothers of Friendship, 1888, rev. 1894), 9. https://archive.org/details/649717102.4767.emory.edu.

26. Brent, White, and Leonard, 9.

27. Brent, White, and Leonard, 10.

28. "Found," *Republican Banner*, January 10, 1873, 2.

29. "Body Snatchers Snatched," *Daily American*, November 25, 1879, 4.

30. "Body of Negro Girl Found," *Nashville American*, August 14, 1899, 5.

31. "'Body Snatchers' Robbed Colored Cemetery Graves," *Knoxville Sentinel*, November 30, 1909, 1.

32. Wright, *Lay Down Body*, 279.

33. Christina Brooks, "Enclosing Their Immortal Souls: A Survey of Two African American Cemeteries in Georgetown, South Carolina," *Southeastern Archaeology* 30, no. 1 (Summer 2011): 177.

CHAPTER 5

1. "Local Paragraphs," *Memphis Daily Appeal*, October 27, 1877, 4.

2. Robinson, "Plans Dat Comed from God," 106.

3. Robinson, "Plans Dat Comed from God," 87.

4. Brian D. Page, "'In the Hands of the Lord': Migrants and Community Politics in the Late Nineteenth Century," in *An Unseen Light: Black Struggles for Freedom in Memphis, Tennessee*, ed. Aram Goudsouzian and Charles W. McKinney Jr. (Lexington: University Press of Kentucky, 2018), 20.

5. Robinson, "Plans Dat Comed from God," 88.

6. "Ledger Lines," *Public Ledger*, October 27, 1877, 3.

7. "Gone to His Rest," *Memphis Daily Appeal*, October 30, 1877, 4.

8. "Gone to His Rest," 4.

9. "Excursion to Nashville, Sept. 21st, under the Direction of the United Sons of Ham, to Attend the Fair and Exposition," *Memphis Daily Appeal*, September 13, 1874, 4.

10. "The Canfield Asylum," *Memphis Daily Appeal*, January 13, 1875, 1.

11. "A Walk Over," *Memphis Daily Appeal*, August 4, 1876, 4.

12. Earnestine Lovelle Jenkins, *Race, Representation & Photography in 19th-Century Memphis: From Slavery to Jim Crow* (New York: Taylor and Francis, 2016), 124–25.

13. "Rev. Morris Henderson Monument," *Memphis Daily Appeal*, May 28, 1881, 1.
14. Jenkins, *Race, Representation & Photography*, 124–25.
15. Heard and Camphor, "Zion Cemetery," sect. 7, p. 2.
16. "Zion Cemetery History," Zion Community Project, accessed December 31, 2019, http://www.zioncommunityproject.org/history.php.
17. Heard and Camphor, "Zion Cemetery," sect. 7, p. 1.
18. "About Us," Zion Community Project, accessed December 31, 2019, http://www.zioncommunityproject.org/about.php.
19. David W. Blight, *Race and Reunion: The Civil War in American Memory* (Boston, MA: Harvard University Press, 2001), 65; see the chapter "Decoration Days" for a fuller discussion of the observance of Decoration Day in relation to the Civil War.
20. Gary S. Foster and William E. Lovekamp, *Cemeteries and the Life of a Smoky Mountain Community: Cades Cove under Foot* (Cham, Switzerland: Palgrave Macmillan, 2019), 30–31; Terry G. Jordan, "'The Roses So Red and Lilies So Fair': Southern Folk Cemeteries in Texas," *Southwestern Historical Quarterly* 83, no. 3 (January 1980): 254; and Terry G. Jordan, "Forest Folk, Prairie Folk: Rural Religious Cultures in North Texas," *Southwestern Historical Quarterly* 80, no. 2 (October 1976): 155.
21. "Nixon," *Savannah Courier*, May 27, 1898, 2.
22. "Decoration Day at Lewisburg," *Nashville American*, May 10, 1898, 6.
23. "Cedar Grove," *Camden Chronicle*, May 20, 1910, 5.
24. "Decoration Day at Head Springs," *Nashville American*, May 10, 1898, 6.
25. "Briersville Notes," *Nashville Globe*, August 2, 1912, 8.
26. "Shelbyville Notes," *Nashville Globe*, May 6, 1910, 6. The article refers to the decoration day celebration as the "sixteenth anniversary decoration of the graves."
27. "Shelbyville Notes," *Nashville Globe*, May 26, 1911, 6.
28. "Decoration Day," *Nashville Globe*, May 29, 1908, 5.
29. Deed from Alfred Miller and wife to Alexander Simmons, William Jordan and other Trustees of Benevolent Lodge No. 11, January 7, 1897, Rutherford County Deed Book 38, pp. 338–39.
30. Anne S. Butler, "Black Fraternal and Benevolent Societies in Nineteenth-Century America," in *African American Fraternities and Sororities*, ed. Tamara L. Brown, Gregory S. Parks, and Clarenda M. Phillips (Louisville: University of Kentucky Press, 2012), 80; Douglas Keister, *Stories in Stone: A Field Guide to Cemetery Symbolism and Iconography* (Salt Lake City, UT: Gibbs Smith, 2004), 197.
31. Keister, *Stories in Stone*, 111.

32. Keister, *Stories in Stone*, 60.
33. Keister, *Stories in Stone*, 113.
34. Keister, *Stories in Stone*, 116, 123.
35. "Murfreesboro Notes," *Nashville Globe*, September 24, 1909, 7.
36. Keister, *Stories in Stone*, 46–47.
37. Vlach, *The Afro-American Tradition*, 139.
38. Skocpol, Liazos, and Ganz, *What a Mighty Power*, 41.
39. Keister, *Stories in Stone*, 108.
40. Vlach, *The Afro-American Tradition*, 139.
41. Vlach, *The Afro-American Tradition*, 145.
42. Charlotte King, "Separated by Death and Color: The African American Cemetery of New Philadelphia, Illinois," *Historical Archaeology* 44, no. 1 (2010): 128.
43. D. Gregory Jeane, "The Upland South Folk Cemetery Complex: Some Suggestions of Origin," in *Cemeteries and Gravemarkers: Voices of American Culture*, ed. Richard E. Meyer (Ann Arbor, MI: UMI Research Press, 1989), 113, 116, 122.
44. Jordan, "'The Roses So Red,'" 232.
45. Vlach, *The Afro-American Tradition*, 139.
46. Carroll Van West, "Sacred Spaces of Faith, Community, and Resistance: Rural African American Churches in Jim Crow Tennessee," in *"We Shall Independent Be": African American Place Making and the Struggle to Claim Space in the United States*, eds. Angel David Nieves and Leslie M. Alexander. (Boulder: University Press of Colorado, 2008), 447.
47. Lynn Rainville, *Hidden History: African American Cemeteries in Central Virginia* (Charlottesville: University of Virginia Press, 2014), 24.
48. Jeane, "The Upland South Folk Cemetery Complex," 116.
49. Baugher and Veit, *The Archaeology of American Cemeteries*, 169; see also Emmeline E. E. Morris, "Gospel Pilgrim's Progress: Rehabilitating an African American Cemetery for the Public," (master's thesis, University of Georgia, 2007), 25–26.
50. Angelica Krüger-Kahloula, "Tributes in Stone and Lapidary Lapses: Commemorating Black People in Eighteenth- and Nineteenth-Century America," *Markers* 6 (1989): 34.
51. "Mount Ararat Cemetery, Find a Grave, www.findagrave.com/cemetery/15897/mount-ararat-cemetery.
52. "Thomas Frank Cassels," *"This Honorable Body": African American Legislators in 19th Century Tennessee*, Tennessee State Library and Archives, accessed July 5, 2020, https://sharetngov.tnsosfiles.com/tsla/exhibits/blackhistory/cassels.htm.

53. "Zion Christian Cemetery Receives Historic Marker for Lynched Victims of 1892," Christian Methodist Episcopal Church, accessed July 5, 2020, https://thecmechurch.org/wp-content/uploads/2019/05/Article-2019-03-Zions-Receives-Additional-Historic-Marker.pdf.
54. Andrew Hurley, *Beyond Preservation: Using Public History to Revitalize Inner Cities* (Philadelphia, PA: Temple University Press, 2010), 33.
55. See Derek Alderman, "'History by the Spoonful' in North Carolina: The Textual Politics of State Highway Historical Markers," *Southeastern Geographer* 52, no. 4 (Winter 2012): 358–59, for a fuller discussion of the ways commemorative markers retell the past.

CHAPTER 6

Epigraph. Ray Stannard Baker, *Following the Colour Line* (New York: Doubleday, Page, 1908), 38.

1. Sanborn Fire Insurance Map from Murfreesboro, Rutherford County, Tennessee. Sanborn Map Company, Aug, 1897. Sheet 1. https://www.loc.gov/item/sanborn08355_003.
2. Carroll Van West, "Port Royal State Historic Area," *Tennessee Encyclopedia*, last updated March 1, 2018, https://tennesseeencyclopedia.net/entries/port-royal-state-historic-area.
3. "Port Royal," *Tennessee State Gazetteer and Business Directory* (Nashville: R. L. Polk, 1876), 341.
4. D. G. Beers & Co., "Map of Montgomery County, Tennessee," (Philadelphia: D. G. Beers, 1877), Library of Congress Geography and Map Division, LCCN 2012586254, https://lccn.loc.gov/2012586254.
5. "The Origination of Benevolent Lodge Order #210," Benevolent Lodge Order #210, accessed June 30, 2019, http://benevolentlodge210.org.
6. *Montgomery County, Tennessee Family History Book 2000*, 47.
7. "Una Notes," *Nashville Globe*, March 19, 1909, 6. The Benevolent Society is referred to in a number of different ways in different sources and different periods. Names include Colored Benevolent Society, Benevolent Society, Benevolent Order, and B.O. Also, Hamilton Church Road is located in the community formerly known as Hamilton Hill.
8. Shay Arthur, "Building with Historical Connections Destroyed in Christmas Morning Fire," WREG NewsChannel 3, December 25, 2018, https://wreg.com/2018/12/25/building-with-historical-connections-destroyed-in-christmas-morning-fire.
9. Shay Arthur, "Property with Connections to Black History in Memphis Is Reborn after Fire," WREG NewsChannel 3, May 22, 2019, https://

wreg.com/2019/05/22/property-with-connections-to-black-history-in-memphis-is-reborn-after-fire.

10. "Suit for $20,000 Damages Filed," *Nashville Tennessean*, April 24, 1908, 3.

11. "Madison Notes," *Nashville Globe*, July 1, 1910, 8.

12. Information from the property listing for the Sons of Ham, Davidson County Property Assessor, accessed July 11, 2020, https://www.padctn.org/prc/property/10734/card/1. The map shows the lodge property as being located west of the cemetery, in what appears to be an overgrown area when the property is visited in person.

13. "Our Story," First Missionary Baptist Church website, accessed April 7, 2020, https://www.fmbgood.com/about.

14. Carroll Van West, "Williamson Chapel CME Church Complex," NPS Form10-900, reference # 06001039. National Register of Historic Places, Digital Archive on NPGallery. National Park Service, Washington, DC. https://npgallery.nps.gov/NRHP, Sections 7 and 8.

15. Osborne, and Hargraves, *Contributions of Blacks to Hamblen County*, 223–24.

16. Robert R. Weyeneth, "The Architecture of Racial Segregation: The Challenges of Preserving the Problematic Past," *Public Historian* 27, no. 4 (Fall 2005): 14, 22.

17. Charles S. Johnson, *Patterns of Negro Segregation* (London: Victor Gollancz, 1944), 77.

18. Brad R. Miller, "Built for the Living: African American Funeral Homes on the Tennessee Landscape" (master's thesis, Middle Tennessee State University, 2012), 32–33.

19. Milton R. Konvitz, "The Extent and Character of Legally-Enforced Segregation," *Journal of Negro Education* 20, no. 3 (Summer 1951): 432; see also Howard N. Rabinowitz, "From Exclusion to Segregation: Southern Race Relations, 1865–1890," *Journal of American History* 63, no. 2 (September 1976): 334, where he notes that Raleigh, North Carolina, also had ordinances related to the burial of African Americans.

20. King, "Separated by Death and Color," 127. King claims that African Americans were only able to purchase marginal land, but it is unclear if this pattern holds true in Tennessee or other places.

21. Du Bois, *Economic Co-operation*, 131–34.

22. W. E. B. Du Bois, *The Souls of Black Folk* (1903; repr., New York: Barnes & Noble Classics, 2003), 119.

23. Lillian Smith, *Killers of the Dream* (1948; repr., New York: W.W. Norton, 1994), 95.

24. "Willow Mount Cemetery," City of Shelbyville, Tennessee, accessed July 2, 2019, https://www.shelbyvilletn.org/departments/willow_mount_cemetery.php.

25. "Cole Cemetery," transcription from the Davidson County Cemetery Survey Project, USGenWeb Archives, accessed July 11, 2020, http://files.usgwarchives.net/tn/davidson/cemeteries/cole.txt.

26. William Rule, ed., *Standard History of Knoxville, Tennessee* (Chicago: Lewis Publishing Company, 1900), 588.

27. "Bethel Confederate Cemetery," Mabry-Hazen House, accessed August 20 2020, http://www.mabryhazen.com/bethel-cemetery.

28. Biles, "'Cotton Fields or Skyscrapers?,'" 224.

29. Ash, *Middle Tennessee Society Transformed*, 210.

30. Rachel Martin and Elizabeth H. Moore, "Promise Land," *Tennessee Encyclopedia*, last updated March 1, 2018, https://tennesseeencyclopedia.net/entries/promise-land.

31. Wali R. Kharif, "Free Hill," last updated March 1, 2018, *Tennessee Encyclopedia*, https://tennesseeencyclopedia.net/entries/free-hill.

32. W. Jerome D. Spence and David L. Spence, *A History of Hickman County* (Nashville: Gospel Advocate Printing Publishing Company, 1900), 332.

33. Robert J. Booker, *An Encyclopedia: Experiences of Black People in Knoxville, Tennessee, 1844–1974* (Knoxville, TN: Russell Printing Options, 2017), 57.

34. *City Directory of Knoxville and Suburbs, 1905* (Knoxville, TN: G. M. Connelly, 1905), 41.

35. Sanborn Fire Insurance Map from Knoxville, Knox County, Tennessee. Sanborn Map Company, 1903. Sheet 25. https://www.loc.gov/item/sanborn08331_0036.

36. *City Directory of Knoxville and Suburbs* (1905), 11–26, 970–71.

37. "Suit for $20,000 Damages Filed," *Nashville Tennessean*, April 24, 1908, 3.

38. "Eight New Schoolhouses to Be Built This Year," *Nashville Globe*, July 9, 1909, 1.

39. "School Named for Dr. Johnson," *Nashville Tennessean*, May 9, 1958, 29.

40. Robin Flowerdew, "Spatial Patterns of Residential Segregation in a Southern City," *Journal of American Studies* 13, no. 1 (April 1979): 96.

41. Flowerdew, "Spatial Patterns," 96.

42. John Kellogg, "Negro Urban Clusters in the Postbellum South," *Geographical Review* 67, no. 3 (July 1977): 313.

CHAPTER 7

Epigraph. Casey Cep, *Furious Hours: Murder, Fraud, and the Last Trial of Harper Lee* (New York: Alfred Knopf, 2019), 242.

1. "Disappearance of Wire Fence: Aroused Citizens of Brierville and Doc Sadler Is Arrested," *Nashville Tennessean,* April 10, 1907, 4.
2. "New Schools for Negroes," *Nashville American,* July 4, 1909, 20.
3. "Brierville Notes," *Nashville Globe,* September 9, 1910, 1.
4. See "Brierville Notes," *Nashville Globe,* February 26, 1909, 8; "Rev. Gilmore in East Tennessee," *Nashville Globe,* September 15, 1911, 7; "Brierville Notes," *Nashville Globe,* January 20, 1911, 3.
5. The change to Briarville Road occurred between 1968 and 1997. The USGS topographical map for this section of Nashville (Nashville East) from 1968 shows Briarville Road in its original configuration. The 1997 USGS topographical map for the same section shows the road as it appears today. Topographical maps accessed at topoView, https://ngmdb.usgs.gov/topoview, an online service of the United State Geological Survey that has free topographical maps available for download.
6. "Negro Hanged in Outskirts of Murfreesboro," *Nashville American,* August 29, 1908, 1, and "Body of Lynched Negro Interred," *Nashville Tennessean,* August 30, 1908, 8.
7. Baugher and Veit, *The Archaeology of American Cemeteries,* 24.
8. Brooks, "Enclosing Their Immortal Souls," 180.
9. Morris, "Gospel Pilgrim's Progress," 19.
10. Harold Hamilton Williams, "A Study of Landscaping in Negro Communities of the Southern States," (master's thesis, Cornell University, 1944), 94, 95.
11. Vlach, *The Afro-American Tradition,* 139.
12. Chicora Foundation, *Grave Matters: The Preservation of African-American Cemeteries* (Columbia, SC: Chicora Foundation, 1996), 5.
13. Chicora Foundation, *Grave Matters,* 10.
14. Melvin Hughes, *A History of Rutherford County's African American Community* (Murfreesboro, TN: Allen Chapel A.M.E. Church, 1996), 157–63.
15. "Benevolent Cemetery," transcription prepared by John Lodl, Rutherford County Archives, Murfreesboro, Tennessee. Undated. https://rutherfordcountytn.gov/archives.
16. "Benevolent Society Church Cemetery," Davidson County Cemetery Survey Project, accessed August 22, 2020, https://web.archive.org/web/20201001003254/www.davidsoncocemeterysurvey.com/home/cemeteries-a-c/benevolent-society-church-cemetery.
17. Rainville, "Protecting Our Shared Heritage," 200.
18. Edward Rothstein, "A Burial Ground and Its Dead Are Given Life," *New York Times,* February 25, 2010, https://www.nytimes.com/2010/02/26/arts/design/26burial.html.

19. Nora McGreevy, "Lost African American Cemetery Found under Florida Parking Lot," *Smithsonian Magazine*, June 17, 2020, https://www.smithsonianmag.com/smart-news/lost-african-american-cemetery-re-discovered-under-florida-parking-lot-180975109.
20. Zoe Nicholson, "Clemson Finds 600 Unmarked Graves on Campus. But Who Were They? Researchers Race to Find Out," *Greenville News*, October 29, 2020, https://www.greenvilleonline.com/story/news/local/south-carolina/2020/10/29/clemson-university-finds-600-unmarked-graves-campus-sc-who-were-they/6009393002.
21. John North and Stephanie Haines, "Hidden in Plain Sight: Historic Cemetery with Thousands of Graves Falls Victim to Decay, Neglect," WBIR 10 News, July 22, 2018, https://www.wbir.com/article/news/local/hidden-in-plain-sight-historic-cemetery-with-thousands-of-graves-falls-victim-to-decay-neglect/51-576460019.

CONCLUSION

Epigraph. Quote from Rebecca D. Williams, "Volunteers, Students Working to Interpret, Renovate East Knoxville Cemeteries," *Knoxville News-Sentinel*, May 11, 2012, http://archive.knoxnews.com/news/local/volunteers-students-working-to-interpret-renovate-east-koxville-cemeteries-ep-360847142-357020151.html.

1. Robert J. Booker, "8th of August Celebrations Marked Johnson Freeing His Slaves," *Knox News-Sentinel*, October 15, 2018, https://www.knoxnews.com/story/opinion/columnists/robert-booker/2018/10/15/8th-august-events-marked-johnson-freeing-slaves-robert-j-booker/1615069002.
2. "Greenwood Park," advertisement, *Nashville Globe*, July 17, 1908, 3.
3. Knoxville History Project, "Emancipation Week: The Backstory of the Eighth of August," *Knoxville Mercury*, August 12, 2016, https://www.knoxmercury.com/2016/08/12/emancipation-week-backstory-eighth-august.
4. McGinnis, *In Everlasting Remembrance*, 75.
5. Katherine Ambroziak, "Odd Fellows Cemetery Reclamation Initiative" portfolio, available from "Odd Fellows Cemetery," University of Tennessee College of Architecture and Design, accessed April 13, 2020, https://archdesign.utk.edu/projects/odd-fellows-cemetery.
6. Shay Arthur, "Fire Destroys Building with Historical Connections," WREG News Channel 3, December 25, 2018, https://wreg.com/news/building-with-historical-connections-destroyed-in-christmas-morning-fire.

7. Shay Arthur, "Property with Connections to Black History."
8. "Our Mission," Benevolent Lodge Order #210, accessed April 19, 2020, http://benevolentlodge210.org.
9. GUOOF National Historian, email to author, May 14, 2020.
10. Beito, *From Mutual Aid to Welfare State*, 234.

GLOSSARY

1. Definitions and information taken from the following: "Terms Used to Describe Cemeteries and Grave Markers," State of Indiana, Dept. of Natural Resources, accessed October 1, 2020, https://www.in.gov/dnr/historic/files/cem_glossary.pdf; Jeanne Hicks, "Types and Explanations of Headstones," Rootsweb, © 2010, accessed October 1, 2020, http://sites.rootsweb.com/~wicemetp/types.htm; "Quick Field Guide to Monument Types," Chicora Foundation, accessed October 1, 2020, https://www.chicora.org/pdfs/Types%20of%20markers.pdf.

BIBLIOGRAPHY

PRIMARY SOURCES

ARCHIVAL SOURCES

Freedmen's Savings & Trust Register. Signatures of Depositors. Nashville
and Memphis, Tennessee, Norfolk, Richmond, Virginia, 1871–1874.
Microfilm Collection, Tennessee State Library and Archives. Nashville,
Tennessee.

*Ladies Benevolent Society No. 2 of Edgefield v. Benevolent Society No. 2 of
Edgefield.* Chancery Court Case No. 7962. Metro Archives, Nashville,
Tennessee.

*Ladies Benevolent Society No. 2 of Edgefield v. Benevolent Society No. 2 of
Edgefield.* Tennessee Supreme Court, 1876, Box 39(a). Tennessee State
Library and Archives, Nashville, Tennessee.

Sons of Relief et al. v. George W. Travis et al. Tennessee Supreme Court,
Middle Division, Box 912. Tennessee State Library and Archives,
Nashville, Tennessee.

Tennessee Secretary of State Charters of Incorporation. Record Group 42.
Tennessee State Library and Archives, Nashville, Tennessee.

Working Peoples Association v. Sons & Daughters of Cyrene. Chancery Court
File. Rutherford County Archives, Murfreesboro, Tennessee.

BOOKS

*Acts of the State of Tennessee, Passed by the First Session of the Thirty-Sixth
General Assembly for the Years 1869–1870.* Nashville, TN: Jones, Purvis, 1870.

Boyd, Dr. R. F. "What Are the Causes of the Great Mortality among the Negroes in the Cities of the South, and How Is That Mortality to be Lessened?" In *Twentieth Century Negro Literature*, edited by D. W. Culp, 214–20. Napierville, IL: J. L. Nichols, 1902.

Brent, Willis N., Morgan T. White, and W. H. Leonard. *Ritual and Degree Book of the United Brothers of Friendship, Containing Forms and Ceremonies of the First, Second, Third, and Fourth Degrees.* Louisville, KY: United Brothers of Friendship, 1888, rev. 1894. https://archive.org/details/649717102.4767.emory.edu

Burial Service of the Independent Order of Good Samaritans and Daughters of Samaria in America. Washington, DC: W. Koch, 1872. https://archive.org/details/burialserviceofi00inde.

Daves, J. H. *A Social Study of the Colored Population of Knoxville, Tennessee.* Knoxville, TN: Free Colored Library, 1926. Calvin M. McClung Digital Collection. https://cmdc.knoxlib.org/digital/collection/p15136coll4/id/1338/rec/1.

Goddard, Frederick B. *Where to Emigrate and Why.* New York: Frederick B. Goddard, Publisher, 1869. https://books.google.com/books?id=650CAAAAMAAJ.

Griggs, Sutton E. *The One Great Question: A Study of Southern Conditions at Close Range.* Nashville, TN: Orion Publishing, 1907. https://archive.org/details/onegreatquestion00grigrich.

Killebrew, J. B. *Introduction to the Resources of Tennessee*, vol. 2. Nashville, TN: Tavel, Eastman and Howell, 1874. https://books.google.com/books?id=5AYoAAAAYAAJ.

Killebrew, J. B. *Tennessee: Its Agricultural and Mineral Wealth.* Nashville, TN: Tavel, Eastman and Howell, 1876. https://books.google.com/books?id=AD0VAAAAYAAJ.

Killebrew, J. B. *West Tennessee: Its Resources and Advantages.* Nashville, TN: Tavel, Eastman and Howell, 1879. https://books.google.com/books?id=VNREAAAAYAAJ.

Proceedings of the Fifty-Eighth Delegated Assembly of the Benevolent Orders of the State of Tennessee. Nashville, TN: J. Ralston Kenan, 1926.

Ritual of Subordinate Lodge of the Independent Order of Good Samaritans and Daughters of Samaria in America. Washington, DC: Supreme Grand Lodge of the I.O.G.S. and D.S. in America, 1872. archive.org/details/ritualofsubordi00inde.

Simmons, William J. *Men of Mark: Eminent, Progressive and Rising.* Cleveland, OH: Geo. M. Rewell, 1887. https://archive.org/details/menmarkeminentp00turngoog.

Tennessee State Gazetteer and Business Directory. Nashville, TN: R. L. Polk & Co., 1876. https://books.google.com/books?id=YusxAQAAMAAJ.

Wilson, Bartow G. *The Knoxville Negro*. Knoxville, TN: Trent Printing, 1929. Calvin M. McClung Digital Collection. https://cmdc.knoxlib.org/digital/collection/p15136coll4/id/2784/rec/1.

CENSUS RECORDS

The following records were accessed through a paid subscription from Ancestry.com; many are also available at the Tennessee State Library and Archives, Nashville, TN, https://sos.tn.gov/products/tsla/tennessee-census-records.

1880 US Census, Knox, County, Tennessee.
1880 US Census, Wilson County, Tennessee.
1900 US Census, Rutherford County, Tennessee.
1900 US Census, Shelby County, Tennessee.
1910 US Census, Rutherford County, Tennessee.
1910 US Census, Shelby County, Tennessee.

CITY DIRECTORIES

1911 Memphis City Directory. Memphis, TN: R. L. Polk, 1911.
Boyle & Chapman's Memphis City Directory. Memphis, TN: Boyle and Chapman, 1872.
Boyle & Chapman's Memphis City Directory. Memphis, TN: Boyle and Chapman, 1874.
City Directory of Chattanooga and Suburbs. Chattanooga, TN: G. M. Connelly, 1902.
City Directory of Knoxville and Suburbs. Knoxville, TN: G. M. Connelly, 1905.
Directory of Jackson, Tennessee. Jackson, TN: Jackson City Directory Co., 1891.
Edwards' Memphis Directory. Memphis, TN: Southern Publishing, 1868.
Helms' Knoxville City Directory. Knoxville, TN: T. Haws, 1869.
Knoxville City Directory 1935. Knoxville, TN: City Directory Co. of Knoxville, 1935.
Knoxville Directory 1882. Nashville, TN: Standard Directory Co., 1882.
Marshall-Bruce-Polk Co's Nashville City Directory. Nashville, TN: Marshall-Bruce-Polk, 1924.
Memphis City Directory 1898. Memphis, TN: R. L. Polk, 1891. https://register.shelby.tn.us/index.php?go=cityDirectories&title=Memphis%20City%20Directories%201849-1943.
Nashville City and Business Directory for 1860–1861. Nashville, TN: L. P. Williams, 1860.

Nashville and Edgefield City Directory for 1878. Nashville, TN: Tavel, Eastman and Howell, 1878.

Nashville City Directory 1890. Nashville, TN: Martin and Bruce, 1890.

Parham's First Annual Directory to the City of Chattanooga. Chattanooga, TN: Lou. L. Parham, 1871.

Sholes' Memphis Directory for 1881. Memphis, TN: Sholes, 1881. https:// register.shelby.tn.us/index.php?go=cityDirectories&title=Memphis%20 City%20Directories%201849-1943.

DEEDS

Davidson County, Tennessee Deed Books. Microfilm Collection. Tennessee State Library and Archives, Nashville, Tennessee.

Giles County, Tennessee Deed Books. Microfilm Collection. Tennessee State Library and Archives, Nashville, Tennessee.

Knox County, Tennessee Deed Books. Microfilm Collection. Tennessee State Library and Archives, Nashville, Tennessee.

Robertson County, Tennessee Deed Books. Microfilm Collection. Tennessee State Library and Archives, Nashville, Tennessee.

Rutherford County, Tennessee Deed Books. Rutherford County Register of Deeds, Murfreesboro, Tennessee.

Wilson County, Tennessee Deed Books. Microfilm Collection. Tennessee State Library and Archives, Nashville, Tennessee.

LODGE SOURCES

Constitution and By-laws of the Edgefield Benevolent Society. Nashville, TN: Union and American Book and Job Print, 1870. Metro Archives, Nashville, TN.

Constitution and General By-Laws of the Colored People's Benevolent Society of Tennessee. Nashville, TN: Chas. LeRoi, 1890

Constitution of the Working People's Labor and Art Association. Nashville, TN: Walden University Press, 1901.

Incorporation, Constitution, By-Laws and Resolutions of the Nashville Order Sons of Relief, No. 1. Nashville: A.M.E. Sunday School Union, 1889.

MAPS

D. G. Beers and Co. "Map of Montgomery County, Tennessee." Philadelphia: D.G. Beers and Co., 1877. Library of Congress Geography and Map Division, LCCN 2012586254, https://lccn.loc.gov/2012586254.

Sanborn Fire Insurance Map from Knoxville, Knox County, Tennessee. Sanborn Map Company, 1903. Sheet 25. https://www.loc.gov/item/sanborn08331_003.

Sanborn Fire Insurance Map from Memphis, Shelby County, Tennessee. Sanborn Map Company, 1888. Sheet 21B. https://www.loc.gov/item/sanborn08348_001.

Sanborn Fire Insurance Map from Murfreesboro, Rutherford County, Tennessee. Sanborn Map Company, August 1897. Sheet 1. https://www.loc.gov/item/sanborn08355_003.

Sanborn Fire Insurance Map from Springfield, Robertson County. Sanborn Map Company, April 1913. Sheet 6. Proquest Digital Sanborn Maps, 1867–1970 database.

NEWSPAPERS AND MAGAZINES

Bolivar Bulletin
Camden Chronicle
Chicago Defender
Daily American (Nashville)
Daily Arkansas Gazette
Daily News Journal (Murfreesboro)
Daily Union and American (Nashville)
Huntsville Mirror
Journal and Tribune (Knoxville)
Knoxville Daily Chronicle
Knoxville Journal
Knoxville Mercury
Knoxville News-Sentinel
Knoxville Sentinel
Knoxville Whig and Chronicle
Memphis Commercial
Memphis Daily Appeal
Memphis World
Milan Exchange
Morristown Gazette
Morristown Gazette Mail
Nashville American
Nashville Banner
Nashville Daily Union
Nashville Globe

Nashville Tennessean
Nashville Tennessean and the Nashville American
Nashville Union and American
Nashville Union & Dispatch
Public Ledger (Memphis)
Pulaski Citizen
Republican Banner (Nashville)
Savannah Courier
The Crisis

SECONDARY SOURCES

Alderman, Derek. "'History by the Spoonful' in North Carolina: The Textual Politics of State Highway Historical Markers." *Southeastern Geographer* 52, no. 4 (Winter 2012): 355–73.

Ambroziak, Katherine. "Odd Fellows Cemetery Reclamation Initiative." Available from "Odd Fellows Cemetery," University of Tennessee College of Architecture and Design. Accessed April 13, 2020. https://archdesign.utk.edu/projects/odd-fellows-cemetery.

Ash, Stephen. *Middle Tennessee Society Transformed 1860–1870: War and Peace in the Upper South*. Baton Rouge: Louisiana State University Press, 1988.

Ayers, Edward L. *The Promise of the New South: Life after Reconstruction.* 1992. Rprt., Oxford, UK: Oxford University Press, 2007.

Baker, John F., Jr. *The Washingtons of Wessyngton Plantation*. New York: Atria Books, 2009.

Baker, Ray Stannard. *Following the Colour Line*. New York: Doubleday, Page, 1908.

Baugher, Sherene, and Richard F. Veit. *The Archaeology of American Cemeteries and Grave Markers*. Gainesville: University of Florida Press, 2014.

Beito, David. *From Mutual Aid to the Welfare State: Fraternal Societies and Social Services, 1890–1967*. Chapel Hill: University of North Carolina Press, 2000.

Bergeron, Paul H., Stephen V. Ash, and Jeanette Keith. *Tennesseans and Their History*. Knoxville: University of Tennessee Press, 1999.

Biles, Roger. "'Cotton Fields or Skyscrapers?' The Case of Memphis, Tennessee." *Historian* 50, no. 2 (February 1988): 210–33.

"Biographies of 19th Century Legislators." *"This Honorable Body": African American Legislators in 19th Century Tennessee*. Tennessee State Library and Archives, 2013, accessed July 5, 2020. https://sharetngov.tnsosfiles.com/tsla/exhibits/blackhistory/cassels.htm.

Blight, David W. *Race and Reunion: The Civil War in American Memory.* Boston, MA: Harvard University Press, 2001.

Blum, Michael Aaron. "'An Island of Peace in a Sea of Racial Strife': The Civil Rights Movement in Knoxville, Tennessee." PhD diss., University of Memphis, 2014.

Booker, Robert J. *An Encyclopedia: Experiences of Black People in Knoxville, Tennessee, 1844–1974.* Knoxville, TN: Russell Printing Options, 2017.

Booker, Robert. *The History of Blacks in Knoxville, Tennessee: The First One Hundred Years, 1791–1891.* Knoxville, TN: Beck Cultural Center 1990.

Brooks, Charles H. *The Official History and Manual of the Grand United Order of Odd Fellows.* Philadelphia, PA: Odd Fellows' Journal Print, 1902.

Brooks, Christina. "Enclosing Their Immortal Souls: A Survey of Two African American Cemeteries in Georgetown, South Carolina." *Southeastern Archaeology* 30, no. 1 (Summer 2011): 176–86.

Brooks, Joanna. "Prince Hall, Freemasonry, and Genealogy." *African American Review* 34, no. 2 (Summer 2000): 197–216.

Brown, Elsa Barkley. "Negotiating and Transforming the Public Sphere: African American Political Life in the Transition from Slavery to Freedom." *Public Culture* 7, no. 1 (Winter 1994): 107–46.

Brown, Elsa Barkley. "To Catch the Vision of Freedom: Reconstructing Southern Black Women's Political History, 1865–1880." In *African American Women and the Vote, 1837–1965,* edited by Ann D. Gordon and Bettye Collier-Thomas, 66–99. Cambridge: University of Massachusetts Press, 1997.

Bucey, Carole Stanford. "Tennessee in the Twentieth Century." *Tennessee Historical Quarterly* 69, no. 3 (Fall 2010): 262–73.

Burrell, W. P., and D. E. Johnson. *Twenty-Five Years History of the Grand Fountain of the United Order of True Reformers 1881–1905.* Richmond, VA: Grand Fountain, United Order of True Reformers, 1909.

Butler, Anne S. "Black Fraternal and Benevolent Societies in Nineteenth Century America." In *African American Fraternities and Sororities,* edited by Tamara L. Brown, Gregory S. Parks, and Clarenda M. Phillips, 75–100. Louisville: University of Kentucky Press, 2012

Butler, J. S. *Entrepreneurship and Self-Help among African Americans.* Albany: State University of New York Press, 1991.

Cartwright, Joseph J. *The Triumph of Jim Crow: Tennessee Race Relations in the 1880s.* Knoxville: University of Tennessee Press, 1976.

Cason, Kevin. "Morristown College." *Tennessee Encyclopedia of History and Culture,* last updated March 1, 2018. https://tennesseeencyclopedia.net/entries/morristown-college.

Cep, Casey. *Furious Hours: Murder, Fraud, and the Last Trial of Harper Lee.* New York: Alfred Knopf, 2019.

Chicora Foundation. *Grave Matters: The Preservation of African-American Cemeteries.* Columbia, SC: Chicora Foundation, 1996.

Commissioner of Insurance. *Annual Report of the Commissioner of Insurance of the State of Alabama for the Year Ending December 31, 1920.* Montgomery, AL: Brown Printing, 1921.

Department of Commerce and Labor, Bureau of the Census. *Thirteenth Census of the United States Taken in the Year 1910: Vol. 3. Population Reports by States, with Statistics for Counties, Cities, and Other Civil Divisions: Nebraska-Wyoming, Alaska, Hawaii, and Porto Rico.* Washington, DC: Government Printing Office, 1913. https://www.census.gov/library/publications/1913/dec/vol-3-population.html.

De Tocqueville, Alexis. *Democracy in America.* Translated by Henry Reeve. New York: George Dearborn, 1838.

Downer, Alan. "Native Americans and Historic Preservation." In *A Richer Heritage: Historic Preservation in the Twenty-First Century,* edited by Robert E. Stipe, 405–21. Chapel Hill: University of North Carolina Press, 2003.

Du Bois, W. E. B. *Black Reconstruction in America 1860–1880.* New York: Free Press, 1998. First published 1935 by Harcourt, Brace (New York).

Du Bois, W. E. B. *Economic Co-operation among Negro Americans.* Atlanta, GA: Atlanta University Press, 1907.

Du Bois, W. E. B. *The Souls of Black Folk.* 1903. Reprint, New York: Barnes & Noble Classics, 2003.

Dunbar, Paul Lawrence. "Hidden in Plain Sight: African American Secret Societies and Black Freemasonry." *Journal of African American Studies* 16, no. 4 (December 2012): 622–37.

Durrett, Jean M., Diane Williams, and Yolanda G. Reid. *Robertson County Tennessee Cemetery Records.* Springfield, TN: Y. G. Reid, 1987.

Edwards, Laura F. *Scarlett Doesn't Live Here Anymore: Southern Women in the Civil War Era.* Urbana: University of Illinois Press, 2000.

El-Amin, Enkeshi Thom. "Chocolate City Way Up South in Appalachia: Black Knoxville at the Intersection of Race, Place, and Region." PhD diss., University of Tennessee, 2019.

Fahey, David M. "United Brothers of Friendship and Sisters of the Mysterious Ten." In *Organizing Black America: An Encyclopedia of African American Associations,* edited by Nina Mjagkij, 577. New York: Garland Publishing, 2001

Fickle, James E. "Industry." *Tennessee Encyclopedia of History and Culture,* last updated March 1, 2018. https://tennesseeencyclopedia.net/entries/industry.

Flowerdew, Robin. "Spatial Patterns of Residential Segregation in a Southern City." *Journal of American Studies* 13, no. 1 (April 1979): 93–107.

Foner, Eric. *Reconstruction: America's Unfinished Revolution, 1863–1877.* New York: Harper Collins, 1988; New York: Perennial Classics, 2002.

Foster, Gary S., and William E. Lovekamp. *Cemeteries and the Life of a Smoky Mountain Community: Cades Cove under Foot.* Cham, Switzerland: Palgrave Macmillan, 2019.

Genovese, Eugene D. *Roll, Jordan, Roll: The World the Slaves Made.* New York: Vintage Books, 1976.

Gibson, W. H. *History of the United Brothers of Friendship and Sisters of the Mysterious Ten.* Louisville, KY: Bradley & Gilbert, 1897.

Giggie, John M. "Mosaic Templars of America." In *Organizing Black America: An Encyclopedia of African American Associations,* edited by Nina Mjagkij, 301. New York: Garland Publishing, 2001

Goings, Kenneth W., and Gerald L. Smith. "'Unhidden' Transcripts: Memphis and African American Agency, 1862–1920." *Journal of Urban History* 21, no. 3 (March 1995): 372–94.

Hamilton, Green Polonius. *The Bright Side of Memphis.* Memphis: G. P. Hamilton, 1908.

Hankins, Caneta Skelley, and Michael Thomas Gavin. *Plowshares and Swords: Tennessee Farm Families Tell Civil War Stories.* Murfreesboro: Center for Historic Preservation at Middle Tennessee State University, 2013.

Harkins, John E. "Memphis." *Tennessee Encyclopedia of History and Culture,* last updated March 1, 2018. https://tennesseeencyclopedia.net/entries/memphis.

Heard, Milbrey, and Zhukov Camphor. "Zion Cemetery." NPS form 10-900, reference # 90000301. National Register of Historic Places, Digital Archive on NPGallery. National Park Service, Washington, DC. https://npgallery.nps.gov/NRHP.

Hughes, Melvin. *A History of Rutherford County's African American Community.* Murfreesboro, TN: Allen Chapel A.M.E. Church, 1996.

Hurley, Andrew. *Beyond Preservation: Using Public History to Revitalize Inner Cities.* Philadelphia, PA: Temple University Press, 2010.

Jeane, D. Gregory. "The Upland South Folk Cemetery Complex: Some Suggestions of Origin." In *Cemeteries and Gravemarkers: Voices of American Culture,* edited by Richard E. Meyer, 107–36. Ann Arbor, MI: UMI Research Press, 1989.

Jenkins, Earnestine Lovelle. *Race, Representation & Photography in 19th-Century Memphis: From Slavery to Jim Crow.* New York: Taylor and Francis, 2016.

Johnson, Charles S. *Patterns of Negro Segregation.* London: Victor Gollancz, 1944.

Jones, Jacqueline. *Labor of Love, Labor of Sorrow: Black Women, Work and Family, from Slavery to the Present.* New York: Vintage Books, 1985.

Jordan, Terry G. "Forest Folk, Prairie Folk: Rural Religious Cultures in North Texas." *Southwestern Historical Quarterly* 80, no. 2 (October 1976): 135–62.

Jordan, Terry G. "'The Roses So Red and Lilies So Fair': Southern Folk Cemeteries in Texas." *Southwestern Historical Quarterly* 83, no. 3 (January 1980): 227–58.

Keister, Douglas. *Stories in Stone: A Field Guide to Cemetery Symbolism and Iconography.* Salt Lake City, UT: Gibbs Smith, 2004.

Kellogg, John. "Negro Urban Clusters in the Postbellum South." *Geographical Review* 67, no. 3 (July 1977): 310–21.

Kharif, Wali R. "Free Hill." *Tennessee Encyclopedia of History and Culture,* last updated March 1, 2018. https://tennesseeencyclopedia.net/entries/free-hill.

King, Charlotte. "Separated by Death and Color: The African American Cemetery of New Philadelphia, Illinois." *Historical Archaeology* 44, no. 1 (2010): 125–37.

Konvitz, Milton R. "The Extent and Character of Legally-Enforced Segregation." *Journal of Negro Education* 20, no. 3 (Summer 1951): 425–35.

Krüger-Kahloula, Angelica. "Tributes in Stone and Lapidary Lapses: Commemorating Black People in Eighteenth- and Nineteenth-Century America." *Markers* 6 (1989): 33–102.

Kuyk, Betty M. "The African Derivation of Black Fraternal Orders in the United States." *Comparative Studies in Society and History* 25, no. 4 (October 1983): 559–92.

Lamon, Lester C. *Black Tennesseans 1900–1930.* Knoxville: University of Tennessee Press, 1977.

LeForge, Judy Bussell. "State Colored Conventions of Tennessee, 1865–1866," *Tennessee Historical Quarterly* 65, no. 3 (Fall 2006): 230–53.

Lockett, Patricia Ward, Mattie McHollin, and Wilson County Black History Committee. *In Their Own Voices: An Account of the Presence of African Americans in Wilson County.* Wilson County, TN: Lebanon Democrat, 1999.

Lovett, Bobby L. *The African-American History of Nashville, Tennessee, 1780–1930: Elites and Dilemmas.* Fayetteville: University of Arkansas Press, 1999.

Lovett, Bobby L. "Benjamin 'Pap' Singleton." *Tennessee Encyclopedia of History and Culture,* last updated March 1, 2018. https://tennesseeencyclopedia.net/entries/benjamin-singleton.

Lovett, Bobby L. *The Civil Rights Movement in Tennessee: A Narrative History.* Knoxville: University of Tennessee Press, 2005.

Martin, Rachel, and Elizabeth H. Moore. "Promise Land." *Tennessee Encyclopedia of History and Culture,* last updated March 1, 2018. https://
tennesseeencyclopedia.net/entries/promise-land.

Martin, Tony. "The Banneker Literary Institute of Philadelphia: African
American Intellectual Activism before the War of the Slaveholders'
Rebellion." *Journal of African American History* 87, no. 3 (Summer
2002): 303–22.

McKenzie, Robert Tracy. "Reconstruction." *Tennessee Encyclopedia of
History and Culture,* last updated March 1, 2018.
https://tennesseeencyclopedia.net/entries/reconstruction.

McGerr, Michael. *A Fierce Discontent: The Rise and Fall of the Progressive
Movement in America 1870–1920.* New York: Free Press, 2003.

McGinnis, Robert A. *Gone and All but Forgotten: The African-American
Cemeteries of Knox County, Tennessee.* Knoxville, TN: Robert A.
McGinnis, 2006.

McGinnis, Robert. *In Everlasting Remembrance, The Cemeteries of the Old
1st and 2nd Districts of Knox County, Tennessee.* Knoxville, TN: Robert
A. McGinnis, 2003.

McGinnis, Robert A. *Loves Lives On: African/American Cemeteries of East
Tennessee.* Knoxville, TN: Robert A. McGinnis, 2017.

Melton, Gloria Brown. "Blacks in Memphis, Tennessee, 1920–1955: A
Historical Study." PhD diss., Washington State University, 1982.

Miller, Brad R. "Built for the Living: African American Funeral Homes on
the Tennessee Landscape." Master's thesis, Middle Tennessee State
University, 2012.

Miller, William D. "Rural Ideals in Memphis Life at the Turn of the Century."
West Tennessee Historical Society Papers 4 (1950): 41–49.

Montgomery County, Tennessee Family History Book 2000. Paducah, KY:
Turner Publishing Company, 2000.

Morris, Emmeline E. E. "Gospel Pilgrim's Progress: Rehabilitating an
African American Cemetery for the Public." Master's thesis, University
of Georgia, 2007.

Myrdal, Gunnar. *An American Dilemma: The Negro Problem and Modern
Democracy.* New York: Harper and Brothers, 1944.

O'Brien, Gail Williams. *The Color of Law: Race, Violence, and Justice in the
Post–World War II South.* Chapel Hill: University of North Carolina
Press, 1999.

Odum, Howard. "Social and Mental Traits of the Negro: Research into the
Conditions of the Negro Race in Southern Towns." PhD diss., Columbia University, 1910.

Osborne, Willie P., Clara L. Osborne, and Luie Hargraves, eds. *Contributions of Blacks to Hamblen County 1796 to 1996.* Morristown, TN:
Progressive Business Association, 1995.

Page, Brian D. "'In the Hands of the Lord': Migrants and Community Politics in the Late Nineteenth Century." In *An Unseen Light: Black Struggles for Freedom in Memphis, Tennessee*, edited by Aram Goudsouzian and Charles W. McKinney Jr., 13–38. Lexington: University Press of Kentucky, 2018.

Page, Brian Daniel. "Local Matters: Race, Place, and Community Politics after the Civil War." PhD diss., Ohio State University, 2009.

Page, Brian D. "'Stand By the Flag': Nationalism and African-American Celebrations of the Fourth of July in Memphis, 1866–1887." *Tennessee Historical Quarterly* 58, no. 4 (Winter 1999): 284–301.

Page, Brian D. "Sutton E. Griggs." *Tennessee Encyclopedia of History and Culture*, last updated March 1, 2018. https://tennesseeencyclopedia. net/entries/sutton-e-griggs.

Palmer, Edward Nelson. "Negro Secret Societies." *Social Forces* 23, no. 2 (December 1944): 207–22.

Pierce, Dan. "Austin Peay." *Tennessee Encyclopedia of History and Culture*, last updated March 1, 2018. https://tennesseeencyclopedia.net/entries/ austin-peay.

Powdermaker, Hortense. *After Freedom: A Cultural Study in the Deep South*. New York: Viking Press, 1939. Reprinted with a new introduction by Brackette P. Williams and Drexel Woodson. Madison: University of Wisconsin Press, 1993.

Rabinowitz, Howard N. "From Exclusion to Segregation: Southern Race Relations, 1865–1890." *Journal of American History* 63, no. 2 (September 1976): 325–50.

Rabinowitz, Howard N. *Race Relations in the Urban South, 1865–1890*, rev. ed. New York: Oxford University Press, 1978; Athens: University of Georgia Press, 1996.

Rainville, Lynn. *Hidden History: African American Cemeteries in Central Virginia*. Charlottesville: University of Virginia Press, 2014.

Rainville, Lynn. "Protecting Our Shared Heritage in African-American Cemeteries." *Journal of Field Archaeology* 34, no. 2 (Summer 2009): 196–206.

Robinson, Armstead L. "Plans Dat Comed from God: Institution Building and the Emergence of Black Leadership in Reconstruction Memphis." In *Church and Community among Black Southerners, 1865–1900*, edited by Donald G. Nieman, 85–116. New York: Garland Publishing, 1994.

Rule, William, ed. *Standard History of Knoxville, Tennessee*. Chicago: Lewis Publishing Company, 1900.

Scruggs, Otey M. "The Economic and Racial Components of Jim Crow." In *Key Issues in the Afro-American Experience*, edited by Nathan I. Huggins, Martin Kilson, and Daniel M. Fox, 70–87. New York: Harcourt Brace Jovanovich, 1971.

Silver, Christopher, and John V. Moeser. *The Separate City: Black Communi-ties in the Urban South 1940–1960*. Lexington: University of Kentucky Press, 2015.

Skocpol, Theda, Ariane Liazos, and Marshall Ganz. *What a Mighty Power We Can Be: African American Fraternal Groups and the Struggle for Racial Equality*. Princeton, NJ: Princeton University Press, 2006.

Smith, Lillian. *Killers of the Dream*. 1948. Reprint, New York: W.W. Norton, 1994.

Spence, W. Jerome D., and David L. Spence. *A History of Hickman County*. Nashville, TN: Gospel Advocate Printing Publishing Company, 1900.

Stevens, Albert C. *The Cyclopaedia of Fraternities*. New York: E. B. Treat and Company, 1907.

Taylor, Alrutheus Ambush. *The Negro in Tennessee, 1865–1880*. Washington, DC: Associated Publishers, 1941.

"Terms Used to Describe Cemeteries and Grave Markers," State of Indiana, Department of Natural Resources, accessed October 1, 2020. https://www.in.gov/dnr/historic/files/cem_glossary.pdf.

"Thomas Frank Cassels." *"This Honorable Body" African American Legislators in 19th Century Tennessee*. Tennessee State Library and Archives, accessed July 5, 2020. https://sharetngov.tnsosfiles.com/tsla/exhibits/blackhistory/cassels.htm.

Vlach, Jon Michael. *By the Work of Their Hands: Studies in Afro-American Folklife*. Ann Arbor, MI: UMI Research Press, 1991.

Vlach, John Michael. *The Afro-American Tradition in Decorative Arts*. Cleveland, OH: Cleveland Museum of Art, 1978.

West, Carroll Van. "Historic Rural African-American Churches in Tennessee, 1850–1970." NPS form 10-900, reference # 64500618. National Register of Historic Places, Digital Archive on NPGallery. National Park Service, Washington, DC. https://npgallery.nps.gov/NRHP.

West, Carroll Van. "Port Royal State Historic Area." *Tennessee Encyclopedia of History and Culture*, last updated March 1, 2018. https://tennesseeencyclopedia.net/entries/port-royal-state-historic-area.

West, Carroll Van. "Sacred Spaces of Faith, Community, and Resistance: Rural African American Churches in Jim Crow Tennessee." In *"We Shall Inde-pendent Be": African American Place Making and the Struggle to Claim Space in the United States*, edited by Angel David Nieves and Leslie M. Alexander, 439–62. Boulder: University Press of Colorado, 2008.

West, Carroll Van. "United Sons and Daughters of Charity Lodge Hall." *Tennessee Encyclopedia of History and Culture*, last up-dated March 1, 2018. https://tennesseeencyclopedia.net/entries/united-sons-and-daughters-of-charity-lodge-hall.

West, Carroll Van. "Williamson Chapel CME Church Complex." NPS Form10-900, reference # 06001039. National Register of Historic Places, Digital Archive on NPGallery. National Park Service, Washington, DC. https://npgallery.nps.gov/NRHP.

Wetherington, Mark V. "Ku Klux Klan." *Tennessee Encyclopedia of History and Culture*, last updated March 1, 2018. https://tennesseeencyclopedia. net/entries/ku-klux-klan.

Weyeneth, Robert R. "The Architecture of Racial Segregation: The Challenges of Preserving the Problematic Past." *Public Historian* 27, no. 4 (Fall 2005): 11–44.

Williams, Harold Hamilton. "A Study of Landscaping in Negro Communities of the Southern States." Master's thesis, Cornell University, 1944.

Williams, Marguerite W. *Cemeteries of Hamblen County, Tennessee*, vol. 3. Morristown, TN: Hamblen County Genealogical Society, 1996.

Wills, Brian S. "Nathan Bedford Forrest." In *Tennessee Encyclopedia of History and Culture*, last updated March 1, 2018. https:// tennesseeencyclopedia.net/entries/nathan-bedford-forrest.

Wolfe, Margaret Ripley Wolfe. "World War I." *Tennessee Encyclopedia of History and Culture*, last updated March 1, 2018. https:// tennesseeencyclopedia.net/entries/world-war-i.

Wood, James L. *The Historical Development of the Negro in Giles County*. Pulaski, TN: J. L. Wood, 2000.

Woodson, C. G. "Insurance Business among Negroes." *Journal of Negro History* 14, no. 2 (April 1929): 202–26.

Wright, Roberta Hughes, and Wilbur B. Hughes. *Lay Down Body: Living History in African American Cemeteries*. Detroit, MI: Visible Ink Press, 1996.

Zebley, Kathleen R. "Freedmen's Bureau." *Tennessee Encyclopedia of History and Culture*, last updated March 1, 2018. https://tennesseeencyclopedia. net/entries/freedmens-bureau.

INDEX